CouchDB: The Definitive Guide

CouchDB: The Definitive Guide

J. Chris Anderson, Jan Lehnardt, and Noah Slater

O'REILLY®

Beijing · Cambridge · Farnham · Köln · Sebastopol · Taipei · Tokyo

CouchDB: The Definitive Guide

by J. Chris Anderson, Jan Lehnardt, and Noah Slater

Published by O'Reilly Media, Inc., 1005 Gravenstein Highway North, Sebastopol, CA 95472.

O'Reilly books may be purchased for educational, business, or sales promotional use. Online editions are also available for most titles (*http://my.safaribooksonline.com*). For more information, contact our corporate/institutional sales department: 800-998-9938 or *corporate@oreilly.com*.

Editor: Mike Loukides
Production Editor: Sarah Schneider
Production Services: Appingo, Inc.

Cover Designer: Karen Montgomery
Interior Designer: David Futato
Illustrator: Robert Romano

Printing History:

January 2010:   First Edition.

RepKover™   This book uses RepKover™, a durable and flexible lay-flat binding.

ISBN: 978-0-596-15589-6

[M]

1263503554

*For the Web, and all the people who helped me
along the way. Thank you.*

—J. Chris

Für Marita und Kalle.

—Jan

For my parents, God and Damien Katz.

—Noah

Table of Contents

Part I. Introduction

Part II.   Developing with CouchDB

Part IV.   Deploying CouchDB

Part VI. Appendixes

Foreword

As the creator of CouchDB, it gives me great pleasure to write this Foreword. This book has been a long time coming. I've worked on CouchDB since 2005, when it was only a vision in my head and only my wife Laura believed I could make it happen.

Now the project has taken on a life of its own, and code is literally running on millions of machines. I couldn't stop it now if I tried.

A great analogy J. Chris uses is that CouchDB has felt like a boulder we've been pushing up a hill. Over time, it's been moving faster and getting easier to push, and now it's moving so fast it's starting to feel like it could get loose and crush some unlucky villagers. Or something. Hey, remember "Tales of the Runaway Boulder" with Robert Wagner on *Saturday Night Live*? Good times.

Well, now we are trying to safely guide that boulder. Because of the villagers. You know what? This boulder analogy just isn't working. Let's move on.

The reason for this book is that CouchDB is a very different way of approaching data storage. A way that isn't inherently better or worse than the ways before—it's just another tool, another way of thinking about things. It's missing some features you might be used to, but it's gained some abilities you've maybe never seen. Sometimes it's an excellent fit for your problems; sometimes it's terrible.

And sometimes you may be thinking about your problems all wrong. You just need to approach them from a different angle.

Hopefully this book will help you understand CouchDB and the approach that it takes, and also understand how and when it can be used for the problems you face.

Otherwise, someday it could become a runaway boulder, being misused and causing disasters that could have been avoided.

And I'll be doing my best Charlton Heston imitation, on the ground, pounding the dirt, yelling, "You maniacs! You blew it up! Ah, damn you! God damn you all to hell!" Or something like that.

—Damien Katz
Creator of CouchDB

Preface

Thanks for purchasing this book! If it was a gift, then congratulations. If, on the other hand, you downloaded it without paying, well, actually, we're pretty happy about that too! This book is available under a free license, and that's important because we want it to serve the community as documentation—and documentation should be free.

So, why pay for a free book? Well, you might like the warm fuzzy feeling you get from holding a book in your hands, as you cosy up on the couch with a cup of coffee. On the couch...get it? Bad jokes aside, whatever your reasons, buying the book helps support us, so we have more time to work on improvements for both the book and CouchDB. So thank you!

We set out to compile the best and most comprehensive collection of CouchDB information there is, and yet we know we failed. CouchDB is a fast-moving target and grew significantly during the time we were writing the book. We were able to adapt quickly and keep things up-to-date, but we also had to draw the line somewhere if we ever hoped to publish it.

At the time of this writing, CouchDB 0.10.1 is the latest release, but you might already be seeing 0.10.2 or even 0.11.0 released or being prepared—maybe even 1.0. Although we have some ideas about how future releases will look, we don't know for certain and didn't want to make any wild guesses. CouchDB is a community project, so ultimately it's up to you, our readers, to help shape the project.

On the plus side, many people successfully run CouchDB 0.10 in production, and you will have more than enough on your hands to run a solid project. Future releases of CouchDB will make things easier in places, but the core features should remain the same. Besides, learning the core features helps you understand and appreciate the shortcuts and allows you to roll your own hand-tailored solutions.

Writing an open book was great fun. We're happy O'Reilly supported our decision in every way possible. The best part—besides giving the CouchDB community early access to the material—was the commenting functionality we implemented on the book's website. It allows anybody to comment on any paragraph in the book with a simple click. We used some simple JavaScript and Google Groups to allow painless commenting. The result was astounding. As of today, 866 people have sent more than 1,100 messages to our little group. Submissions have ranged from pointing out small typos to deep technical discussions. Feedback on our original first chapter led us to a complete rewrite in order to make sure the points we wanted to get across did, indeed, get across. This system allowed us to clearly formulate what we wanted to say in a way that worked for you, our readers.

Overall, the book has become so much better because of the help of hundreds of volunteers who took the time to send in their suggestions. We understand the immense value this model has, and we want to keep it up. New features in CouchDB should make it into the book without us necessarily having to do a reprint every thee months. The publishing industry is not ready for that yet, but we want to continue to release new and revised content and listen closely to the feedback. The specifics of how we'll do this are still in flux, but we'll be posting the information to the book's website the first moment we know it. That's a promise! So make sure to visit the book's website at *http://books.couchdb.org/relax* to keep up-to-date.

Before we let you dive into the book, we want to make sure you're well prepared. CouchDB is written in Erlang, but you don't need to know anything about Erlang to use CouchDB. CouchDB also heavily relies on web technologies like HTTP and JavaScript, and some experience with those does help when following the examples throughout the book. If you have built a website before—simple or complex—you should be ready to go.

If you are an experienced developer or systems architect, the introduction to CouchDB should be comforting, as you already know everything involved—all you need to learn are the ways CouchDB puts them together. Toward the end of the book, we ramp up the experience level to help you get as comfortable building large-scale CouchDB systems as you are with personal projects.

If you are a beginning web developer, don't worry—by the time you get to the later parts of the book, you should be able to follow along with the harder stuff.

Now, sit back, relax, and enjoy the ride through the wonderful world of CouchDB.

Using Code Examples

This book is here to help you get your job done. In general, you may use the code in this book in your programs and documentation. You do not need to contact us for permission unless you're reproducing a significant portion of the code. For example, writing a program that uses several chunks of code from this book does not require permission. Selling or distributing a CD-ROM of examples from O'Reilly books does require permission. Answering a question by citing this book and quoting example code does not require permission. Incorporating a significant amount of example code from this book into your product's documentation does require permission.

This work is licensed under the Creative Commons Attribution License. To view a copy of this license, visit *http://creativecommons.org/licenses/by/2.0/legalcode* or send a letter to Creative Commons, 171 2nd Street, Suite 300, San Francisco, California, 94105, USA.

An attribution usually includes the title, author, publisher, and ISBN. For example: "*CouchDB: The Definitive Guide* by J. Chris Anderson, Jan Lehnardt, and Noah Slater. Copyright 2010 J. Chris Anderson, Jan Lehnardt, and Noah Slater, 978-0-596-15589-6."

If you feel your use of code examples falls outside fair use or the permission given above, feel free to contact us at *permissions@oreilly.com*.

Conventions Used in This Book

The following typographical conventions are used in this book:

Italic
> Indicates new terms, URLs, email addresses, filenames, and file extensions.

`Constant width`
> Used for program listings, as well as within paragraphs to refer to program elements such as variable or function names, databases, data types, environment variables, statements, and keywords.

`Constant width bold`
> Shows commands or other text that should be typed literally by the user.

`Constant width italic`
> Shows text that should be replaced with user-supplied values or by values determined by context.

 This icon signifies a tip, suggestion, or general note.

 This icon indicates a warning or caution.

Safari® Books Online

 Safari Books Online is an on-demand digital library that lets you easily search over 7,500 technology and creative reference books and videos to find the answers you need quickly.

With a subscription, you can read any page and watch any video from our library online. Read books on your cell phone and mobile devices. Access new titles before they are available for print, and get exclusive access to manuscripts in development and post feedback for the authors. Copy and paste code samples, organize your favorites, download chapters, bookmark key sections, create notes, print out pages, and benefit from tons of other time-saving features.

O'Reilly Media has uploaded this book to the Safari Books Online service. To have full digital access to this book and others on similar topics from O'Reilly and other publishers, sign up for free at *http://my.safaribooksonline.com*.

How to Contact Us

Please address comments and questions concerning this book to the publisher:

O'Reilly Media, Inc.
1005 Gravenstein Highway North
Sebastopol, CA 95472
800-998-9938 (in the United States or Canada)
707-829-0515 (international or local)
707-829-0104 (fax)

We have a web page for this book, where we list errata, examples, and any additional information. You can access this page at:

http://www.oreilly.com/catalog/9780596155896

To comment or ask technical questions about this book, send email to:

bookquestions@oreilly.com

For more information about our books, conferences, Resource Centers, and the O'Reilly Network, see our website at:

http://www.oreilly.com

Acknowledgments

J. Chris

I would like to acknowledge all the committers of CouchDB, the people sending patches, and the rest of the community. I couldn't have done it without my wife, Amy, who helps me think about the big picture; without the patience and support of my coauthors and O'Reilly; nor without the help of everyone who helped us hammer out book content details on the mailing lists. And a shout-out to the copyeditor, who was awesome!

Jan

I would like to thank the CouchDB community. Special thanks go out to a number of nice people all over the place who invited me to attend or talk at a conference, who let me sleep on their couches (pun most definitely intended), and who made sure I had a good time when I was abroad presenting CouchDB. There are too many to name, but all of you in Dublin, Portland, Lisbon, London, Zurich, San Francisco, Mountain View, Dortmund, Stockholm, Hamburg, Frankfurt, Salt Lake City, Blacksburg, San Diego, and Amsterdam: you know who you are—thanks!

To my family, friends, and coworkers: thanks you for your support and your patience with me over the last year. You won't hear, "I've got to leave early, I have a book to write" from me anytime soon, promise!

Anna, you believe in me; I couldn't have done this without you.

Noah

I would like to thank O'Reilly for their enthusiasm in CouchDB and for realizing the importance of free documentation. And of course, I'd like to thank Jan and J. Chris for being so great to work with. But a special thanks goes out to the whole CouchDB community, for making everything so fun and rewarding. Without you guys, none of this would be possible. And if you're reading this, that means you!

PART I

Introduction

CHAPTER 1

Why CouchDB?

Apache CouchDB is one of a new breed of database management systems. This chapter explains why there's a need for new systems as well as the motivations behind building CouchDB.

As CouchDB developers, we're naturally very excited to be using CouchDB. In this chapter we'll share with you the reasons for our enthusiasm. We'll show you how CouchDB's schema-free document model is a better fit for common applications, how the built-in query engine is a powerful way to use and process your data, and how CouchDB's design lends itself to modularization and scalability.

Relax

If there's one word to describe CouchDB, it is *relax*. It is in the title of this book, it is the byline to CouchDB's official logo, and when you start CouchDB, you see:

```
Apache CouchDB has started. Time to relax.
```

Why is relaxation important? Developer productivity roughly doubled in the last five years. The chief reason for the boost is more powerful tools that are easier to use. Take Ruby on Rails as an example. It is an infinitely complex framework, but it's easy to get started with. Rails is a success story because of the core design focus on ease of use. This is one reason why CouchDB is relaxing: learning CouchDB and understanding its core concepts should feel natural to most everybody who has been doing any work on the Web. And it is still pretty easy to explain to non-technical people.

Getting out of the way when creative people try to build specialized solutions is in itself a core feature and one thing that CouchDB aims to get right. We found existing tools too cumbersome to work with during development or in production, and decided to focus on making CouchDB easy, even a pleasure, to use. Chapters 3 and 4 will demonstrate the intuitive HTTP-based REST API.

Another area of relaxation for CouchDB users is the production setting. If you have a live running application, CouchDB again goes out of its way to avoid troubling you.

Its internal architecture is fault-tolerant, and failures occur in a controlled environment and are dealt with gracefully. Single problems do not cascade through an entire server system but stay isolated in single requests.

CouchDB's core concepts are simple (yet powerful) and well understood. Operations teams (if you have a team; otherwise, that's you) do not have to fear random behavior and untraceable errors. If anything should go wrong, you can easily find out what the problem is—but these situations are rare.

CouchDB is also designed to handle varying traffic gracefully. For instance, if a website is experiencing a sudden spike in traffic, CouchDB will generally absorb a lot of concurrent requests without falling over. It may take a little more time for each request, but they all get answered. When the spike is over, CouchDB will work with regular speed again.

The third area of relaxation is growing and shrinking the underlying hardware of your application. This is commonly referred to as *scaling*. CouchDB enforces a set of limits on the programmer. On first look, CouchDB might seem inflexible, but some features are left out by design for the simple reason that if CouchDB supported them, it would allow a programmer to create applications that couldn't deal with scaling up or down. We'll explore the whole matter of scaling CouchDB in Part IV, *Deploying CouchDB*.

In a nutshell: CouchDB doesn't let you do things that would get you in trouble later on. This sometimes means you'll have to unlearn best practices you might have picked up in your current or past work. Chapter 24 contains a list of common tasks and how to solve them in CouchDB.

A Different Way to Model Your Data

We believe that CouchDB will drastically change the way you build document-based applications. CouchDB combines an intuitive document storage model with a powerful query engine in a way that's so simple you'll probably be tempted to ask, "Why has no one built something like this before?"

> Django may be built *for* the Web, but CouchDB is built *of* the Web. I've never seen software that so completely embraces the philosophies behind HTTP. CouchDB makes Django look old-school in the same way that Django makes ASP look outdated.
>
> —Jacob Kaplan-Moss, Django developer

CouchDB's design borrows heavily from web architecture and the concepts of resources, methods, and representations. It augments this with powerful ways to query, map, combine, and filter your data. Add fault tolerance, extreme scalability, and incremental replication, and CouchDB defines a sweet spot for document databases.

A Better Fit for Common Applications

We write software to improve our lives and the lives of others. Usually this involves taking some mundane information—such as contacts, invoices, or receipts—and manipulating it using a computer application. CouchDB is a great fit for common applications like this because it embraces the natural idea of evolving, self-contained documents as the very core of its data model.

Self-Contained Data

An invoice contains all the pertinent information about a single transaction—the seller, the buyer, the date, and a list of the items or services sold. As shown in Figure 1-1, there's no abstract reference on this piece of paper that points to some other piece of paper with the seller's name and address. Accountants appreciate the simplicity of having everything in one place. And given the choice, programmers appreciate that, too.

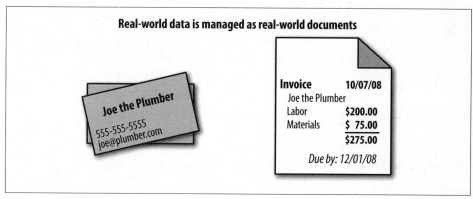

Figure 1-1. Self-contained documents

Yet using references is exactly how we model our data in a relational database! Each invoice is stored in a table as a row that refers to other rows in other tables—one row for seller information, one for the buyer, one row for each item billed, and more rows still to describe the item details, manufacturer details, and so on and so forth.

This isn't meant as a detraction of the relational model, which is widely applicable and extremely useful for a number of reasons. Hopefully, though, it illustrates the point that sometimes your model may not "fit" your data in the way it occurs in the real world.

Let's take a look at the humble contact database to illustrate a different way of modeling data, one that more closely "fits" its real-world counterpart—a pile of business cards. Much like our invoice example, a business card contains all the important information, right there on the cardstock. We call this "self-contained" data, and it's an important concept in understanding document databases like CouchDB.

Syntax and Semantics

Most business cards contain roughly the same information—someone's identity, an affiliation, and some contact information. While the exact form of this information can vary between business cards, the general information being conveyed remains the same, and we're easily able to recognize it as a business card. In this sense, we can describe a business card as a *real-world document*.

Jan's business card might contain a phone number but no fax number, whereas J. Chris's business card contains both a phone and a fax number. Jan does not have to make his lack of a fax machine explicit by writing something as ridiculous as "Fax: None" on the business card. Instead, simply omitting a fax number implies that he doesn't have one.

We can see that real-world documents of the same type, such as business cards, tend to be very similar in *semantics*—the sort of information they carry—but can vary hugely in *syntax*, or how that information is structured. As human beings, we're naturally comfortable dealing with this kind of variation.

While a traditional relational database requires you to model your data *up front*, CouchDB's schema-free design unburdens you with a powerful way to aggregate your data *after the fact*, just like we do with real-world documents. We'll look in depth at how to design applications with this underlying storage paradigm.

Building Blocks for Larger Systems

CouchDB is a storage system useful on its own. You can build many applications with the tools CouchDB gives you. But CouchDB is designed with a bigger picture in mind. Its components can be used as building blocks that solve storage problems in slightly different ways for larger and more complex systems.

Whether you need a system that's crazy fast but isn't too concerned with reliability (think logging), or one that guarantees storage in two or more physically separated locations for reliability, but you're willing to take a performance hit, CouchDB lets you build these systems.

There are a multitude of knobs you could turn to make a system work better in one area, but you'll affect another area when doing so. One example would be the CAP theorem discussed in the next chapter. To give you an idea of other things that affect storage systems, see Figures 1-2 and 1-3.

By reducing latency for a given system (and that is true not only for storage systems), you affect concurrency and throughput capabilities.

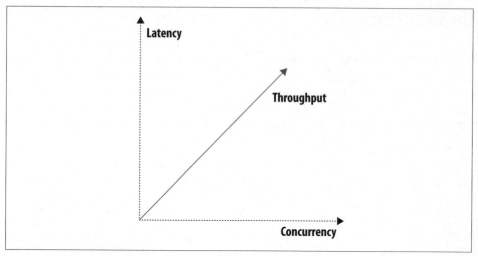

Figure 1-2. Throughput, latency, or concurrency

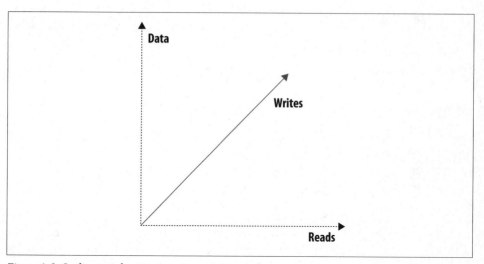

Figure 1-3. Scaling: read requests, write requests, or data

When you want to scale out, there are three distinct issues to deal with: scaling read requests, write requests, and data. Orthogonal to all three and to the items shown in Figures 1-2 and 1-3 are many more attributes like reliability or simplicity. You can draw many of these graphs that show how different features or attributes pull into different directions and thus shape the system they describe.

CouchDB is very flexible and gives you enough building blocks to create a system shaped to suit your exact problem. That's not saying that CouchDB can be bent to solve any problem—CouchDB is no silver bullet—but in the area of data storage, it can get you a long way.

CouchDB Replication

CouchDB replication is one of these building blocks. Its fundamental function is to synchronize two or more CouchDB databases. This may sound simple, but the simplicity is key to allowing replication to solve a number of problems: reliably synchronize databases between multiple machines for redundant data storage; distribute data to a cluster of CouchDB instances that share a subset of the total number of requests that hit the cluster (load balancing); and distribute data between physically distant locations, such as one office in New York and another in Tokyo.

CouchDB replication uses the same REST API all clients use. HTTP is ubiquitous and well understood. Replication works incrementally; that is, if during replication anything goes wrong, like dropping your network connection, it will pick up where it left off the next time it runs. It also only transfers data that is needed to synchronize databases.

A core assumption CouchDB makes is that things can go wrong, like network connection troubles, and it is designed for graceful error recovery instead of assuming all will be well. The replication system's incremental design shows that best. The ideas behind "things that can go wrong" are embodied in the Fallacies of Distributed Computing:[*]

1. The network is reliable.
2. Latency is zero.
3. Bandwidth is infinite.
4. The network is secure.
5. Topology doesn't change.
6. There is one administrator.
7. Transport cost is zero.
8. The network is homogeneous.

Existing tools often try to hide the fact that there is a network and that any or all of the previous conditions don't exist for a particular system. This usually results in fatal error scenarios when something finally goes wrong. In contrast, CouchDB doesn't try to hide the network; it just handles errors gracefully and lets you know when actions on your end are required.

Local Data Is King

CouchDB takes quite a few lessons learned from the Web, but there is one thing that could be improved about the Web: latency. Whenever you have to wait for an application to respond or a website to render, you almost always wait for a network con-

---

[*] http://en.wikipedia.org/wiki/Fallacies_of_Distributed_Computing

nection that isn't as fast as you want it at that point. Waiting a few seconds instead of milliseconds greatly affects user experience and thus user satisfaction.

What do you do when you are offline? This happens all the time—your DSL or cable provider has issues, or your iPhone, G1, or Blackberry has no bars, and no connectivity means no way to get to your data.

CouchDB can solve this scenario as well, and this is where scaling is important again. This time it is scaling down. Imagine CouchDB installed on phones and other mobile devices that can synchronize data with centrally hosted CouchDBs when they are on a network. The synchronization is not bound by user interface constraints like subsecond response times. It is easier to tune for high bandwidth and higher latency than for low bandwidth and very low latency. Mobile applications can then use the local CouchDB to fetch data, and since no remote networking is required for that, latency is low by default.

Can you really use CouchDB on a phone? Erlang, CouchDB's implementation language has been designed to run on embedded devices magnitudes smaller and less powerful than today's phones.

Wrapping Up

The next chapter further explores the distributed nature of CouchDB. We should have given you enough bites to whet your interest. Let's go!

CHAPTER 2

Eventual Consistency

In the previous chapter, we saw that CouchDB's flexibility allows us to evolve our data as our applications grow and change. In this chapter, we'll explore how working "with the grain" of CouchDB promotes simplicity in our applications and helps us naturally build scalable, distributed systems.

Working with the Grain

A *distributed system* is a system that operates robustly over a wide network. A particular feature of network computing is that network links can potentially disappear, and there are plenty of strategies for managing this type of network segmentation. CouchDB differs from others by accepting eventual consistency, as opposed to putting absolute consistency ahead of raw availability, like RDBMS or Paxos. What these systems have in common is an awareness that data acts differently when many people are accessing it simultaneously. Their approaches differ when it comes to which aspects of *consistency*, *availability*, or *partition tolerance* they prioritize.

Engineering distributed systems is tricky. Many of the caveats and "gotchas" you will face over time aren't immediately obvious. We don't have all the solutions, and CouchDB isn't a panacea, but when you work with CouchDB's grain rather than against it, the path of least resistance leads you to naturally scalable applications.

Of course, building a distributed system is only the beginning. A website with a database that is available only half the time is next to worthless. Unfortunately, the traditional relational database approach to consistency makes it very easy for application programmers to rely on global state, global clocks, and other high availability no-nos, without even realizing that they're doing so. Before examining how CouchDB promotes scalability, we'll look at the constraints faced by a distributed system. After we've seen the problems that arise when parts of your application can't rely on being in constant contact with each other, we'll see that CouchDB provides an intuitive and useful way for modeling applications around high availability.

The CAP Theorem

The CAP theorem describes a few different strategies for distributing application logic across networks. CouchDB's solution uses replication to propagate application changes across participating nodes. This is a fundamentally different approach from consensus algorithms and relational databases, which operate at different intersections of consistency, availability, and partition tolerance.

The CAP theorem, shown in Figure 2-1, identifies three distinct concerns:

Consistency
    All database clients see the same data, even with concurrent updates.

Availability
    All database clients are able to access some version of the data.

Partition tolerance
    The database can be split over multiple servers.

Pick two.

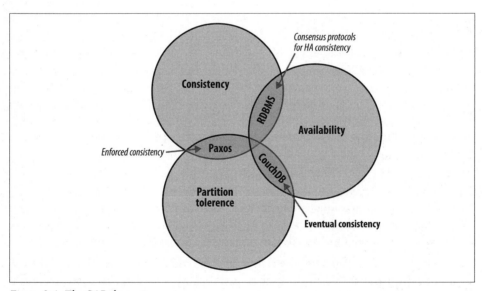

Figure 2-1. The CAP theorem

When a system grows large enough that a single database node is unable to handle the load placed on it, a sensible solution is to add more servers. When we add nodes, we have to start thinking about how to partition data between them. Do we have a few databases that share exactly the same data? Do we put different sets of data on different database servers? Do we let only certain database servers write data and let others handle the reads?

Regardless of which approach we take, the one problem we'll keep bumping into is that of keeping all these database servers in synchronization. If you write some information to one node, how are you going to make sure that a read request to another database server reflects this newest information? These events might be milliseconds apart. Even with a modest collection of database servers, this problem can become extremely complex.

When it's absolutely critical that all clients see a consistent view of the database, the users of one node will have to wait for any other nodes to come into agreement before being able to read or write to the database. In this instance, we see that *availability* takes a backseat to *consistency*. However, there are situations where availability trumps consistency:

> Each node in a system should be able to make decisions purely based on local state. If you need to do something under high load with failures occurring and you need to reach agreement, you're lost. If you're concerned about scalability, any algorithm that forces you to run agreement will eventually become your bottleneck. Take that as a given.
>
> —Werner Vogels, Amazon CTO and Vice President

If availability is a priority, we can let clients write data to one node of the database without waiting for other nodes to come into agreement. If the database knows how to take care of reconciling these operations between nodes, we achieve a sort of "eventual consistency" in exchange for high availability. This is a surprisingly applicable trade-off for many applications.

Unlike traditional relational databases, where each action performed is necessarily subject to database-wide consistency checks, CouchDB makes it really simple to build applications that sacrifice immediate consistency for the huge performance improvements that come with simple distribution.

Local Consistency

Before we attempt to understand how CouchDB operates in a cluster, it's important that we understand the inner workings of a single CouchDB node. The CouchDB API is designed to provide a convenient but thin wrapper around the database core. By taking a closer look at the structure of the database core, we'll have a better understanding of the API that surrounds it.

The Key to Your Data

At the heart of CouchDB is a powerful *B-tree* storage engine. A B-tree is a sorted data structure that allows for searches, insertions, and deletions in logarithmic time. As Figure 2-2 illustrates, CouchDB uses this B-tree storage engine for all internal data, documents, and views. If we understand one, we will understand them all.

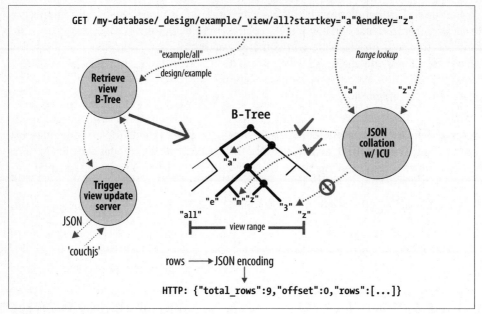

Figure 2-2. Anatomy of a view request

CouchDB uses MapReduce to compute the results of a view. MapReduce makes use of two functions, "map" and "reduce," which are applied to each document in isolation. Being able to isolate these operations means that view computation lends itself to parallel and incremental computation. More important, because these functions produce key/value pairs, CouchDB is able to insert them into the B-tree storage engine, sorted by key. Lookups by key, or key range, are extremely efficient operations with a B-tree, described in *big O notation* as *O(log N)* and *O(log N + K)*, respectively.

In CouchDB, we access documents and view results by key or key range. This is a direct mapping to the underlying operations performed on CouchDB's B-tree storage engine. Along with document inserts and updates, this direct mapping is the reason we describe CouchDB's API as being a thin wrapper around the database core.

Being able to access results by key alone is a very important restriction because it allows us to make huge performance gains. As well as the massive speed improvements, we can partition our data over multiple nodes, without affecting our ability to query each node in isolation. *BigTable*, *Hadoop*, *SimpleDB*, and *memcached* restrict object lookups by key for exactly these reasons.

No Locking

A table in a relational database is a single data structure. If you want to modify a table—say, update a row—the database system must ensure that nobody else is trying to update that row and that nobody can read from that row while it is being updated. The common way to handle this uses what's known as a *lock*. If multiple clients want to access a table, the first client gets the lock, making everybody else wait. When the first client's request is processed, the next client is given access while everybody else waits, and so on. This serial execution of requests, even when they arrived in parallel, wastes a significant amount of your server's processing power. Under high load, a relational database can spend more time figuring out who is allowed to do what, and in which order, than it does doing any actual work.

Instead of locks, CouchDB uses *Multi-Version Concurrency Control (MVCC)* to manage concurrent access to the database. Figure 2-3 illustrates the differences between MVCC and traditional locking mechanisms. MVCC means that CouchDB can run at full speed, all the time, even under high load. Requests are run in parallel, making excellent use of every last drop of processing power your server has to offer.

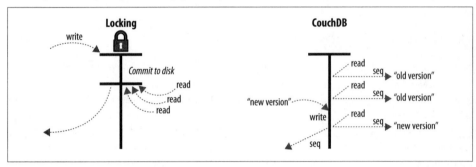

Figure 2-3. MVCC means no locking

Documents in CouchDB are versioned, much like they would be in a regular version control system such as Subversion. If you want to change a value in a document, you create an entire new version of that document and save it over the old one. After doing this, you end up with two versions of the same document, one old and one new.

How does this offer an improvement over locks? Consider a set of requests wanting to access a document. The first request reads the document. While this is being processed, a second request changes the document. Since the second request includes a completely new version of the document, CouchDB can simply append it to the database without having to wait for the read request to finish.

When a third request wants to read the same document, CouchDB will point it to the new version that has just been written. During this whole process, the first request could still be reading the original version.

A read request will always see the most recent snapshot of your database.

Validation

As application developers, we have to think about what sort of input we should accept and what we should reject. The expressive power to do this type of validation over complex data *within* a traditional relational database leaves a lot to be desired. Fortunately, CouchDB provides a powerful way to perform per-document validation from within the database.

CouchDB can validate documents using JavaScript functions similar to those used for MapReduce. Each time you try to modify a document, CouchDB will pass the validation function a copy of the existing document, a copy of the new document, and a collection of additional information, such as user authentication details. The validation function now has the opportunity to approve or deny the update.

By working with the grain and letting CouchDB do this for us, we save ourselves a tremendous amount of CPU cycles that would otherwise have been spent serializing object graphs from SQL, converting them into domain objects, and using those objects to do application-level validation.

Distributed Consistency

Maintaining consistency within a single database node is relatively easy for most databases. The real problems start to surface when you try to maintain consistency between multiple database servers. If a client makes a write operation on server *A*, how do we make sure that this is consistent with server *B*, or *C*, or *D*? For relational databases, this is a very complex problem with entire books devoted to its solution. You could use multi-master, master/slave, partitioning, sharding, write-through caches, and all sorts of other complex techniques.

Incremental Replication

Because CouchDB operations take place within the context of a single document, if you want to use two database nodes, you no longer have to worry about them staying in constant communication. CouchDB achieves *eventual consistency* between databases by using incremental replication, a process where document changes are periodically copied between servers. We are able to build what's known as a *shared nothing* cluster of databases where each node is independent and self-sufficient, leaving no single point of contention across the system.

Need to scale out your CouchDB database cluster? Just throw in another server.

As illustrated in Figure 2-4, with CouchDB's incremental replication, you can synchronize your data between any two databases however you like and whenever you like. After replication, each database is able to work independently.

You could use this feature to synchronize database servers within a cluster or between data centers using a job scheduler such as *cron*, or you could use it to synchronize data with your laptop for offline work as you travel. Each database can be used in the usual fashion, and changes between databases can be synchronized later in both directions.

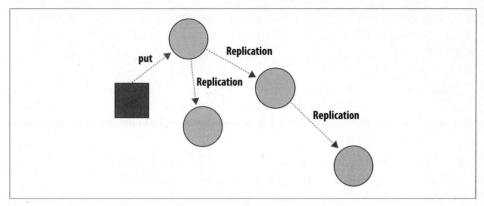

Figure 2-4. Incremental replication between CouchDB nodes

What happens when you change the same document in two different databases and want to synchronize these with each other? CouchDB's replication system comes with automatic conflict detection *and* resolution. When CouchDB detects that a document has been changed in both databases, it flags this document as being in conflict, much like they would be in a regular version control system.

This isn't as troublesome as it might first sound. When two versions of a document conflict during replication, the *winning* version is saved as the most recent version in the document's history. Instead of throwing the *losing* version away, as you might expect, CouchDB saves this as a previous version in the document's history, so that you can access it if you need to. This happens automatically and consistently, so both databases will make exactly the same choice.

It is up to you to handle conflicts in a way that makes sense for your application. You can leave the chosen document versions in place, revert to the older version, or try to merge the two versions and save the result.

Case Study

Greg Borenstein, a friend and coworker, built a small library for converting Songbird playlists to JSON objects and decided to store these in CouchDB as part of a backup application. The completed software uses CouchDB's MVCC and document revisions to ensure that Songbird playlists are backed up robustly between nodes.

 Songbird is a free software media player with an integrated web browser, based on the Mozilla XULRunner platform. Songbird is available for Microsoft Windows, Apple Mac OS X, Solaris, and Linux.

Let's examine the workflow of the Songbird backup application, first as a user backing up from a single computer, and then using Songbird to synchronize playlists between multiple computers. We'll see how document revisions turn what could have been a hairy problem into something that *just works*.

The first time we use this backup application, we feed our playlists to the application and initiate a backup. Each playlist is converted to a JSON object and handed to a CouchDB database. As illustrated in Figure 2-5, CouchDB hands back the document ID and revision of each playlist as it's saved to the database.

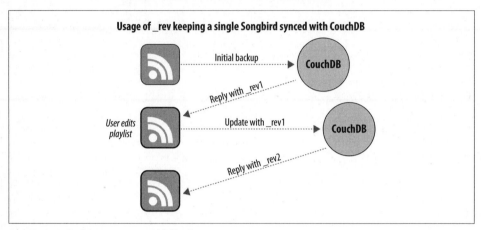

Figure 2-5. Backing up to a single database

After a few days, we find that our playlists have been updated and we want to back up our changes. After we have fed our playlists to the backup application, it fetches the latest versions from CouchDB, along with the corresponding document revisions. When the application hands back the new playlist document, CouchDB requires that the document revision is included in the request.

CouchDB then makes sure that the document revision handed to it in the request matches the current revision held in the database. Because CouchDB updates the revision with every modification, if these two are out of synchronization it suggests that someone else has made changes to the document between the time we requested it from the database and the time we sent our updates. Making changes to a document after someone else has modified it without first inspecting those changes is usually a bad idea.

Forcing clients to hand back the correct document revision is the heart of CouchDB's optimistic concurrency.

We have a laptop we want to keep synchronized with our desktop computer. With all our playlists on our desktop, the first step is to "restore from backup" onto our laptop. This is the first time we've done this, so afterward our laptop should hold an exact replica of our desktop playlist collection.

After editing our Argentine Tango playlist on our laptop to add a few new songs we've purchased, we want to save our changes. The backup application replaces the playlist document in our laptop CouchDB database and a new document revision is generated. A few days later, we remember our new songs and want to copy the playlist across to our desktop computer. As illustrated in Figure 2-6, the backup application copies the new document and the new revision to the desktop CouchDB database. Both CouchDB databases now have the same document revision.

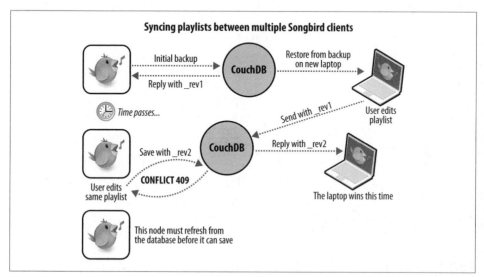

Figure 2-6. Synchronizing between two databases

Because CouchDB tracks document revisions, it ensures that updates like these will work only if they are based on current information. If we had made modifications to the playlist backups between synchronization, things wouldn't go as smoothly.

We back up some changes on our laptop and forget to synchronize. A few days later, we're editing playlists on our desktop computer, make a backup, and want to synchronize this to our laptop. As illustrated in Figure 2-7, when our backup application tries to replicate between the two databases, CouchDB sees that the changes being sent from our desktop computer are modifications of out-of-date documents and helpfully informs us that there has been a conflict.

Recovering from this error is easy to accomplish from an application perspective. Just download CouchDB's version of the playlist and provide an opportunity to merge the changes or save local modifications into a new playlist.

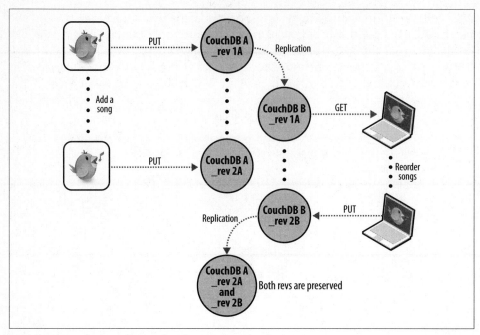

Figure 2-7. Synchronization conflicts between two databases

Wrapping Up

CouchDB's design borrows heavily from web architecture and the lessons learned deploying massively distributed systems on that architecture. By understanding why this architecture works the way it does, and by learning to spot which parts of your application can be easily distributed and which parts cannot, you'll enhance your ability to design distributed and scalable applications, with CouchDB or without it.

We've covered the main issues surrounding CouchDB's consistency model and hinted at some of the benefits to be had when you work *with* CouchDB and not against it. But enough theory—let's get up and running and see what all the fuss is about!

CHAPTER 3

Getting Started

In this chapter, we'll take a quick tour of CouchDB's features, familiarizing ourselves with *Futon*, the built-in administration interface. We'll create our first document and experiment with CouchDB views. Before we start, skip to Appendix D and look for your operating system. You will need to follow those instructions and get CouchDB installed before you can progress.

All Systems Are Go!

We'll have a very quick look at CouchDB's bare-bones *Application Programming Interface (API)* by using the command-line utility `curl`. Please note that this is only one way of talking to CouchDB. We will show you plenty more throughout the rest of the book. What's interesting about `curl` is that it gives you control over raw HTTP requests, and you can see exactly what is going on "underneath the hood" of your database.

Make sure CouchDB is still running, and then do:

```
curl http://127.0.0.1:5984/
```

This issues a `GET` request to your newly installed CouchDB instance.

The reply should look something like:

```
{"couchdb":"Welcome","version":"0.10.1"}
```

Not all that spectacular. CouchDB is saying "hello" with the running version number.

Next, we can get a list of databases:

```
curl -X GET http://127.0.0.1:5984/_all_dbs
```

All we added to the previous request is the `_all_dbs` string.

The response should look like:

```
[]
```

Oh, that's right, we didn't create any databases yet! All we see is an empty list.

The `curl` command issues `GET` requests by default. You can issue `POST` requests using `curl -X POST`. To make it easy to work with our terminal history, we usually use the `-X` option even when issuing `GET` requests. If we want to send a `POST` next time, all we have to change is the method.

HTTP does a bit more under the hood than you can see in the examples here. If you're interested in every last detail that goes over the wire, pass in the `-v` option (e.g., `curl -vX GET`), which will show you the server `curl` tries to connect to, the request headers it sends, and response headers it receives back. Great for debugging!

Let's create a database:

```
curl -X PUT http://127.0.0.1:5984/baseball
```

CouchDB will reply with:

```
{"ok":true}
```

Retrieving the list of databases again shows some useful results this time:

```
curl -X GET http://127.0.0.1:5984/_all_dbs
```

```
["baseball"]
```

We should mention *JavaScript Object Notation (JSON)* here, the data format CouchDB speaks. JSON is a lightweight data interchange format based on JavaScript syntax. Because JSON is natively compatible with JavaScript, your web browser is an ideal client for CouchDB.

Brackets ([ ]) represent ordered lists, and curly braces ({}) represent key/value dictionaries. Keys must be strings, delimited by quotes ("), and values can be strings, numbers, booleans, lists, or key/value dictionaries. For a more detailed description of JSON, see Appendix E.

Let's create another database:

```
curl -X PUT http://127.0.0.1:5984/baseball
```

CouchDB will reply with:

```
{"error":"file_exists","reason":"The database could not be created, the file
already exists."}
```

We already have a database with that name, so CouchDB will respond with an error. Let's try again with a different database name:

```
curl -X PUT http://127.0.0.1:5984/plankton
```

CouchDB will reply with:

```
{"ok":true}
```

Retrieving the list of databases yet again shows some useful results:

```
curl -X GET http://127.0.0.1:5984/_all_dbs
```

CouchDB will respond with:

```
["baseball", "plankton"]
```

To round things off, let's delete the second database:

```
curl -X DELETE http://127.0.0.1:5984/plankton
```

CouchDB will reply with:

```
{"ok":true}
```

The list of databases is now the same as it was before:

```
curl -X GET http://127.0.0.1:5984/_all_dbs
```

CouchDB will respond with:

```
["baseball"]
```

For brevity, we'll skip working with documents, as the next section covers a different and potentially easier way of working with CouchDB that should provide experience with this. As we work through the example, keep in mind that "under the hood" everything is being done by the application exactly as you have been doing here manually. Everything is done using GET, PUT, POST, and DELETE with a URI.

Welcome to Futon

After having seen CouchDB's raw API, let's get our feet wet by playing with Futon, the built-in administration interface. Futon provides full access to all of CouchDB's features and makes it easy to work with some of the more complex ideas involved. With Futon we can create and destroy databases; view and edit documents; compose and run MapReduce views; and trigger replication between databases.

To load Futon in your browser, visit:

```
http://127.0.0.1:5984/_utils/
```

If you're running version 0.9 or later, you should see something similar to Figure 3-1. In later chapters, we'll focus on using CouchDB from server-side languages such as Ruby and Python. As such, this chapter is a great opportunity to showcase an example of natively serving up a dynamic web application using nothing more than CouchDB's integrated web server, something you may wish to do with your own applications.

The first thing we should do with a fresh installation of CouchDB is run the test suite to verify that everything is working properly. This assures us that any problems we may run into aren't due to bothersome issues with our setup. By the same token, failures in the Futon test suite are a red flag, telling us to double-check our installation before attempting to use a potentially broken database server, saving us the confusion when nothing seems to be working quite like we expect!

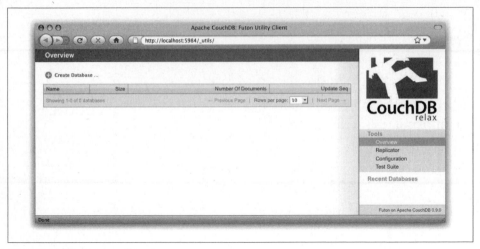

Figure 3-1. The Futon welcome screen

 Some common network configurations cause the replication test to fail when accessed via the `localhost` address. You can fix this by accessing CouchDB via *http://127.0.0.1:5984/_utils/*.

Navigate to the test suite by clicking "Test Suite" on the Futon sidebar, then click "run all" at the top to kick things off. Figure 3-2 shows the Futon test suite running some tests.

Because the test suite is run from the browser, not only does it test that CouchDB is functioning properly, it also verifies that your browser's connection to the database is properly configured, which can be very handy for diagnosing misbehaving proxies or other HTTP middleware.

 If the test suite has an inordinate number of failures, you'll need to see the troubleshooting section in Appendix D for the next steps to fix your installation.

Now that the test suite is finished, you've verified that your CouchDB installation is successful and you're ready to see what else Futon has to offer.

Your First Database and Document

Creating a database in Futon is simple. From the overview page, click "Create Database." When asked for a name, enter `hello-world` and click the Create button.

After your database has been created, Futon will display a list of all its documents. This list will start out empty (Figure 3-3), so let's create our first document. Click the "Create

Figure 3-2. The Futon test suite running some tests

Document" link and then the Create button in the pop up. Make sure to leave the document ID blank, and CouchDB will generate a UUID for you.

For demoing purposes, having CouchDB assign a UUID is fine. When you write your first programs, we recommend assigning your own UUIDs. If your rely on the server to generate the UUID and you end up making two POST requests because the first POST request bombed out, you might generate two docs and never find out about the first one because only the second one will be reported back. Generating your own UUIDs makes sure that you'll never end up with duplicate documents.

Futon will display the newly created document, with its `_id` and `_rev` as the only fields. To create a new field, click the "Add Field" button. We'll call the new field `hello`. Click the green check icon (or hit the Enter key) to finalize creating the `hello` field. Double-click the `hello` field's value (default `null`) to edit it.

If you try to enter `world` as the new value, you'll get an error when you click the value's green check icon. CouchDB values must be entered as valid JSON. Instead, enter `"world"` (with quotes) because this is a valid JSON string. You should have no problems saving it. You can experiment with other JSON values; e.g., `[1, 2, "c"]` or `{"foo":"bar"}`. Once you've entered your values into the document, make a note of its `_rev` attribute and click "Save Document." The result should look like Figure 3-4.

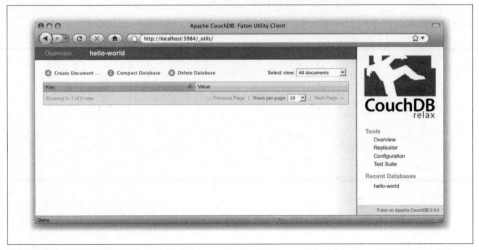

Figure 3-3. An empty database in Futon

Figure 3-4. A "hello world" document in Futon

You'll notice that the document's _rev has changed. We'll go into more detail about this in later chapters, but for now, the important thing to note is that _rev acts like a safety feature when saving a document. As long as you and CouchDB agree on the most recent _rev of a document, you can successfully save your changes.

Futon also provides a way to display the underlying JSON data, which can be more compact and easier to read, depending on what sort of data you are dealing with. To see the JSON version of our "hello world" document, click the Source tab. The result should look like Figure 3-5.

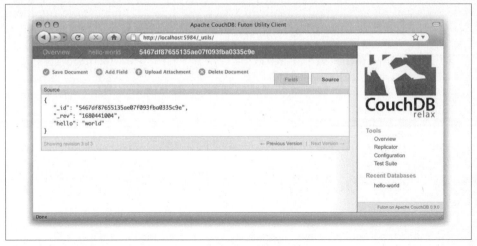

Figure 3-5. The JSON source of a "hello world" document in Futon

Running a Query Using MapReduce

Traditional relational databases allow you to run any queries you like as long as your data is structured correctly. In contrast, CouchDB uses predefined *map* and *reduce* functions in a style known as MapReduce. These functions provide great flexibility because they can adapt to variations in document structure, and indexes for each document can be computed independently and in parallel. The combination of a map and a reduce function is called a *view* in CouchDB terminology.

> For experienced relational database programmers, MapReduce can take some getting used to. Rather than declaring which rows from which tables to include in a result set and depending on the database to determine the most efficient way to run the query, reduce queries are based on simple range requests against the indexes generated by your map functions.

Map functions are called once with each document as the argument. The function can choose to skip the document altogether or *emit* one or more view rows as key/value pairs. Map functions may not depend on any information outside of the document. This independence is what allows CouchDB views to be generated incrementally and in parallel.

CouchDB views are stored as rows that are kept sorted by key. This makes retrieving data from a range of keys efficient even when there are thousands or millions of rows. When writing CouchDB map functions, your primary goal is to build an index that stores related data under nearby keys.

Before we can run an example MapReduce view, we'll need some data to run it on. We'll create documents carrying the price of various supermarket items as found at different stores. Let's create documents for apples, oranges, and bananas. (Allow CouchDB to generate the `_id` and `_rev` fields.) Use Futon to create documents that have a final JSON structure that looks like this:

```
{
    "_id" : "bc2a41170621c326ec68382f846d5764",
    "_rev" : "2612672603",
    "item" : "apple",
    "prices" : {
        "Fresh Mart" : 1.59,
        "Price Max" : 5.99,
        "Apples Express" : 0.79
    }
}
```

This document should look like Figure 3-6 when entered into Futon.

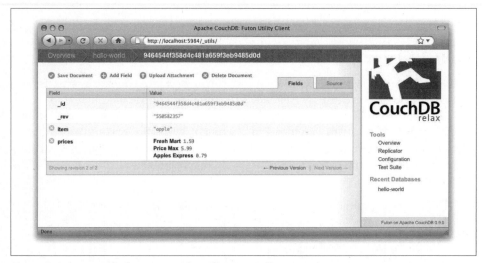

Figure 3-6. An example document with apple prices in Futon

OK, now that that's done, let's create the document for oranges:

```
{
    "_id" : "bc2a41170621c326ec68382f846d5764",
    "_rev" : "2612672603",
    "item" : "orange",
    "prices" : {
        "Fresh Mart" : 1.99,
        "Price Max" : 3.19,
        "Citrus Circus" : 1.09
    }
}
```

And finally, the document for bananas:

```
{
    "_id" : "bc2a41170621c326ec68382f846d5764",
    "_rev" : "2612672603",
    "item" : "banana",
    "prices" : {
        "Fresh Mart" : 1.99,
        "Price Max" : 0.79,
        "Banana Montana" : 4.22
    }
}
```

Imagine we're catering a big luncheon, but the client is very price-sensitive. To find the lowest prices, we're going to create our first view, which shows each fruit sorted by price. Click "hello-world" to return to the hello-world overview, and then from the "select view" menu choose "Temporary view…" to create a new view. The result should look something like Figure 3-7.

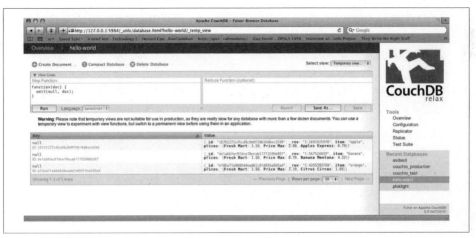

Figure 3-7. A temporary view in Futon

Edit the map function, on the left, so that it looks like the following:

```
function(doc) {
    var store, price, value;
    if (doc.item && doc.prices) {
        for (store in doc.prices) {
            price = doc.prices[store];
            value = [doc.item, store];
            emit(price, value);
        }
    }
}
```

This is a *JavaScript* function that CouchDB runs for each of our documents as it computes the view. We'll leave the reduce function blank for the time being.

Click "Run" and you should see result rows like in Figure 3-8, with the various items sorted by price. This map function could be even more useful if it grouped the items by type so that all the prices for bananas were next to each other in the result set. CouchDB's key sorting system allows any valid JSON object as a key. In this case, we'll emit an array of [`item, price`] so that CouchDB groups by item type and price.

Figure 3-8. The results of running a view in Futon

Let's modify the view function so that it looks like this:

```
function(doc) {
    var store, price, key;
    if (doc.item && doc.prices) {
        for (store in doc.prices) {
            price = doc.prices[store];
            key = [doc.item, price];
            emit(key, store);
        }
    }
}
```

Here, we first check that the document has the fields we want to use. CouchDB recovers gracefully from a few isolated map function failures, but when a map function fails regularly (due to a missing required field or other JavaScript exception), CouchDB shuts off its indexing to prevent any further resource usage. For this reason, it's important to check for the existence of any fields before you use them. In this case, our map function will skip the first "hello world" document we created without emitting any rows or encountering any errors. The result of this query should look like Figure 3-9.

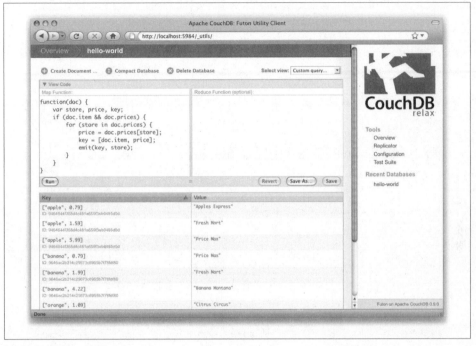

Figure 3-9. The results of running a view after grouping by item type and price

Once we know we've got a document with an item type and some prices, we iterate over the item's prices and emit key/values pairs. The key is an array of the item and the price, and forms the basis for CouchDB's sorted index. In this case, the value is the name of the store where the item can be found for the listed price.

View rows are sorted by their keys—in this example, first by item, then by price. This method of complex sorting is at the heart of creating useful indexes with CouchDB.

 MapReduce can be challenging, especially if you've spent years working with relational databases. The important things to keep in mind are that map functions give you an opportunity to sort your data using any key you choose, and that CouchDB's design is focused on providing fast, efficient access to data within a range of keys.

Triggering Replication

Futon can trigger replication between two local databases, between a local and remote database, or even between two remote databases. We'll show you how to replicate data from one local database to another, which is a simple way of making backups of your databases as we're working through the examples.

First we'll need to create an empty database to be the target of replication. Return to the overview and create a database called `hello-replication`. Now click "Replicator" in the sidebar and choose `hello-world` as the source and `hello-replication` as the target. Click "Replicate" to replicate your database. The result should look something like Figure 3-10.

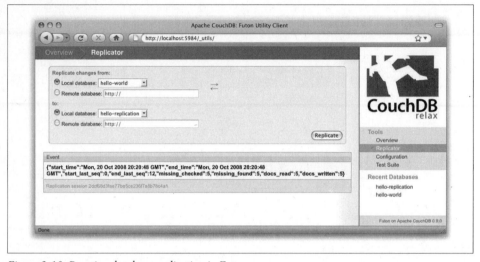

Figure 3-10. Running database replication in Futon

 For larger databases, replication can take much longer. It is important to leave the browser window open while replication is taking place. As an alternative, you can trigger replication via `curl` or some other HTTP client that can handle long-running connections. If your client closes the connection before replication finishes, you'll have to retrigger it. Luckily, CouchDB's replication can take over from where it left off instead of starting from scratch.

Wrapping Up

Now that you've seen most of Futon's features, you'll be prepared to dive in and inspect your data as we build our example application in the next few chapters. Futon's pure JavaScript approach to managing CouchDB shows how it's possible to build a fully featured web application using only CouchDB's HTTP API and integrated web server.

But before we get there, we'll have another look at CouchDB's HTTP API—now with a magnifying glass. Let's *curl* on the couch and relax.

CHAPTER 4

The Core API

This chapter explores the CouchDB in minute detail. It shows all the nitty-gritty and clever bits. We show you best practices and guide you around common pitfalls.

We start out by revisiting the basic operations we ran in the last chapter, looking behind the scenes. We also show what Futon needs to do behind its user interface to give us the nice features we saw earlier.

This chapter is both an introduction to the core CouchDB API as well as a reference. If you can't remember how to run a particular request or why some parameters are needed, you can always come back here and look things up (we are probably the heaviest users of this chapter).

While explaining the API bits and pieces, we sometimes need to take a larger detour to explain the reasoning for a particular request. This is a good opportunity for us to tell you why CouchDB works the way it does.

The API can be subdivided into the following sections. We'll explore them individually:

- Server
- Databases
- Documents
- Replication

Server

This one is basic and simple. It can serve as a sanity check to see if CouchDB is running at all. It can also act as a safety guard for libraries that require a certain version of CouchDB. We're using the `curl` utility again:

```
curl http://127.0.0.1:5984/
```

CouchDB replies, all excited to get going:

```
{"couchdb":"Welcome","version":"0.10.1"}
```

You get back a JSON string, that, if parsed into a native object or data structure of your programming language, gives you access to the welcome string and version information.

This is not terribly useful, but it illustrates nicely the way CouchDB behaves. You send an HTTP request and you receive a JSON string in the HTTP response as a result.

Databases

Now let's do something a little more useful: create databases. For the strict, CouchDB is a *database management system* (DMS). That means it can hold multiple *databases*. A database is a bucket that holds "related data." We'll explore later what that means exactly. In practice, the terminology is overlapping—often people refer to a DMS as "a database" and also a database within the DMS as "a database." We might follow that slight oddity, so don't get confused by it. In general, it should be clear from the context if we are talking about the whole of CouchDB or a single database within CouchDB.

Now let's make one! We want to store our favorite music albums, and we creatively give our database the name albums. Note that we're now using the -X option again to tell curl to send a PUT request instead of the default GET request:

```
curl -X PUT http://127.0.0.1:5984/albums
```

CouchDB replies:

```
{"ok":true}
```

That's it. You created a database and CouchDB told you that all went well. What happens if you try to create a database that already exists? Let's try to create that database again:

```
curl -X PUT http://127.0.0.1:5984/albums
```

CouchDB replies:

```
{"error":"file_exists","reason":"The database could not be created, the file
already exists."}
```

We get back an error. This is pretty convenient. We also learn a little bit about how CouchDB works. CouchDB stores each database in a single file. Very simple. This has some consequences down the road, but we'll skip the details for now and explore the underlying storage system in Appendix F.

Let's create another database, this time with curl's -v (for "verbose") option. The verbose option tells curl to show us not only the essentials—the HTTP response body—but all the underlying request and response details:

```
curl -vX PUT http://127.0.0.1:5984/albums-backup
```

curl elaborates:

```
* About to connect() to 127.0.0.1 port 5984 (#0)
*   Trying 127.0.0.1... connected
```

```
* Connected to 127.0.0.1 (127.0.0.1) port 5984 (#0)
> PUT /albums-backup HTTP/1.1
> User-Agent: curl/7.16.3 (powerpc-apple-darwin9.0) libcurl/7.16.3 OpenSSL/0.9.7l
zlib/1.2.3
> Host: 127.0.0.1:5984
> Accept: */*
>
< HTTP/1.1 201 Created
< Server: CouchDB/0.9.0 (Erlang OTP/R12B)
< Date: Sun, 05 Jul 2009 22:48:28 GMT
< Content-Type: text/plain;charset=utf-8
< Content-Length: 12
< Cache-Control: must-revalidate
<
{"ok":true}
* Connection #0 to host 127.0.0.1 left intact
* Closing connection #0
```

What a mouthful. Let's step through this line by line to understand what's going on and find out what's important. Once you've seen this output a few times, you'll be able to spot the important bits more easily.

```
* About to connect() to 127.0.0.1 port 5984 (#0)
```

This is `curl` telling us that it is going to establish a *TCP* connection to the CouchDB server we specified in our request URI. Not at all important, except when debugging networking issues.

```
*    Trying 127.0.0.1... connected
* Connected to 127.0.0.1 (127.0.0.1) port 5984 (#0)
```

`curl` tells us it successfully connected to CouchDB. Again, not important if you aren't trying to find problems with your network.

The following lines are prefixed with > and < characters. > means the line was sent to CouchDB verbatim (without the actual >). < means the line was sent back to `curl` by CouchDB.

```
> PUT /albums-backup HTTP/1.1
```

This initiates an HTTP request. Its *method* is PUT, the *URI* is /albums-backup, and the HTTP version is HTTP/1.1. There is also HTTP/1.0, which is simpler in some cases, but for all practical reasons you should be using HTTP/1.1.

Next, we see a number of *request headers*. These are used to provide additional details about the request to CouchDB.

```
> User-Agent: curl/7.16.3 (powerpc-apple-darwin9.0) libcurl/7.16.3 OpenSSL/0.9.7l
zlib/1.2.3
```

The User-Agent header tell CouchDB which piece of client software is doing the HTTP request. We don't learn anything new: it's `curl`. This header is often useful in web development when there are known errors in client implementations that a server might want to prepare the response for. It also helps to determine which platform a user is on. This information can be used for technical and statistical reasons. For CouchDB, the User-Agent header is irrelevant.

```
> Host: 127.0.0.1:5984
```

The Host header is required by HTTP 1.1. It tells the server the hostname that came with the request.

```
> Accept: */*
```

The Accept header tells CouchDB that curl accepts any media type. We'll look into why this is useful a little later.

```
>
```

An empty line denotes that the request headers are now finished and the rest of the request contains data we're sending to the server. In this case, we're not sending any data, so the rest of the curl output is dedicated to the HTTP response.

```
< HTTP/1.1 201 Created
```

The first line of CouchDB's HTTP response includes the HTTP version information (again, to acknowledge that the requested version could be processed), an HTTP *status code*, and a *status code message*. Different requests trigger different response codes. There's a whole range of them telling the client (curl in our case) what effect the request had on the server. Or, if an error occurred, what kind of error. RFC 2616 (the HTTP 1.1 specification) defines clear behavior for response codes. CouchDB fully follows the RFC.

The *201 Created* status code tells the client that the resource the request was made against was successfully created. No surprise here, but if you remember that we got an error message when we tried to create this database twice, you now know that this response could include a different response code. Acting upon responses based on response codes is a common practice. For example, all response codes of 400 or larger tell you that some error occurred. If you want to shortcut your logic and immediately deal with the error, you could just check a >= 400 response code.

```
< Server: CouchDB/0.10.1 (Erlang OTP/R13B)
```

The Server header is good for diagnostics. It tells us which CouchDB version and which underlying Erlang version we are talking to. In general, you can ignore this header, but it is good to know it's there if you need it.

```
< Date: Sun, 05 Jul 2009 22:48:28 GMT
```

The Date header tells you the time of the server. Since client and server time are not necessary synchronized, this header is purely informational. You shouldn't build any critical application logic on top of this!

```
< Content-Type: text/plain;charset=utf-8
```

The Content-Type header tells you which MIME type the HTTP response body is and its encoding. We already know CouchDB returns JSON strings. The appropriate

Content-Type header is application/json. Why do we see text/plain? This is where pragmatism wins over purity. Sending an application/json Content-Type header will make a browser offer you the returned JSON for download instead of just displaying it. Since it is extremely useful to be able to test CouchDB from a browser, CouchDB sends a text/plain content type, so all browsers will display the JSON as text.

There are some browser extensions that make your browser JSON-aware, but they are not installed by default.

Do you remember the Accept request header and how it is set to */* -> */* to express interest in any MIME type? If you send Accept: application/json in your request, CouchDB knows that you can deal with a pure JSON response with the proper Content-Type header and will use it instead of text/plain.

```
< Content-Length: 12
```

The Content-Length header simply tells us how many bytes the response body has.

```
< Cache-Control: must-revalidate
```

This Cache-Control header tells you, or any proxy server between CouchDB and you, not to cache this response.

```
<
```

This empty line tells us we're done with the response headers and what follows now is the response body.

```
{"ok":true}
```

We've seen this before.

```
* Connection #0 to host 127.0.0.1 left intact
* Closing connection #0
```

The last two lines are curl telling us that it kept the TCP connection it opened in the beginning open for a moment, but then closed it after it received the entire response.

Throughout the book, we'll show more requests with the -v option, but we'll omit some of the headers we've seen here and include only those that are important for the particular request.

Creating databases is all fine, but how do we get rid of one? Easy—just change the HTTP method:

```
> curl -vX DELETE http://127.0.0.1:5984/albums-backup
```

This deletes a CouchDB database. The request will remove the file that the database contents are stored in. There is no "Are you sure?" safety net or any "Empty the trash" magic you've got to do to delete a database. Use this command with care. Your data will be deleted without a chance to bring it back easily if you don't have a backup copy.

This section went knee-deep into HTTP and set the stage for discussing the rest of the core CouchDB API. Next stop: documents.

Documents

Documents are CouchDB's central data structure. The idea behind a document is, unsurprisingly, that of a real-world document—a sheet of paper such as an invoice, a recipe, or a business card. We already learned that CouchDB uses the JSON format to store documents. Let's see how this storing works at the lowest level.

Each document in CouchDB has an *ID*. This ID is unique per database. You are free to choose any string to be the ID, but for best results we recommend a UUID (or GUID), i.e., a Universally (or Globally) Unique IDentifier. UUIDs are random numbers that have such a low collision probability that everybody can make thousands of UUIDs a minute for millions of years without ever creating a duplicate. This is a great way to ensure two independent people cannot create two different documents with the same ID. Why should you care what somebody else is doing? For one, that somebody else could be you at a later time or on a different computer; secondly, CouchDB replication lets you share documents with others and using UUIDs ensures that it all works. But more on that later; let's make some documents:

```
curl -X PUT http://127.0.0.1:5984/albums/6e1295ed6c29495e54cc05947f18c8af \
-d '{"title":"There is Nothing Left to Lose","artist":"Foo Fighters"}'
```

CouchDB replies:

```
{"ok":true,"id":"6e1295ed6c29495e54cc05947f18c8af","rev":"1-2902191555"}
```

The `curl` command appears complex, but let's break it down. First, `-X PUT` tells `curl` to make a PUT request. It is followed by the URL that specifies your CouchDB IP address and port. The resource part of the URL `/albums/6e1295ed6c29495e54cc05947f18c8af` specifies the location of a document inside our `albums` database. The wild collection of numbers and characters is a UUID. This UUID is your document's ID. Finally, the `-d` flag tells `curl` to use the following string as the body for the PUT request. The string is a simple JSON structure including `title` and `artist` attributes with their respective values.

If you don't have a UUID handy, you can ask CouchDB to give you one (in fact, that is what we did just now without showing you). Simply send a GET request to /_uuids:

```
curl -X GET http://127.0.0.1:5984/_uuids
```

CouchDB replies:

```
{"uuids":["6e1295ed6c29495e54cc05947f18c8af"]}
```

Voilá, a UUID. If you need more than one, you can pass in the `?count=10` HTTP parameter to request 10 UUIDs, or really, any number you need.

To double-check that CouchDB isn't lying about having saved your document (it usually doesn't), try to retrieve it by sending a GET request:

```
curl -X GET http://127.0.0.1:5984/albums/6e1295ed6c29495e54cc05947f18c8af
```

We hope you see a pattern here. Everything in CouchDB has an address, a URI, and you use the different HTTP methods to operate on these URIs.

CouchDB replies:

```
{"_id":"6e1295ed6c29495e54cc05947f18c8af",
    "_rev":"1-2902191555",
    "title":"There is Nothing Left to Lose",
    "artist":"Foo Fighters"}
```

This looks a lot like the document you asked CouchDB to save, which is good. But you should notice that CouchDB added two fields to your JSON structure. The first is _id, which holds the UUID we asked CouchDB to save our document under. We always know the ID of a document if it is included, which is very convenient.

The second field is _rev. It stands for *revision*.

Revisions

If you want to change a document in CouchDB, you don't tell it to go and find a field in a specific document and insert a new value. Instead, you load the full document out of CouchDB, make your changes in the JSON structure (or object, when you are doing actual programming), and save the entire new revision (or version) of that document back into CouchDB. Each revision is identified by a new _rev value.

If you want to update or delete a document, CouchDB expects you to include the _rev field of the revision you wish to change. When CouchDB accepts the change, it will generate a new revision number. This mechanism ensures that, in case somebody else made a change unbeknownst to you before you got to request the document update, CouchDB will not accept your update because you are likely to overwrite data you didn't know existed. Or simplified: whoever saves a change to a document first, wins. Let's see what happens if we don't provide a _rev field (which is equivalent to providing a outdated value):

```
curl -X PUT http://127.0.0.1:5984/albums/6e1295ed6c29495e54cc05947f18c8af \
-d '{"title":"There is Nothing Left to Lose","artist":"Foo Fighters","year":"1997"}'
```

CouchDB replies:

```
{"error":"conflict","reason":"Document update conflict."}
```

If you see this, add the latest revision number of your document to the JSON structure:

```
curl -X PUT http://127.0.0.1:5984/albums/6e1295ed6c29495e54cc05947f18c8af \
-d '{"_rev":"1-2902191555","title":"There is Nothing Left to Lose",
"artist":"Foo Fighters","year":"1997"}'
```

Now you see why it was handy that CouchDB returned that _rev when we made the initial request. CouchDB replies:

```
{"ok":true,"id":"6e1295ed6c29495e54cc05947f18c8af","rev":"2-2739352689"}
```

CouchDB accepted your write and also generated a new revision number. The revision number is the md5 hash of the transport representation of a document with an N- prefix denoting the number of times a document got updated. This is useful for replication. See Chapter 17 for more information.

There are multiple reasons why CouchDB uses this revision system, which is also called Multi-Version Concurrency Control (MVCC). They all work hand-in-hand, and this is a good opportunity to explain some of them.

One of the aspects of the HTTP protocol that CouchDB uses is that it is *stateless*. What does that mean? When talking to CouchDB you need to *make requests*. Making a request includes opening a network connection to CouchDB, exchanging bytes, and closing the connection. This is done every time you make a request. Other protocols allow you to open a connection, exchange bytes, keep the connection open, exchange more bytes later—maybe depending on the bytes you exchanged at the beginning—and eventually close the connection. Holding a connection open for later use requires the server to do extra work. One common pattern is that for the lifetime of a connection, the client has a consistent and static view of the data on the server. Managing huge amounts of parallel connections is a significant amount of work. HTTP connections are usually short-lived, and making the same guarantees is a lot easier. As a result, CouchDB can handle many more concurrent connections.

Another reason CouchDB uses MVCC is that this model is simpler conceptually and, as a consequence, easier to program. CouchDB uses less code to make this work, and less code is always good because the ratio of defects per lines of code is static.

The revision system also has positive effects on replication and storage mechanisms, but we'll explore these later in the book.

 The terms *version* and *revision* might sound familiar (if you are programming without version control, drop this book right now and start learning one of the popular systems). Using new versions for document changes works a lot like version control, but there's an important difference: CouchDB does *not* guarantee that older versions are kept around.

Documents in Detail

Now let's have a closer look at our document creation requests with the `curl -v` flag that was helpful when we explored the database API earlier. This is also a good opportunity to create more documents that we can use in later examples.

We'll add some more of our favorite music albums. Get a fresh UUID from the /_uuids resource. If you don't remember how that works, you can look it up a few pages back.

```
curl -vX PUT http://127.0.0.1:5984/albums/70b50bfa0a4b3aed1f8aff9e92dc16a0 \
-d '{"title":"Blackened Sky","artist":"Biffy Clyro","year":2002}'
```

 By the way, if you happen to know more information about your favorite albums, don't hesitate to add more properties. And don't worry about not knowing all the information for all the albums. CouchDB's schema-less documents can contain whatever you know. After all, you should relax and not worry about data.

Now with the -v option, CouchDB's reply (with only the important bits shown) looks like this:

```
> PUT /albums/70b50bfa0a4b3aed1f8aff9e92dc16a0 HTTP/1.1
>
< HTTP/1.1 201 Created
< Location: http://127.0.0.1:5984/albums/70b50bfa0a4b3aed1f8aff9e92dc16a0
< Etag: "1-2248288203"
<
{"ok":true,"id":"70b50bfa0a4b3aed1f8aff9e92dc16a0","rev":"1-2248288203"}
```

We're getting back the 201 Created HTTP status code in the response headers, as we saw earlier when we created a database. The Location header gives us a full URL to our newly created document. And there's a new header. An Etag in HTTP-speak identifies a specific version of a resource. In this case, it identifies a specific version (the first one) of our new document. Sound familiar? Yes, conceptually, an Etag is the same as a CouchDB document revision number, and it shouldn't come as a surprise that CouchDB uses revision numbers for Etags. Etags are useful for caching infrastructures. We'll learn how to use them in Chapter 8.

Attachments

CouchDB documents can have attachments just like an email message can have attachments. An attachment is identified by a name and includes its MIME type (or Content-Type) and the number of bytes the attachment contains. Attachments can be any data. It is easiest to think about attachments as files attached to a document. These files can be text, images, Word documents, music, or movie files. Let's make one.

Attachments get their own URL where you can upload data. Say we want to add the album artwork to the 6e1295ed6c29495e54cc05947f18c8af document ("There is Nothing Left to Lose"), and let's also say the artwork is in a file *artwork.jpg* in the current directory:

```
> curl -vX PUT http://127.0.0.1:5984/albums/6e1295ed6c29495e54cc05947f18c8af/ \
artwork.jpg?rev=2-2739352689 --data-binary @artwork.jpg -H "Content-Type: image/jpg"
```

The `-d@` option tells `curl` to read a file's contents into the HTTP request body. We're using the `-H` option to tell CouchDB that we're uploading a JPEG file. CouchDB will keep this information around and will send the appropriate header when requesting this attachment; in case of an image like this, a browser will render the image instead of offering you the data for download. This will come in handy later. Note that you need to provide the current revision number of the document you're attaching the artwork to, just as if you would update the document. Because, after all, attaching some data is changing the document.

You should now see your artwork image if you point your browser to *http://127.0.0.1:5984/albums/6e1295ed6c29495e54cc05947f18c8af/artwork.jpg*.

If you request the document again, you'll see a new member:

```
curl http://127.0.0.1:5984/albums/6e1295ed6c29495e54cc05947f18c8af
```

CouchDB replies:

```
{"_id":"6e1295ed6c29495e54cc05947f18c8af","_rev":"3-131533518","title":
"There is Nothing Left to Lose","artist":"Foo Fighters","year":"1997","_attachments":
{"artwork.jpg":{"stub":true,"content_type":"image/jpg","length":52450}}}
```

`_attachments` is a list of keys and values where the values are JSON objects containing the attachment metadata. `stub=true` tells us that this entry is just the metadata. If we use the `?attachments=true` HTTP option when requesting this document, we'd get a Base64-encoded string containing the attachment data.

We'll have a look at more document request options later as we explore more features of CouchDB, such as replication, which is the next topic.

Replication

CouchDB replication is a mechanism to synchronize databases. Much like `rsync` synchronizes two directories locally or over a network, replication synchronizes two databases locally or remotely.

In a simple POST request, you tell CouchDB the *source* and the *target* of a replication and CouchDB will figure out which documents and new document revisions are on *source* that are not yet on *target*, and will proceed to move the missing documents and revisions over.

We'll take an in-depth look at replication later in the book; in this chapter, we'll just show you how to use it.

First, we'll create a target database. Note that CouchDB won't automatically create a target database for you, and will return a replication failure if the target doesn't exist (likewise for the source, but that mistake isn't as easy to make):

```
curl -X PUT http://127.0.0.1:5984/albums-replica
```

Now we can use the database `albums-replica` as a replication target:

```
curl -vX POST http://127.0.0.1:5984/_replicate \
-d '{"source":"albums","target":"albums-replica"}'
```

 As of version 0.11, CouchDB supports the option `"create_tar get":true` placed in the JSON POSTed to the `_replicate` URL. It implicitly creates the target database if it doesn't exist.

CouchDB replies (this time we formatted the output so you can read it more easily):

```
{
  "history": [
    {
      "start_last_seq": 0,
      "missing_found": 2,
      "docs_read": 2,
      "end_last_seq": 5,
      "missing_checked": 2,
      "docs_written": 2,
      "doc_write_failures": 0,
      "end_time": "Sat, 11 Jul 2009 17:36:21 GMT",
      "start_time": "Sat, 11 Jul 2009 17:36:20 GMT"
    }
  ],
  "source_last_seq": 5,
  "session_id": "924e75e914392343de89c99d29d06671",
  "ok": true
}
```

CouchDB maintains a *session history* of replications. The response for a replication request contains the history entry for this *replication session*. It is also worth noting that the request for replication will stay *open* until replication closes. If you have a lot of documents, it'll take a while until they are all replicated and you won't get back the replication response until all documents are replicated. It is important to note that replication replicates the database only as it was at the point in time when replication was started. So, any additions, modifications, or deletions subsequent to the start of replication will not be replicated.

We'll punt on the details again—the `"ok": true` at the end tells us all went well. If you now have a look at the `albums-replica` database, you should see all the documents that you created in the `albums` database. Neat, eh?

What you just did is called *local replication* in CouchDB terms. You created a local copy of a database. This is useful for backups or to keep snapshots of a specific state of your data around for later. You might want to do this if you are developing your applications but want to be able to roll back to a stable version of your code and data.

There are more types of replication useful in other situations. The `source` and `target` members of our replication request are actually links (like in HTML) and so far we've seen links relative to the server we're working on (hence *local*). You can also specify a remote database as the target:

```
curl -vX POST http://127.0.0.1:5984/_replicate \
-d '{"source":"albums","target":"http://127.0.0.1:5984/albums-replica"}'
```

Using a local **source** and a remote **target** database is called *push replication*. We're pushing changes to a remote server.

 Since we don't have a second CouchDB server around just yet, we'll just use the absolute address of our single server, but you should be able to infer from this that you can put any remote server in there.

This is great for sharing local changes with remote servers or buddies next door.

You can also use a remote **source** and a local **target** to do a *pull replication*. This is great for getting the latest changes from a server that is used by others:

```
curl -vX POST http://127.0.0.1:5984/_replicate \
-d '{"source":"http://127.0.0.1:5984/albums-replica","target":"albums"}'
```

Finally, you can run *remote replication*, which is mostly useful for management operations:

```
curl -vX POST http://127.0.0.1:5984/_replicate \
-d '{"source":"http://127.0.0.1:5984/albums",
"target":"http://127.0.0.1:5984/albums-replica"}'
```

CouchDB and REST

CouchDB prides itself on having a *RESTful API*, but these replication requests don't look very RESTy to the trained eye. What's up with that? While CouchDB's core database, document, and attachment API are RESTful, not all of CouchDB's API is. The replication API is one example. There are more, as we'll see later in the book.

Why are there RESTful and non-RESTful APIs mixed up here? Have the developers been too lazy to go REST all the way? Remember, REST is an architectural style that lends itself to certain architectures (such as the CouchDB document API). But it is not a one-size-fits-all. Triggering an event like replication does not make a whole lot of sense in the REST world. It is more like a traditional remote procedure call. And there is nothing wrong with this.

We very much believe in the "use the right tool for the job" philosophy, and REST does not fit every job. For support, we refer to Leonard Richardson and Sam Ruby who wrote *RESTful Web Services* (O'Reilly), as they share our view.

Wrapping Up

This is still not the full CouchDB API, but we discussed the essentials in great detail. We're going to fill in the blanks as we go. For now, we believe you're ready to start building CouchDB applications.

Developing with CouchDB

Design Documents

Design documents are a special type of CouchDB document that contains application code. Because it runs inside a database, the application API is highly structured. We've seen JavaScript views and other functions in the previous chapters. In this section, we'll take a look at the function APIs, and talk about how functions in a design document are related within applications.

This part (Part II, Chapters Chapter 5 through Chapter 9) lays the foundation for Part III, where we take what we've learned and build a small blog application to further develop an understanding of how CouchDB applications are built. The application is called Sofa, and on a few occasions we discuss it this part. If you are unclear on what we are referring to, do not worry, we'll get to it in Part III.

Document Modeling

In our experience, there are two main kinds of documents. The first kind is like something a word processor would save, or a user profile. With that sort of data, you want to denormalize as much as you possibly can. Basically, you want to be able to load the document in one request and get something that makes sense enough to display.

A technique exists for creating "virtual" documents by using views to collate data together. You could use this to store each attribute of your user profiles in a different document, but I wouldn't recommend it. Virtual documents are useful in cases where the presented view will be created by merging the work of different authors; for instance, the reference example, a blog post, and its comments in one query. A blog post titled "CouchDB Joins," by Christopher Lenz, covers this in more detail.[*]

This virtual document idea takes us to the other kind of document—the event log. Use this in cases where you don't trust user input or where you need to trigger an asynchronous job. This records the user action as an event, so only minimal validation needs

---

[*] *http://www.cmlenz.net/archives/2007/10/couchdb-joins*

to occur at save time. It's when you load the document for further work that you'd check for complex relational-style constraints.

You can treat documents as state machines, with a combination of user input and background processing managing document state. You'd use a view by state to pull out the relevant document—changing its state would move it in the view.

This approach is also useful for logging—combined with the `batch=ok` performance hint, CouchDB should make a fine log store, and reduce views are ideal for finding things like average response time or highly active users.

The Query Server

CouchDB's default query server (the software package that executes design document functions) is written in JavaScript, but there are views servers available for nearly any language you can imagine. Implementing a new language is a matter of handling a few JSON commands from a simple line-based program.

In this section, we'll review existing functionality like MapReduce views, update validation functions, and show and list transforms. We'll also briefly describe capabilities available on CouchDB's roadmap, like replication filters, update handlers for parsing non-JSON input, and a rewrite handler for making application URLs more palatable. Since CouchDB is an open source project, we can't really say when each planned feature will become available, but it's our hope that everything described here is available by the time you read this. We'll make it clear in the text when we're talking about things that aren't yet in the CouchDB trunk.

Applications Are Documents

CouchDB is designed to work best when there is a one-to-one correspondence between applications and design documents.

A *design document* is a CouchDB document with an `id` that begins with `_design/`. For instance, the example blog application, Sofa, is stored in a design document with the ID `_design/sofa` (see Figure 5-1). Design documents are just like any other CouchDB document—they replicate along with the other documents in their database and track edit conflicts with the `rev` parameter.

As we've seen, design documents are normal JSON documents, denoted by the fact that their DocID is prefixed with `_design/`.

CouchDB looks for views and other application functions here. The static HTML pages of our application are served as attachments to the design document. Views and validations, however, aren't stored as attachments; rather, they are directly included in the design document's JSON body.

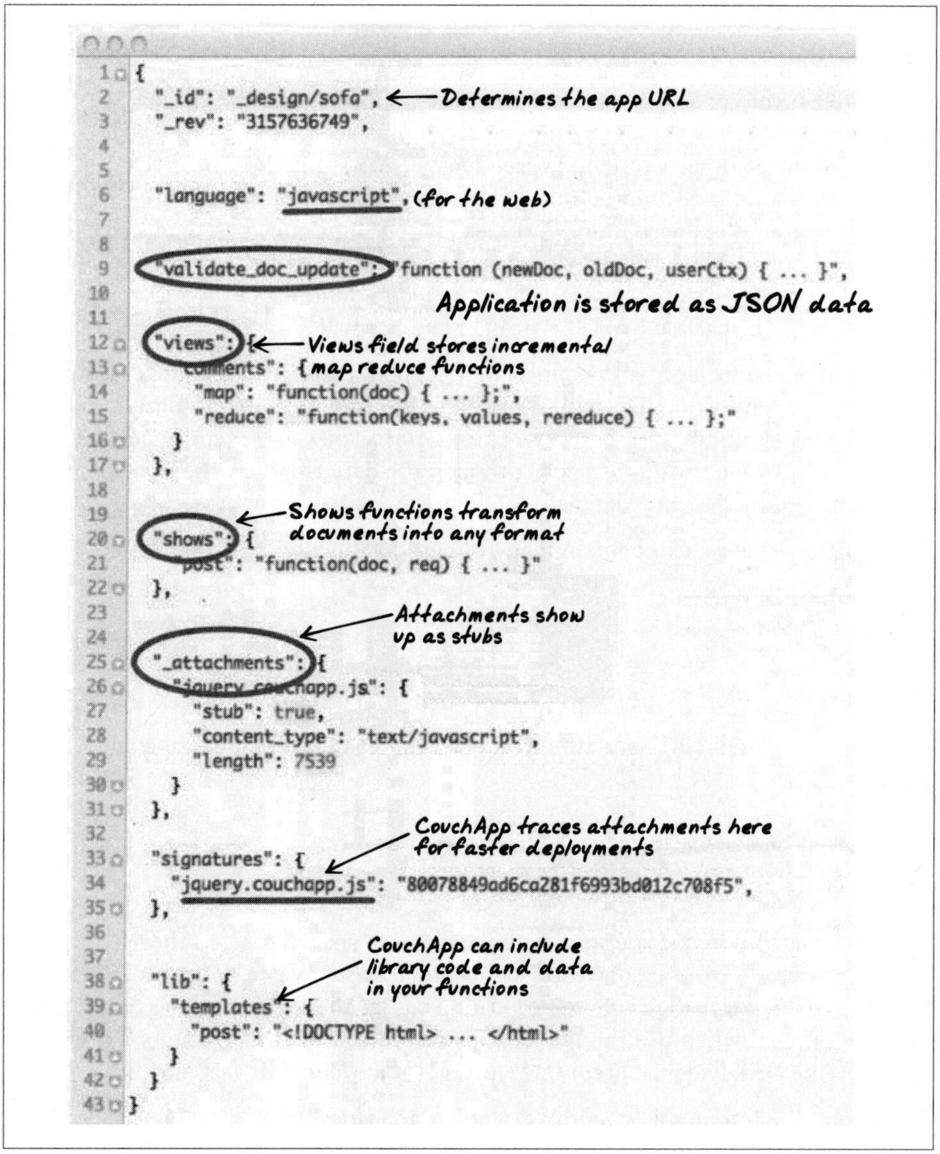

```
1  {
2    "_id": "_design/sofa",    ← Determines the app URL
3    "_rev": "3157636749",
4
5
6    "language": "javascript", (for the web)
7
8
9    "validate_doc_update": "function (newDoc, oldDoc, userCtx) { ... }",
10
11                    Application is stored as JSON data
12   "views": {    ← Views field stores incremental
13     "recents": { map reduce functions
14       "map": "function(doc) { ... };",
15       "reduce": "function(keys, values, rereduce) { ... };"
16     }
17   },
18
19                 Shows functions transform
20   "shows": {    documents into any format
21     "post": "function(doc, req) { ... }"
22   },
23
24                 Attachments show
25   "_attachments": {    up as stubs
26     "jquery.couchapp.js": {
27       "stub": true,
28       "content_type": "text/javascript",
29       "length": 7539
30     }
31   },
32                     CouchApp traces attachments here
33   "signatures": {    for faster deployments
34     "jquery.couchapp.js": "80078849ad6ca281f6993bd012c708f5",
35   },
36
37                    CouchApp can include
38   "lib": {    library code and data
39     "templates": {    in your functions
40       "post": "<!DOCTYPE html> ... </html>"
41     }
42   }
43 }
```

Figure 5-1. Anatomy of our design document

CouchDB's MapReduce queries are stored in the **views** field. This is how Futon displays and allows you to edit MapReduce queries. View indexes are stored on a per–design document basis, according to a fingerprint of the function's text contents. This means that if you edit attachments, validations, or any other non-view (or language) fields on the design document, the views will not be regenerated. However, if you change a map or a reduce function, the view index will be deleted and a new index built for the new view functions.

CouchDB has the capability to render responses in formats other than raw JSON. The design doc fields `show` and `list` contain functions used to transform raw JSON into HTML, XML, or other Content-Types. This allows CouchDB to serve Atom feeds without any additional middleware. The `show` and `list` functions are a little like "actions" in traditional web frameworks—they run some code based on a request and render a response. However, they differ from actions in that they may not have side effects. This means that they are largely restricted to handling `GET` requests, but it also means they can be cached by HTTP proxies like Varnish.

Because application logic is contained in a single document, code upgrades can be accomplished with CouchDB replication. This also opens the possibility for a single database to host multiple applications. The interface a newspaper editor needs is vastly different from what a reader desires, although the data is largely the same. They can both be hosted by the same database, in different design documents.

A CouchDB database can contain many design documents. Example design DocIDs are:

```
_design/calendar
_design/contacts
_design/blog
_design/admin
```

In the full CouchDB URL structure, you'd be able to `GET` the design document JSON at URLs like:

```
http://localhost:5984/mydb/_design/calendar
http://127.0.0.1:5984/mydb/_design/contacts
http://127.0.0.1:5984/mydb/_design/blog
http://127.0.0.1:5984/mydb/_design/admin
```

We show this to note that design documents have a special case, as they are the only documents whose URLs can be used with a literal slash. We've done this because nobody likes to see `%2F` in their browser's location bar. In all other cases, a slash in a DocID must be escaped when used in a URL. For instance, the DocID `movies/jaws` would appear in the URL like this: `http://127.0.0.1:5984/mydb/movies%2Fjaws`.

We'll build the first iteration of the example application without using `show` or `list`, because writing Ajax queries against the JSON API is a better way to teach CouchDB as a database. The APIs we explore in the first iteration are the same APIs you'd use to analyze log data, archive assets, or manage persistent queues.

In the second iteration, we'll upgrade our example blog so that it can function with client-side JavaScript turned off. For now, sticking to Ajax queries gives more transparency into how CouchDB's JSON/HTTP API works. JSON is a subset of JavaScript, so working with it in JavaScript keeps the impedance mismatch low, while the browser's *XMLHttpRequest (XHR)* object handles the HTTP details for us.

CouchDB uses the `validate_doc_update` function to prevent invalid or unauthorized document updates from proceeding. We use it in the example application to ensure that blog posts can be authored only by logged-in users. CouchDB's validation functions also can't have any side effects, and they have the opportunity to block not only end user document saves, but also replicated documents from other nodes. We'll talk about validation in depth in Part III.

The raw images, JavaScript, CSS, and HTML assets needed by Sofa are stored in the `_attachments` field, which is interesting in that by default it shows only the stubs, rather than the full content of the files. Attachments are available on all CouchDB documents, not just design documents, so asset management applications have as much flexibility as they could need. If a set of resources is required for your application to run, they should be attached to the design document. This means that a new user can easily bootstrap your application on an empty database.

The other fields in the design document shown in Figure 5-1 (and in the design documents we'll be using) are used by CouchApp's upload process (see Chapter 10 for more information on CouchApp). The `signatures` field allows us to avoid updating attachments that have not changed between the disk and the database. It does this by comparing file content hashes. The `lib` field is used to hold additional JavaScript code and JSON data to be inserted at deploy time into view, show, and validation functions. We'll explain CouchApp in the next chapter.

A Basic Design Document

In the next section we'll get into advanced techniques for working with design documents, but before we finish here, let's look at a very basic design document. All we'll do is define a single view, but it should be enough to show you how design documents fit into the larger system.

First, add the following text (or something like it) to a text file called *mydesign.json* using your editor:

```
{
  "_id" : "_design/example",
  "views" : {
    "foo" : {
      "map" : "function(doc){ emit(doc._id, doc._rev)}"
    }
  }
}
```

Now use `curl` to PUT the file to CouchDB (we'll create a database first for good measure):

```
curl -X PUT http://127.0.0.1:5984/basic
curl -X PUT http://127.0.0.1:5984/basic/_design/example -d @mydesign.json
```

From the second request, you should see a response like:

```
{"ok":true,"id":"_design/example","rev":"1-230141dfa7e07c3dbfef0789bf11773a"}
```

Now we can query the view we've defined, but before we do that, we should add a few documents to the database so we have something to view. Running the following command a few times will add empty documents:

```
curl -X POST http://127.0.0.1:5984/basic -d '{}'
```

Now to query the view:

```
curl http://127.0.0.1:5984/basic/_design/example/_view/foo
```

This should give you a list of all the documents in the database (except the design document). You've created and used your first design document!

Looking to the Future

There are other design document functions that are being introduced at the time of this writing, including _update and _filter that we aren't covering in depth here. Filter functions are covered in Chapter 20. Imagine a web service that POSTs an XML blob at a URL of your choosing when particular events occur. PayPal's instant payment notification is one of these. With an _update handler, you can POST these directly in CouchDB and it can parse the XML into a JSON document and save it. The same goes for CSV, multi-part form, or any other format.

The bigger picture we're working on is like an app server, but different in one crucial regard: rather than let the developer do whatever he wants (loop a list of DocIDs and make queries, make queries based on the results of other queries, etc.), we're defining "safe" transformations, such as view, show, list, and update. By safe, we mean that they have well-known performance characteristics and otherwise fit into CouchDB's architecture in a streamlined way.

The goal here is to provide a way to build standalone apps that can also be easily indexed by search engines and used via screen readers. Hence, the push for plain old HTML. You can pretty much rely on JavaScript getting executed (except when you can't). Having HTML resources means CouchDB is suitable for public-facing web apps.

On the horizon are a rewrite handler and a database event handler, as they seem to flesh out the application capabilities nicely. A rewrite handler would allow your application to present its own URL space, which would make integration into existing systems a bit easier. An event handler would allow you to run asynchronous processes when the database changes, so that, for instance, a document update can trigger a workflow, multi-document validation, or message queue.

CHAPTER 6

Finding Your Data with Views

Views are useful for many purposes:

- Filtering the documents in your database to find those relevant to a particular process.
- Extracting data from your documents and presenting it in a specific order.
- Building efficient indexes to find documents by any value or structure that resides in them.
- Use these indexes to represent relationships among documents.
- Finally, with views you can make all sorts of calculations on the data in your documents. For example, a view can answer the question of what your company's spending was in the last week, month, or year.

What Is a View?

Let's go through the different use cases. First is extracting data that you might need for a special purpose in a specific order. For a front page, we want a list of blog post titles sorted by date. We'll work with a set of example documents as we walk through how views work:

```
{
  "_id":"biking",
  "_rev":"AE19EBC7654",

  "title":"Biking",
  "body":"My biggest hobby is mountainbiking. The other day...",
  "date":"2009/01/30 18:04:11"
}

{
  "_id":"bought-a-cat",
  "_rev":"4A3BBEE711",
```

```
  "title":"Bought a Cat",
  "body":"I went to the the pet store earlier and brought home a little kitty...",
  "date":"2009/02/17 21:13:39"
}

{
  "_id":"hello-world",
  "_rev":"43FBA4E7AB",

  "title":"Hello World",
  "body":"Well hello and welcome to my new blog...",
  "date":"2009/01/15 15:52:20"
}
```

Three will do for the example. Note that the documents are sorted by "**_id**", which is how they are stored in the database. Now we define a view. Chapter 3 showed you how to create a view in Futon, the CouchDB administration client. Bear with us without an explanation while we show you some code:

```
function(doc) {
  if(doc.date && doc.title) {
    emit(doc.date, doc.title);
  }
}
```

This is a *map function*, and it is written in JavaScript. If you are not familiar with Java-Script but have used C or any other C-like language such as Java, PHP, or C#, this should look familiar. It is a simple function definition.

You provide CouchDB with view functions as strings stored inside the **views** field of a design document. You don't run it yourself. Instead, when you *query your view*, CouchDB takes the source code and runs it for you on every document in the database your view was defined in. You *query your view* to retrieve the *view result*.

All map functions have a single parameter **doc**. This is a single document in the database. Our map function checks whether our document has a **date** and a **title** attribute—luckily, all of our documents have them—and then calls the built-in **emit()** function with these two attributes as arguments.

The **emit()** function always takes two arguments: the first is **key**, and the second is **value**. The **emit(key, value)** function creates an entry in our *view result*. One more thing: the **emit()** function can be called multiple times in the map function to create multiple entries in the view results from a single document, but we are not doing that yet.

CouchDB takes whatever you pass into the **emit()** function and puts it into a list (see Table 6-1). Each row in that list includes the **key** and **value**. More importantly, the list is sorted by **key** (by **doc.date** in our case). The most important feature of a view result is that it is sorted by **key**. We will come back to that over and over again to do neat things. Stay tuned.

Table 6-1. View results

Key	Value
"2009/01/15 15:52:20"	"Hello World"
"2009/01/30 18:04:11"	"Biking"
"2009/02/17 21:13:39"	"Bought a Cat"

If you read carefully over the last few paragraphs, one part stands out: "When you query your view, CouchDB takes the source code and runs it for you on every document in the database." If you have a lot of documents, that takes quite a bit of time and you might wonder if it is not horribly inefficient to do this. Yes, it would be, but CouchDB is designed to avoid any extra costs: it only runs through all documents once, when you *first* query your view. If a document is changed, the map function is only run once, to recompute the keys and values for that single document.

The view result is stored in a B-tree, just like the structure that is responsible for holding your documents. View B-trees are stored in their own file, so that for high-performance CouchDB usage, you can keep views on their own disk. The B-tree provides very fast lookups of rows by key, as well as efficient streaming of rows in a key range. In our example, a single view can answer all questions that involve time: "Give me all the blog posts from last week" or "last month" or "this year." Pretty neat. Read more about how CouchDB's B-trees work in Appendix F.

When we query our view, we get back a list of all documents sorted by date. Each row also includes the post title so we can construct links to posts. Figure 6-1 is just a graphical representation of the view result. The actual result is JSON-encoded and contains a little more metadata:

```
{
  "total_rows": 3,
  "offset": 0,
  "rows": [
    {
      "key": "2009/01/15 15:52:20",
      "id": "hello-world",
      "value": "Hello World"
    },

    {
      "key": "2009/02/17 21:13:39",
      "id": "bought-a-cat",
      "value": "Bought a Cat"
    },

    {
      "key": "2009/01/30 18:04:11",
      "id": "biking",
      "value": "Biking"
    }
```

```
        ]
    }
```

Now, the actual result is not as nicely formatted and doesn't include any superfluous whitespace or newlines, but this is better for you (and us!) to read and understand. Where does that `"id"` member in the result rows come from? That wasn't there before. That's because we omitted it earlier to avoid confusion. CouchDB automatically includes the document ID of the document that created the entry in the view result. We'll use this as well when constructing links to the blog post pages.

Efficient Lookups

Let's move on to the second use case for views: "building efficient indexes to find documents by any value or structure that resides in them." We already explained the efficient indexing, but we skipped a few details. This is a good time to finish this discussion as we are looking at map functions that are a little more complex.

First, back to the B-trees! We explained that the B-tree that backs the key-sorted view result is built only once, when you first query a view, and all subsequent queries will just read the B-tree instead of executing the map function for all documents again. What happens, though, when you change a document, add a new one, or delete one? Easy: CouchDB is smart enough to find the rows in the view result that were created by a specific document. It marks them *invalid* so that they no longer show up in view results. If the document was deleted, we're good—the resulting B-tree reflects the state of the database. If a document got updated, the new document is run through the map function and the resulting new lines are inserted into the B-tree at the correct spots. New documents are handled in the same way. Appendix F demonstrates that a B-tree is a very efficient data structure for our needs, and the crash-only design of CouchDB databases is carried over to the view indexes as well.

To add one more point to the efficiency discussion: usually multiple documents are updated between view queries. The mechanism explained in the previous paragraph gets applied to all changes in the database since the last time the view was queried in a batch operation, which makes things even faster and is generally a better use of your resources.

Find One

On to more complex map functions. We said "find documents by any value or structure that resides in them." We already explained how to extract a value by which to sort a list of views (our `date` field). The same mechanism is used for fast lookups. The URI to query to get a view's result is `/database/_design/designdocname/_view/viewname`. This gives you a list of all rows in the view. We have only three documents, so things are small, but with thousands of documents, this can get long. You can add *view parameters* to the URI to constrain the result set. Say we know the date of a blog post. To find a single document, we would use /blog/_design/docs/_view/by_date?key="2009/01/30 18:04:11" to get the "Biking" blog post. Remember that you can place whatever you like in the key parameter to the emit() function. Whatever you put in there, we can now use to look up exactly—and fast.

Note that in the case where multiple rows have the same key (perhaps we design a view where the key is the name of the post's author), key queries can return more than one row.

Find Many

We talked about "getting all posts for last month." If it's February now, this is as easy as /blog/_design/docs/_view/by_date?startkey="2010/01/01 00:00:00"&end key="2010/02/00 00:00:00". The startkey and endkey parameters specify an inclusive range on which we can search.

To make things a little nicer and to prepare for a future example, we are going to change the format of our date field. Instead of a string, we are going to use an array, where individual members are part of a timestamp in decreasing significance. This sounds fancy, but it is rather easy. Instead of:

```
{
    "date": "2009/01/31 00:00:00"
}
```

we use:

```
"date": [2009, 1, 31, 0, 0, 0]
```

Our map function does not have to change for this, but our view result looks a little different. See Table 6-2.

Table 6-2. New view results

Key	Value
[2009, 1, 15, 15, 52, 20]	"Hello World"
[2009, 2, 17, 21, 13, 39]	"Biking"
[2009, 1, 30, 18, 4, 11]	"Bought a Cat"

And our queries change to /blog/_design/docs/_view/by_date?key=[2009, 1, 1, 0, 0, 0] and /blog/_design/docs/_view/by_date?key=[2009, 01, 31, 0, 0, 0]. For all you care, this is just a change in syntax, not meaning. But it shows you the power of views. Not only can you construct an index with scalar values like strings and integers, you can also use JSON structures as keys for your views. Say we tag our documents with a list of tags and want to see all tags, but we don't care for documents that have not been tagged.

```
{
  ...
  tags: ["cool", "freak", "plankton"],
  ...
}
{
  ...
  tags: [],
  ...
}
function(doc) {
  if(doc.tags.length > 0) {
    for(var idx in doc.tags) {
      emit(doc.tags[idx], null);
    }
  }
}
```

This shows a few new things. You can have conditions on structure (if(doc.tags.length > 0)) instead of just values. This is also an example of how a map function calls emit() multiple times per document. And finally, you can pass null instead of a value to the value parameter. The same is true for the key parameter. We'll see in a bit how that is useful.

Reversed Results

To retrieve view results in reverse order, use the descending=true query parameter. If you are using a startkey parameter, you will find that CouchDB returns different rows or no rows at all. What's up with that?

It's pretty easy to understand when you see how view query options work under the hood. A view is stored in a tree structure for fast lookups. Whenever you query a view, this is how CouchDB operates:

1. Starts reading at the top, or at the position that startkey specifies, if present.
2. Returns one row at a time until the end or until it hits endkey, if present.

If you specify descending=true, the reading direction is reversed, *not* the sort order of the rows in the view. In addition, the same two-step procedure is followed.

Say you have a view result that looks like this:

Key	Value
0	"foo"
1	"bar"
2	"baz"

Here are potential query options: ?startkey=1&descending=true. What will CouchDB do? See #1 above: it jumps to startkey, which is the row with the key 1, and starts reading backward until it hits the end of the view. So the particular result would be:

Key	Value
1	"bar"
0	"foo"

This is very likely not what you want. To get the rows with the indexes 1 and 2 in reverse order, you need to switch the startkey to endkey: endkey=1&descending=true:

Key	Value
2	"baz"
1	"bar"

Now that looks a lot better. CouchDB started reading at the bottom of the view and went backward until it hit endkey.

The View to Get Comments for Posts

We use an array key here to support the group_level reduce query parameter. CouchDB's views are stored in the B-tree file structure (which will be described in more detail later on). Because of the way B-trees are structured, we can cache the intermediate reduce results in the non-leaf nodes of the tree, so reduce queries can be computed along arbitrary key ranges in logarithmic time. See Figure 6-1.

In the blog app, we use group_level reduce queries to compute the count of comments both on a per-post and total basis, achieved by querying the same view index with different methods. With some array keys, and assuming each key has the value 1:

```
["a","b","c"]
["a","b","e"]
["a","c","m"]
["b","a","c"]
["b","a","g"]
```

the reduce view:

```
function(keys, values, rereduce) {
  return sum(values)
}
```

returns the total number of rows between the start and end key. So with start key=["a","b"]&endkey=["b"] (which includes the first three of the above keys) the result would equal 3. The effect is to count rows. If you'd like to count rows without depending on the row value, you can switch on the rereduce parameter:

```
function(keys, values, rereduce) {
  if (rereduce) {
    return sum(values);
  } else {
    return values.length;
  }
}
```

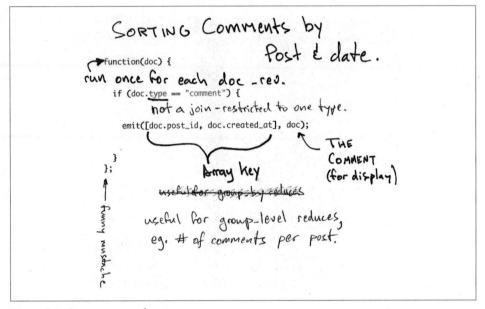

Figure 6-1. Comments map function

This is the reduce view used by the example app to count comments, while utilizing the map to output the comments, which are more useful than just 1 over and over. It pays to spend some time playing around with map and reduce functions. Futon is OK for this, but it doesn't give full access to all the query parameters. Writing your own test code for views in your language of choice is a great way to explore the nuances and capabilities of CouchDB's incremental MapReduce system.

Anyway, with a `group_level` query, you're basically running a series of reduce range queries: one for each *group* that shows up at the *level* you query. Let's reprint the key list from earlier, grouped at level 1:

```
["a"]   3
["b"]   2
```

And at group_level=2:

```
["a","b"]   2
["a","c"]   1
["b","a"]   2
```

Using the parameter `group=true` makes it behave as though it were `group_level=Exact`, so in the case of our current example, it would give the number 1 for each key, as there are no exactly duplicated keys.

Reduce/Rereduce

We briefly talked about the `rereduce` parameter to your reduce function. We'll explain what's up with it in this section. By now, you should have learned that your view result is stored in B-tree index structure for efficiency. The existence and use of the `rere duce` parameter is tightly coupled to how the B-tree index works.

Consider the map result shown in Example 6-1.

Example 6-1. Example view result (mmm, food)

```
"afrikan", 1
"afrikan", 1
"chinese", 1
"chinese", 1
"chinese", 1
"chinese", 1
"french", 1
"italian", 1
"italian", 1
"spanish", 1
"vietnamese", 1
"vietnamese", 1
```

When we want to find out how many dishes there are per origin, we can reuse the simple reduce function shown earlier:

```
function(keys, values, rereduce) {
    return sum(values);
}
```

Figure 6-2 shows a simplified version of what the B-tree index looks like. We abbreviated the key strings.

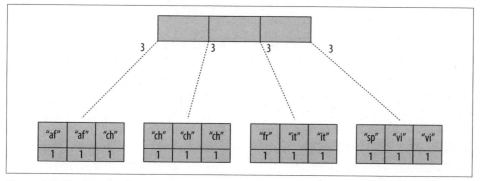

Figure 6-2. The B-tree index

The view result is what computer science grads call a "pre-order" walk through the tree. We look at each element in each node starting from the left. Whenever we see that there is a subnode to descend into, we descend and start reading the elements in that subnode. When we have walked through the entire tree, we're done.

You can see that CouchDB stores both keys and values inside each leaf node. In our case, it is simply always 1, but you might have a value where you count other results and then all rows have a different value. What's important is that CouchDB runs all elements that are within a node into the reduce function (setting the **rereduce** parameter to **false**) and stores the result inside the parent node along with the edge to the subnode. In our case, each edge has a **3** representing the reduce value for the node it points to.

In reality, nodes have more than 1,600 elements in them. CouchDB computes the result for all the elements in multiple iterations over the elements in a single node, not all at once (which would be disastrous for memory consumption).

Now let's see what happens when we run a query. We want to know how many **"chinese"** entries we have. The query option is simple: **?key="chinese"**. See Figure 6-3.

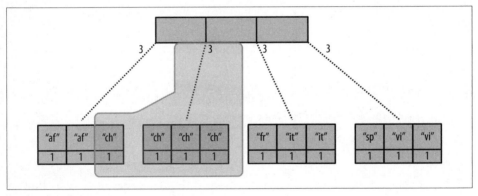

Figure 6-3. The B-tree index reduce result

CouchDB detects that all values in the subnode include the **"chinese"** key. It concludes that it can take just the **3** value associated with that node to compute the final result. It then finds the node left to it and sees that it's a node with keys outside the requested range (key= requests a range where the beginning and the end are the same value). It concludes that it has to use the **"chinese"** element's value and the other node's value and run them through the reduce function with the **rereduce** parameter set to **true**.

The reduce function effectively calculates **3 + 1** on query time and returns the desired result. Example 6-2 shows some pseudocode that shows the last invocation of the reduce function with actual values.

Example 6-2. The result is 4

```
function(null, [3, 1], true) {
  return sum([3, 1]);
}
```

Now, we said your reduce function must actually reduce your values. If you see the B-tree, it should become obvious what happens when you don't reduce your values. Consider the following map result and reduce function. This time we want to get a list of all the unique labels in our view:

```
"abc", "afrikan"
"cef", "afrikan"
"fhi", "chinese"
"hkl", "chinese"
"ino", "chinese"
"lqr", "chinese"
"mtu", "french"
"owx", "italian"
"qza", "italian"
"tdx", "spanish"
"xfg", "vietnamese"
"zul", "vietnamese"
```

We don't care for the key here and only list all the labels we have. Our reduce function removes duplicates; see Example 6-3.

Example 6-3. Don't use this, it's an example broken on purpose

```
function(keys, values, rereduce) {
  var unique_labels = {};
  values.forEach(function(label) {
    if(!unique_labels[label]) {
      unique_labels[label] = true;
    }
  });

  return unique_labels;
}
```

This translates to Figure 6-4.

We hope you get the picture. The way the B-tree storage works means that if you don't actually reduce your data in the reduce function, you end up having CouchDB copy huge amounts of data around that grow linearly, if not faster with the number of rows in your view.

CouchDB will be able to compute the final result, but only for views with a few rows. Anything larger will experience a ridiculously slow view build time. To help with that, CouchDB since version 0.10.0 will throw an error if your reduce function does not reduce its input values.

See Chapter 21 for an example of how to compute unique lists with views.

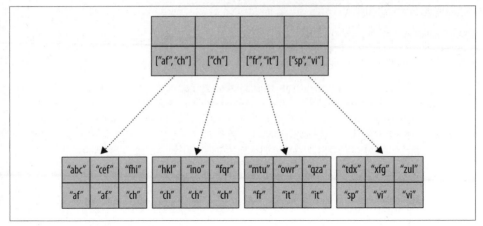

Figure 6-4. An overflowing reduce index

Lessons Learned

- If you don't use the key field in the map function, you are probably doing it wrong.
- If you are trying to make a list of values unique in the reduce functions, you are probably doing it wrong.
- If you don't reduce your values to a single scalar value or a small fixed-sized object or array with a fixed number of scalar values of small sizes, you are probably doing it wrong.

Wrapping Up

Map functions are side effect–free functions that take a document as argument and emit key/value pairs. CouchDB stores the *emitted rows* by constructing a sorted B-tree index, so row lookups by key, as well as streaming operations across a range of rows, can be accomplished in a small memory and processing footprint, while writes avoid seeks. Generating a view takes O(N), where N is the total number of rows in the view. However, querying a view is very quick, as the B-tree remains shallow even when it contains many, many keys.

Reduce functions operate on the sorted rows emitted by map view functions. CouchDB's reduce functionality takes advantage of one of the fundamental properties of B-tree indexes: for every leaf node (a sorted row), there is a chain of internal nodes reaching back to the root. Each leaf node in the B-tree carries a few rows (on the order of tens, depending on row size), and each internal node may link to a few leaf nodes or other internal nodes.

The reduce function is run on every node in the tree in order to calculate the final reduce value. The end result is a reduce function that can be incrementally updated upon changes to the map function, while recalculating the reduction values for a minimum number of nodes. The initial reduction is calculated once per each node (inner and leaf) in the tree.

When run on leaf nodes (which contain actual map rows), the reduce function's third parameter, `reduce`, is false. The arguments in this case are the keys and values as output by the map function. The function has a single returned reduction value, which is stored on the inner node that a working set of leaf nodes have in common, and is used as a cache in future reduce calculations.

When the reduce function is run on inner nodes, the `reduce` flag is `true`. This allows the function to account for the fact that it will be receiving its own prior output. When `reduce` is `true`, the values passed to the function are intermediate reduction values as cached from previous calculations. When the tree is more than two levels deep, the reduce phase is repeated, consuming chunks of the previous level's output until the final reduce value is calculated at the root node.

A common mistake new CouchDB users make is attempting to construct complex aggregate values with a reduce function. Full reductions should result in a scalar value, like **5**, and not, for instance, a JSON hash with a set of unique keys and the count of each. The problem with this approach is that you'll end up with a very large final value. The number of unique keys can be nearly as large as the number of total keys, even for a large set. It is fine to combine a few scalar calculations into one reduce function; for instance, to find the total, average, and standard deviation of a set of numbers in a single function.

If you're interested in pushing the edge of CouchDB's incremental reduce functionality, have a look at Google's paper on Sawzall (*http://labs.google.com/papers/sawzall.html*), which gives examples of some of the more exotic reductions that can be accomplished in a system with similar constraints.

CHAPTER 7

Validation Functions

In this chapter, we look closely at the individual components of Sofa's validation function. Sofa has the basic set of validation features you'll want in your apps, so understanding its validation function will give you a good foundation for others you may write in the future.

CouchDB uses the `validate_doc_update` function to prevent invalid or unauthorized document updates from proceeding. We use it in the example application to ensure that blog posts can be authored only by logged-in users. CouchDB's validation functions—like map and reduce functions—can't have any side effects; they run in isolation of a request. They have the opportunity to block not only end-user document saves, but also replicated documents from other CouchDBs.

Document Validation Functions

To ensure that users may save only documents that provide these fields, we can validate their input by adding another member to the `_design/` document: the `validate_doc_update` function. This is the first time you've seen CouchDB's external process in action. CouchDB sends functions and documents to a JavaScript interpreter. This mechanism is what allows us to write our document validation functions in JavaScript. The `validate_doc_update` function gets executed for each document you want to create or update. If the validation function raises an exception, the update is denied; when it doesn't, the updates are accepted.

Document validation is optional. If you don't create a validation function, no checking is done and documents with any content or structure can be written into your CouchDB database. If you have multiple design documents, each with a `validate_doc_update` function, all of those functions are called upon each incoming write request. Only if all of them pass does the write succeed. The order of the validation execution is not defined. Each validation function must act on its own. See Figure 7-1.

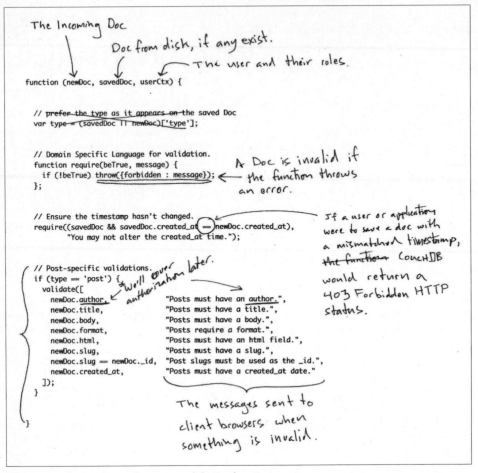

The Incoming Doc

Doc from disk, if any exist.

The user and their roles.

```
function (newDoc, savedDoc, userCtx) {

  // prefer the type as it appears on the saved Doc
  var type = (savedDoc || newDoc)['type'];

  // Domain Specific Language for validation.
  function require(beTrue, message) {
    if (!beTrue) throw({forbidden : message});
  };

  // Ensure the timestamp hasn't changed.
  require((savedDoc && savedDoc.created_at == newDoc.created_at),
          "You may not alter the created_at time.");

  // Post-specific validations.
  if (type == 'post') {
    validate([
      newDoc.author,              "Posts must have an author.",
      newDoc.title,               "Posts must have a title.",
      newDoc.body,                "Posts must have a body.",
      newDoc.format,              "Posts require a format.",
      newDoc.html,                "Posts must have an html field.",
      newDoc.slug,                "Posts must have a slug.",
      newDoc.slug == newDoc._id,  "Post slugs must be used as the _id.",
      newDoc.created_at,          "Posts must have a created_at date."
    ]);
  }
}
```

A Doc is invalid if the function throws an error.

If a user or application were to save a doc with a mismatched timestamp, ~~the function~~ CouchDB would return a 403 Forbidden HTTP status.

We'll cover authorization later.

The messages sent to client browsers when something is invalid.

Figure 7-1. The JavaScript document validation function

Validation functions can cancel document updates by throwing errors. To throw an error in such a way that the user will be asked to authenticate, before retrying the request, use JavaScript code like:

```
throw({unauthorized : message});
```

When you're trying to prevent an authorized user from saving invalid data, use this:

```
throw({forbidden : message});
```

This function throws forbidden errors when a post does not contain the necessary fields. In places it uses a validate() helper to clean up the JavaScript. We also use simple JavaScript conditionals to ensure that the doc._id is set to be the same as doc.slug for the sake of pretty URLs.

If no exceptions are thrown, CouchDB expects the incoming document to be valid and will write it to the database. By using JavaScript to validate JSON documents, we can deal with any structure a document might have. Given that you can just make up document structure as you go, being able to validate what you come up with is pretty flexible and powerful. Validation can also be a valuable form of documentation.

Validation's Context

Before we delve into the details of our validation function, let's talk about the context in which they run and the effects they can have.

Validation functions are stored in *design documents* under the `validate_doc_update` field. There is only one per design document, but there can be many design documents in a database. In order for a document to be saved, it must pass validations on all design documents in the database (the order in which multiple validations are executed is left undefined). In this chapter, we'll assume you are working in a database with only one validation function.

Writing One

The function declaration is simple. It takes three arguments: the proposed document update, the current version of the document on disk, and an object corresponding to the user initiating the request.

```
function(newDoc, oldDoc, userCtx) {}
```

Above is the simplest possible validation function, which, when deployed, would allow all updates regardless of content or user roles. The converse, which never lets anyone do anything, looks like this:

```
function(newDoc, oldDoc, userCtx) {
  throw({forbidden : 'no way'});
}
```

Note that if you install this function in your database, you won't be able to perform any other document operations until you remove it from the design document or delete the design document. Admins can create and delete design documents despite the existence of this extreme validation function.

We can see from these examples that the return value of the function is ignored. Validation functions prevent document updates by raising errors. When the validation function passes without raising errors, the update is allowed to proceed.

Type

The most basic use of validation functions is to ensure that documents are properly formed to fit your application's expectations. Without validation, you need to check for the existence of all fields on a document that your MapReduce or user-interface code needs to function. With validation, you know that any saved documents meet whatever criteria you require.

A common pattern in most languages, frameworks, and databases is using types to distinguish between subsets of your data. For instance, in Sofa we have a few document types, most prominently `post` and `comment`.

CouchDB itself has no notion of types, but they are a convenient shorthand for use in your application code, including MapReduce views, display logic, and user interface code. The convention is to use a field called `type` to store document types, but many frameworks use other fields, as CouchDB itself doesn't care which field you use. (For instance, the CouchRest Ruby client uses `couchrest-type`).

Here's an example validation function that runs only on posts:

```
function(newDoc, oldDoc, userCtx) {
  if (newDoc.type == "post") {
    // validation logic goes here
  }
}
```

Since CouchDB stores only one validation function per design document, you'll end up validating multiple types in one function, so the overall structure becomes something like:

```
function(newDoc, oldDoc, userCtx) {
  if (newDoc.type == "post") {
    // validation logic for posts
  }
  if (newDoc.type == "comment") {
    // validation logic for comments
  }
  if (newDoc.type == "unicorn") {
    // validation logic for unicorns
  }
}
```

It bears repeating that `type` is a completely optional field. We present it here as a helpful technique for managing validations in CouchDB, but there are other ways to write validation functions. Here's an example that uses *duck typing* instead of an explicit `type` attribute:

```
function(newDoc, oldDoc, userCtx) {
  if (newDoc.title && newDoc.body) {
    // validate that the document has an author
  }
}
```

This validation function ignores the `type` attribute altogether and instead makes the somewhat simpler requirement that any document with both a title and a body must have an author. For some applications, typeless validations are simpler. For others, it can be a pain to keep track of which sets of fields are dependent on one another.

In practice, many applications end up using a mix of typed and untyped validations. For instance, Sofa uses document types to track which fields are required on a given document, but it also uses duck typing to validate the structure of particular named fields. We don't care what sort of document we're validating. If the document has a created_at field, we ensure that the field is a properly formed timestamp. Similarly, when we validate the author of a document, we don't care what type of document it is; we just ensure that the author matches the user who saved the document.

Required Fields

The most fundamental validation is ensuring that particular fields are available on a document. The proper use of required fields can make writing MapReduce views much simpler, as you don't have to test for all the properties before using them—you know all documents will be well-formed.

Required fields also make display logic much simpler. Nothing says amateur like the word undefined showing up throughout your application. If you know for certain that all documents will have a field, you can avoid lengthy conditional statements to render the display differently depending on document structure.

Sofa requires a different set of fields on posts and comments. Here's a subset of the Sofa validation function:

```
function(newDoc, oldDoc, userCtx) {
  function require(field, message) {
    message = message || "Document must have a " + field;
    if (!newDoc[field]) throw({forbidden : message});
  };

  if (newDoc.type == "post") {
    require("title");
    require("created_at");
    require("body");
    require("author");
  }
  if (newDoc.type == "comment") {
    require("name");
    require("created_at");
    require("comment", "You may not leave an empty comment");
  }
}
```

This is our first look at actual validation logic. You can see that the actual error throwing code has been wrapped in a helper function. Helpers like the require function just shown go a long way toward making your code clean and readable. The require function is simple. It takes a field name and an optional message, and it ensures that the field is not empty or blank.

Once we've declared our helper function, we can simply use it in a type-specific way. Posts require a title, a timestamp, a body, and an author. Comments require a name, a timestamp, and the comment itself. If we wanted to require that every single document contained a created_at field, we could move that declaration outside of any type conditional logic.

Timestamps

Timestamps are an interesting problem in validation functions. Because validation functions are run at replication time as well as during normal client access, we can't require that timestamps be set close to the server's system time. We can require two things: that timestamps do not change after they are initially set, and that they are well formed. What it means to be well formed depends on your application. We'll look at Sofa's particular requirements here, as well as digress a bit about other options for timestamp formats.

First, let's look at a validation helper that does not allow fields, once set, to be changed on subsequent updates:

```
function(newDoc, oldDoc, userCtx) {
  function unchanged(field) {
    if (oldDoc && toJSON(oldDoc[field]) != toJSON(newDoc[field]))
      throw({forbidden : "Field can't be changed: " + field});
  }
  unchanged("created_at");
}
```

The unchanged helper is a little more complex than the require helper, but not much. The first line of the function prevents it from running on initial updates. The unchanged helper doesn't care at all what goes into a field the first time it is saved. However, if there exists an already-saved version of the document, the unchanged helper requires that whatever fields it is used on are the same between the new and the old version of the document.

JavaScript's equality test is not well suited to working with deeply nested objects. We use CouchDB's JavaScript runtime's built-in toJSON function in our equality test, which is better than testing for raw equality. Here's why:

```
js> [] == []
false
```

JavaScript considers these arrays to be different because it doesn't look at the contents of the array when making the decision. Since they are distinct objects, JavaScript must consider them not equal. We use the toJSON function to convert objects to a string representation, which makes comparisons more likely to succeed in the case where two objects have the same contents. This is not guaranteed to work for deeply nested objects, as toJSON may serialize objects.

The js command gets installed when you install CouchDB's Spider-Monkey dependency. It is a command-line application that lets you parse, evaluate, and run JavaScript code. js lets you quickly test JavaScript code snippets like the one previously shown. You can also run a syntax check of your JavaScript code using js file.js. In case CouchDB's error messages are not helpful, you can resort to testing your code standalone and get a useful error report.

Authorship

Authorship is an interesting question in distributed systems. In some environments, you can trust the server to ascribe authorship to a document. Currently, CouchDB has a simple built-in validation system that manages *node admins*. There are plans to add a database admin role, as well as other roles. The authentication system is pluggable, so you can integrate with existing services to authenticate users to CouchDB using an HTTP layer, using LDAP integration, or through other means.

Sofa uses the built-in node admin account system and so is best suited for single or small groups of authors. Extending Sofa to store author credentials in CouchDB itself is an exercise left to the reader.

Sofa's validation logic says that documents saved with an author field must be saved by the author listed on that field:

```
function(newDoc, oldDoc, userCtx) {
  if (newDoc.author) {
    enforce(newDoc.author == userCtx.name,
      "You may only update documents with author " + userCtx.name);
  }
}
```

Wrapping Up

Validation functions are a powerful tool to ensure that only documents you expect end up in your databases. You can test writes to your database by content, by structure, and by user who is making the document request. Together, these three angles let you build sophisticated validation routines that will stop anyone from tampering with your database.

Of course, validation functions are no substitute for a full security system, although they go a long way and work well with CouchDB's other security mechanisms. Read more about CouchDB's security in Chapter 22.

CHAPTER 8

Show Functions

CouchDB's JSON documents are great for programmatic access in most environments. Almost all languages have HTTP and JSON libraries, and in the unlikely event that yours doesn't, writing them is fairly simple. However, there is one important use case that JSON documents don't cover: building plain old HTML web pages. Browsers are powerful, and it's exciting that we can build Ajax applications using only CouchDB's JSON and HTTP APIs, but this approach is not appropriate for most public-facing websites.

HTML is the *lingua franca* of the web, for good reasons. By rendering our JSON documents into HTML pages, we make them available and accessible for a wider variety of uses. With the pure Ajax approach, visually impaired visitors to our blog stand a chance of not seeing any useful content at all, as popular screen-reading browsers have a hard time making sense of pages when the content is changed on the fly via JavaScript. Another important concern for authors is that their writing be indexed by search engines. Maintaining a high-quality blog doesn't do much good if readers can't find it via a web search. Most search engines do not execute JavaScript found within a page, so to them an Ajax blog looks devoid of content. We also mustn't forget that HTML is likely more friendly as an archive format in the long term than the platform-specific JavaScript and JSON approach we used in previous chapters. Also, by serving plain HTML, we make our site snappier, as the browser can render meaningful content with fewer round-trips to the server. These are just a few of the reasons it makes sense to provide web content as HTML.

The traditional way to accomplish the goal of rendering HTML from database records is by using a middle-tier application server, such as Ruby on Rails or Django, which loads the appropriate records for a user request, runs a template function using them, and returns the resulting HTML to the visitor's browser. The basics of this don't change in CouchDB's case; wrapping JSON views and documents with an application server is relatively straightforward. Rather than using browser-side JavaScript to load JSON from CouchDB and rendering dynamic pages, Rails or Django (or your framework of choice) could make those same HTTP requests against CouchDB, render the output to HTML, and return it to the browser. We won't cover this approach in this book, as it is specific to particular languages and frameworks, and surveying the different options would take more space than you want to read.

CouchDB includes functionality designed to make it possible to do most of what an application tier would do, without relying on additional software. The appeal of this approach is that CouchDB can serve the whole application without dependencies on a complex environment such as might be maintained on a production web server. Because CouchDB is designed to run on client computers, where the environment is out of the control of application developers, having some built-in templating capabilities greatly expands the potential uses of these applications. When your application can be served by a standard CouchDB instance, you gain deployment ease and flexibility.

The Show Function API

Show functions, as they are called, have a constrained API designed to ensure cacheability and side effect–free operation. This is in stark contrast to other application servers, which give the programmer the freedom to run any operation as the result of any request. Let's look at a few example show functions.

The most basic show function looks something like this:

```
function(doc, req) {
  return '<h1>' + doc.title + '</h1>';
}
```

When run with a document that has a field called `title` with the content "Hello World," this function will send an HTTP response with the default Content-Type of `text/html`, the UTF-8 character encoding, and the body `<h1>Hello World</h1>`.

The simplicity of the request/response cycle of a show function is hard to overstate. The most common question we hear is, "How can I load another document so that I can render its content as well?" The short answer is that you can't. The longer answer is that for some applications you might use a list function to render a view result as HTML, which gives you the opportunity to use more than one document as the input of your function.

The basic function from a document and a request to a response, with no side effects and no alternative inputs, stays the same even as we start using more advanced features. Here's a more complex show function illustrating the ability to set custom headers:

```
function(doc, req) {
  return {
    body : '<foo>' + doc.title + '</foo>',
    headers : {
      "Content-Type" : "application/xml",
      "X-My-Own-Header": "you can set your own headers"
    }
  }
}
```

If this function were called with the same document as we used in the previous example, the response would have a Content-Type of `application/xml` and the body `<foo>Hello World</foo>`. You should be able to see from this how you'd be able to use show functions to generate any output you need, from any of your documents.

Popular uses of show functions are for outputting HTML page, CSV files, or XML needed for compatibility with a particular interface. The CouchDB test suite even illustrates using show functions to output a PNG image. To output binary data, there is the option to return a Base64-encoded string, like this:

```
function(doc, req) {
  return {
    base64 :
      ["iVBORw0KGgoAAAANSUhEUgAAABAAAAAQCAMAAAAoLQ9TAAAAsV",
       "BMVEUAAAD///////////////////5ur3rEBn/////////////wDBL/",
       "AADuBAe9EB3IEBz/7+//X1/qBQn2AgP/f3/ilpzsDxfpChDtDhXeCA76AQH/v7",
       "/84eLyWV/uc3bJPEf/Dw/uw8bRWmP1h4zxSlD6YGHuQof6g4XyQkXvCA36MDH6",
       "wMH/z8/yAwX640Deh47BHiv/Ly/20dLQLTj98PDXWmP/Pz//39/wGyJ7Iy9JAA",
       "AADHRSTlMAbw8vf08/bz+Pv19jK/W3AAAAgolEQVR4Xp3LRQ4DQRBDOQqTm4Y5",
       "zMxw/40leiJlHeUtv2X6RbNO1Uqj9g0RMCuQ0OovBIg4vMFeOpCWIWmDOw82fZx",
       "vaND1c80G4vrdOqD8YwgpDYDxRgkSm5rwuOnQVBJuMg++pLXZyr5jnc1BaH4GT",
       "LvEliY253nA3pVhQqdPtOf/erJkMGMB8xucAAAAASUVORK5CYII="].join(''),
    headers : {
      "Content-Type" : "image/png"
    }
  };
}
```

This function outputs a 16×16 pixel version of the CouchDB logo. The JavaScript code necessary to generate images from document contents would likely be quite complex, but the ability to send Base64-encoded binary data means that query servers written in other languages like C or PHP have the ability to output any data type.

Side Effect–Free

We've mentioned that a key constraint of show functions is that they are side effect–free. This means that you can't use them to update documents, kick off background processes, or trigger any other function. In the big picture, this is a *good thing*, as it allows CouchDB to give performance and reliability guarantees that standard web frameworks can't. Because a show function will always return the same result given the same input and can't change anything about the environment in which it runs, its output can be cached and intelligently reused. In a high-availability deployment with proper caching, this means that a given show function will be called only once for any particular document, and the CouchDB server may not even be contacted for subsequent requests.

Working without side effects can be a little bit disorienting for developers who are used to the anything-goes approach offered by most application servers. It's considered best practice to ensure that actions run in response to GET requests are side effect–free and cacheable, but rarely do we have the discipline to achieve that goal. CouchDB takes a different tack: because it's a database, not an application server, we think it's more important to enforce best practices (and ensure that developers don't write functions that adversely effect the database server) than offer absolute flexibility. Once you're used to working within these constraints, they start to make a lot of sense. (There's a reason they are considered best practices.)

Design Documents

Before we look into show functions themselves, we'll quickly review how they are stored in design documents. CouchDB looks for show functions stored in a top-level field called shows, which is named like this to be parallel with views, lists, and filters. Here's an example design document that defines two show functions:

```
{
  "_id" : "_design/show-function-examples",
  "shows" : {
    "summary" : "function(doc, req){ ... }",
    "detail" : "function(doc, req){ ... }"
  }
}
```

There's not much to note here except the fact that design documents can define multiple show functions. Now let's see how these functions are run.

Querying Show Functions

We've described the show function API, but we haven't yet seen how these functions are run.

The show function lives inside a design document, so to invoke it we append the name of the function to the design document itself, and then the ID of the document we want to render:

```
GET /mydb/_design/mydesign/_show/myshow/72d43a93eb74b5f2
```

Because show functions (and the others like list, etc.) are available as resources within the design document path, all resources provided by a particular design document can be found under a common root, which makes custom application proxying simpler. We'll see an example of this in Part III.

If the document with ID 72d43a93eb74b5f2 does not exist, the request will result in an HTTP 500 Internal Server Error response. This seems a little harsh; why does it happen? If we query a show function with a document ID that doesn't point to an existing document, the doc argument in the function is null. Then the show function tries to access it, and the JavaScript interpreter doesn't like that. So it bails out. To secure against these errors, or to handle non-existing documents in a custom way (e.g., a wiki could display a "create new page" page), you can wrap the code in our function with `if(doc !== null) { ... }`.

However, show functions can also be called without a document ID at all, like this:

```
GET /mydb/_design/mydesign/_show/myshow
```

In this case, the `doc` argument to the function has the value `null`. This option is useful in cases where the show function can make sense without a document. For instance, in the example application we'll explore in Part III, we use the same show function to provide for editing existing blog posts when a DocID is given, as well as for composing new blog posts when no DocID is given. The alternative would be to maintain an alternate resource (likely a static HTML attachment) with parallel functionality. As programmers, we strive not to repeat ourselves, which motivated us to give show functions the ability to run without a document ID.

Design Document Resources

In addition to the ability to run show functions, other resources are available within the design document path. This combination of features within the design document resource means that applications can be deployed without exposing the full CouchDB API to visitors, with only a simple proxy to rewrite the paths. We won't go into full detail here, but the gist of it is that end users would run the previous query from a path like this:

```
GET /_show/myshow/72d43a93eb74b5f2
```

Under the covers, an HTTP proxy can be programmed to prepend the database and design document portion of the path (in this case, */mydb/_design/mydesign*) so that CouchDB sees the standard query. With such a system in place, end users can access the application only via functions defined on the design document, so developers can enforce constraints and prevent access to raw JSON document and view data. While it doesn't provide 100% security, using custom rewrite rules is an effective way to control the access end users have to a CouchDB application. This technique has been used in production by a few websites at the time of this writing.

Query Parameters

The request object (including helpfully parsed versions of query parameters) is available to show functions as well. By way of illustration, here's a show function that returns different data based on the URL query parameters:

```
function(req, doc) {
  return "<p>Aye aye, " + req.parrot + "!</p>";
}
```

Requesting this function with a query parameter will result in the query parameter being used in the output:

```
GET /mydb/_design/mydesign/_show/myshow?parrot=Captain
```

In this case, we'll see the output: `<p>Aye aye, Captain!</p>`

Allowing URL parameters into the function does not affect cacheability, as each unique invocation results in a distinct URL. However, making heavy use of this feature will lower your cache effectiveness. Query parameters like this are most useful for doing things like switching the mode or the format of the show function output. It's recommended that you avoid using them for things like inserting custom content (such as requesting the user's nickname) into the response, as that will mean each users's data must be cached separately.

Accept Headers

Part of the HTTP spec allows for clients to give hints to the server about which media types they are capable of accepting. At this time, the JavaScript query server shipped with CouchDB 0.10.0 contains helpers for working with Accept headers. However, web browser support for Accept headers is *very poor*, which has prompted frameworks such as Ruby on Rails to remove their support for them. CouchDB may or may not follow suit here, but the fact remains that you are discouraged from relying on Accept headers for applications that will be accessed via web browsers.

There is a suite of helpers for Accept headers present that allow you to specify the format in a query parameter as well. For instance:

```
GET /db/_design/app/_show/post
Accept: application/xml
```

is equivalent to a similar URL with mismatched Accept headers. This is because browsers don't use sensible Accept headers for feed URLs. Browsers 1, Accept headers 0. Yay browsers.

```
GET /db/_design/app/_show/post?format=xml
Accept: x-foo/whatever
```

The request function allows developers to switch response Content-Types based on the client's request. The next example adds the ability to return either HTML, XML, or a developer-designated media type: `x-foo/whatever`.

CouchDB's *main.js* library provides the (`"format"`, `render_function`) function, which makes it easy for developers to handle client requests for multiple MIME types in one form function.

This function also shows off the use of `registerType(name, mime_types)`, which adds new types to mapping objects used by `respondWith`. The end result is ultimate flexibility for developers, with an easy interface for handling different types of requests. *main.js* uses a JavaScript port of *Mimeparse*, an open source reference implementation, to provide this service.

Etags

We've mentioned that show function requests are side effect–free and cacheable, but we haven't discussed the mechanism used to accomplish this. *Etags* are a standard HTTP mechanism for indicating whether a cached copy of an HTTP response is still current. Essentially, when the client makes its first request to a resource, the response is accompanied by an Etag, which is an opaque string token unique to the version of the resource requested. The second time the client makes a request against the same resource, it sends along the original Etag with the request. If the server determines that the Etag still matches the resource, it can avoid sending the full response, instead replying with a message that essentially says, "You have the latest version already."

When implemented properly, the use of Etags can cut down significantly on server load. CouchDB provides an Etag header, so that by using an HTTP proxy cache like Squid, you'll instantly remove load from CouchDB.

Functions and Templates

CouchDB's process runner looks only at the functions stored under `show`, but we'll want to keep the template HTML separate from the content negotiation logic. The `couchapp` script handles this for us, using the `!code` and `!json` handlers.

Let's follow the show function logic through the files that Sofa splits it into. Here's Sofa's `edit` show function:

```
function(doc, req) {
  // !json templates.edit
  // !json blog
  // !code vendor/couchapp/path.js
  // !code vendor/couchapp/template.js

  // we only show html
  return template(templates.edit, {
    doc : doc,
    docid : toJSON((doc && doc._id) || null),
    blog : blog,
    assets : assetPath(),
    index : listPath('index','recent-posts',{descending:true,limit:8})
  });
}
```

This should look pretty straightforward. First, we have the function's *head*, or *signature*, that tells us we are dealing with a function that takes two arguments: `doc` and `req`.

The next four lines are comments, as far as JavaScript is concerned. But these are special documents. The CouchApp upload script knows how to read these special comments on top of the show function. They include *macros*; a macro starts with a bang (!) and a name. Currently, CouchApp supports the two macros `!json` and `!code`.

The !json Macro

The `!json` macro takes one argument: the path to a file in the CouchApp directory hierarchy in the *dot notation*. Instead of a slash (/) or backslash (\), you use a dot (.). The `!json` macro then reads the contents of the file and puts them into a variable that has the same name as the file's path in dot notation.

For example, if you use the macro like this:

```
// !json template.edit
```

CouchDB will read the file *template/edit.* * and place its contents into a variable:

```
var template.edit = "contents of edit.*"
```

When specifying the path, you omit the file's extension. That way you can read *.json*, *.js*, or *.html* files, or any other files into variables in your functions. Because the macro matches files with any extensions, you can't have two files with the same name but different extensions.

In addition, you can specify a directory and CouchApp will load all the files in this directory and any subdirectory. So this:

```
// !json template
```

creates:

```
var template.edit = "contents of edit.*"
var teplate.post = "contents of post.*"
```

Note that the macro also takes care of creating the top-level `template` variable. We just omitted that here for brevity. The `!json` macro will generate only valid JavaScript.

The !code Macro

The `!code` macro is similar to the `!json` macro, but it serves a slightly different purpose. Instead of making the contents of one or more files available as variables in your functions, it replaces itself with the contents of the file referenced in the argument to the macro.

This is useful for sharing library functions between CouchDB functions (map/reduce/show/list/validate) without having to maintain their source code in multiple places.

Our example shows this line:

```
// !code vendor/couchapp/path.js
```

If you look at the CouchApp sources, there is a file in *vendor/couchapp/path.js* that includes a bunch of useful function related to the URL path of a request. In the example just shown, CouchApp will replace the line with the contents of *path.js*, making the functions locally available to the show function.

The `!code` macro can load only a single file at a time.

Learning Shows

Before we dig into the full code that will render the post permalink pages, let's look at some *Hello World* form examples. The first one shows just the function arguments and the simplest possible return value. See Figure 8-1.

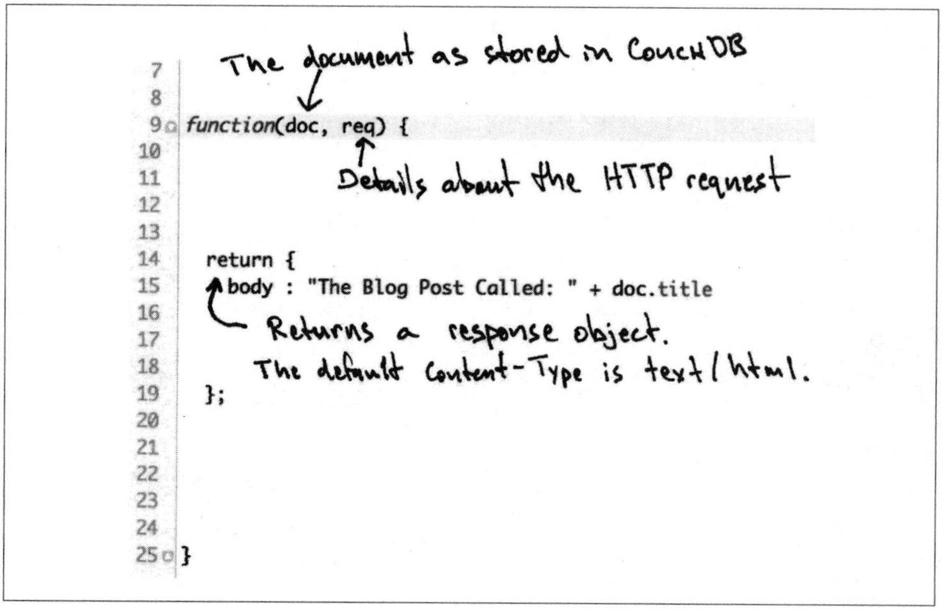

```
 7
 8
 9   function(doc, req) {
10
11
12
13
14     return {
15       body : "The Blog Post Called: " + doc.title
16
17
18
19     };
20
21
22
23
24
25   }
```

The document as stored in CouchDB

Details about the HTTP request

Returns a response object. The default Content-Type is text/html.

Figure 8-1. *Basic form function*

A *show function* is a JavaScript function that converts a document and some details about the HTTP request into an HTTP response. Typically it will be used to construct HTML, but it is also capable of returning Atom feeds, images, or even just filtered JSON. The document argument is just like the documents passed to map functions.

Using Templates

The only thing missing from the show function development experience is the ability to render HTML without ruining your eyes looking at a whole lot of string manipulation, among other unpleasantries. Most programming environments solve this problem with templates; for example, documents that look like HTML but have portions of their content filled out dynamically.

Dynamically combining template strings and data in JavaScript is a solved problem. However, it hasn't caught on, partly because JavaScript doesn't have very good support for multi-line "heredoc" strings. After all, once you get through escaping quotes and leaving out newlines, it's not much fun to edit HTML templates inlined into JavaScript code. We'd much rather keep our templates in separate files, where we can avoid all the escaping work, and they can be syntax-highlighted by our editor.

The couchapp script has a couple of helpers to make working with templates and library code stored in design documents less painful. In the function shown in Figure 8-2, we use them to load a blog post template, as well as the JavaScript function responsible for rendering it.

```
 1  <!DOCTYPE html>      ☺ HTML 5
 2  <html>
 3    <head>
 4      <title>CouchDB Example Blog</title>
 5      <link rel="stylesheet" href="<%= attachRoot %>/screen.css" type="text/css">
 6    </head>
 7
 8    <body>                          assets
 9      <div id="header">
10        <h2><a href="<%= attachRoot %>/index.html">List Recent Posts</a></h2>
11      </div>
12
13      <div id="content">
14                                Blog Post Data
15        <h1><%= title %></h1>
16
17        <div id="post">
18
19          <span class="date"><%= date %></span>  ← The date comes
20                                                    out as an ugly JSON
21          <div class="body"><%= body %></div>      timestamp.
22
23        </div>
24
25      </div>
26
27    </body>
28    <script src="/_utils/script/json2.js"></script>
29    <script src="/_utils/script/jquery.js?1.2.6"></script>
30    <script src="/_utils/script/jquery.couch.js?0.8.0"></script>
31    <script src="<%= attachRoot %>/jquery.couchapp.js"></script>
32    <script src="<%= attachRoot %>/blog.js"></script>
33    <script type="text/javascript" charset="utf-8">
34        ... see next figure ...
35    </script>
36  </html>
```

Figure 8-2. The blog post template

As you can see, we take the opportunity in the function to strip JavaScript tags from the form post. That regular expression is not secure, and the blogging application is meant to be written to only by its owners, so we should probably drop the regular expression and simplify the function to avoid transforming the document, instead passing it directly to the template. Or we should port a known-good sanitization routine from another language and provide it in the templates library.

Writing Templates

Working with templates, instead of trying to cram all the presentation into one file, makes editing forms a little more relaxing. The templates are stored in their own file, so you don't have to worry about JavaScript or JSON encoding, and your text editor can highlight the template's HTML syntax. CouchDB's JavaScript query server includes the E4X extensions for JavaScript, which can be helpful for XML templates but do not work well for HTML. We'll explore E4X templates in Chapter 14 when we cover forms for views, which makes providing an Atom feed of view results easy and memory efficient.

Trust us when we say that looking at this HTML page is much more relaxing than trying to understand what a raw JavaScript one is trying to do. The template library we're using in the example blog is by John Resig and was chosen for simplicity. It could easily be replaced by one of many other options, such as the Django template language, available in JavaScript.

This is a good time to note that CouchDB's architecture is designed to make it simple to swap out languages for the query servers. With a query server written in Lisp, Python, or Ruby (or any language that supports JSON and *stdio*), you could have an even wider variety of templating options. However, the CouchDB team recommends sticking with JavaScript as it provides the highest level of support and interoperability, though other options are available.

CHAPTER 9

Transforming Views with List Functions

Just as show functions convert documents to arbitrary output formats, CouchDB *list functions* allow you to render the output of view queries in any format. The powerful iterator API allows for flexibility to filter and aggregate rows on the fly, as well as output raw transformations for an easy way to make Atom feeds, HTML lists, CSV files, config files, or even just modified JSON.

List functions are stored under the `lists` field of a design document. Here's an example design document that contains two list functions:

```
{
  "_id" : "_design/foo",
  "_rev" : "1-67at7bg",
  "lists" : {
    "bar" : "function(head, req) { var row; while (row = getRow()) { ... } }",
    "zoom" : "function() { return 'zoom!' }",
  }
}
```

Arguments to the List Function

The function is called with two arguments, which can sometimes be ignored, as the row data itself is loaded during function execution. The first argument, `head`, contains information about the view. Here's what you might see looking at a JSON representation of `head`:

```
{total_rows:10, offset:0}
```

The request itself is a much richer data structure. This is the same request object that is available to show, update, and filter functions. We'll go through it in detail here as a reference. Here's the example `req` object:

```
{
  "info": {
    "db_name": "test_suite_db","doc_count": 11,"doc_del_count": 0,
    "update_seq": 11,"purge_seq": 0,"compact_running": false,"disk_size": 4930,
    "instance_start_time": "1250046852578425","disk_format_version": 4},
```

The database information, as available in an information request against a database's
URL, is included in the request parameters. This allows you to stamp rendered rows
with an update sequence and know the database you are working with.

```
  "method": "GET",
  "path": ["test_suite_db","_design","lists","_list","basicJSON","basicView"],
```

The HTTP method and the path in the client from the client request are useful, especially for rendering links to other resources within the application.

```
  "query": {"foo":"bar"},
```

If there are parameters in the query string (in this case corresponding to ?foo=bar), they
will be parsed and available as a JSON object at req.query.

```
  "headers":
    {"Accept": "text/html,application/xhtml+xml ,application/xml;q=0.9,*/*;q=0.8",
     "Accept-Charset": "ISO-8859-1,utf-8;q=0.7,*;q=0.7","Accept-Encoding":
     "gzip,deflate","Accept-Language": "en-us,en;q=0.5","Connection": "keep-alive",
     "Cookie": "_x=95252s.sd25; AuthSession=","Host": "127.0.0.1:5984",
     "Keep-Alive": "300",
     "Referer": "http://127.0.0.1:5984/_utils/couch_tests.html?script/couch_tests.js",
     "User-Agent": "Mozilla/5.0 Gecko/20090729 Firefox/3.5.2"},
  "cookie": {"_x": "95252s.sd25","AuthSession": ""},
```

Headers give list and show functions the ability to provide the Content-Type response
that the client prefers, as well as other nifty things like cookies. Note that cookies are
also parsed into a JSON representation. Thanks, MochiWeb!

```
  "body": "undefined",
  "form": {},
```

In the case where the method is POST, the request body (and a form-decoded JSON
representation of it, if applicable) are available as well.

```
  "userCtx": {"db": "test_suite_db","name": null,"roles": ["_admin"]}
}
```

Finally, the userCtx is the same as that sent to the validation function. It provides access
to the database the user is authenticated against, the user's name, and the roles they've
been granted. In the previous example, you see an anonymous user working with a
CouchDB node that is in "admin party" mode. Unless an admin is specified, everyone
is an admin.

That's enough about the arguments to list functions. Now it's time to look at the
mechanics of the function itself.

An Example List Function

Let's put this knowledge to use. In the chapter introduction, we mentioned using lists to generate config files. One fun thing about this is that if you keep your configuration information in CouchDB and generate it with lists, you don't have to worry about being able to regenerate it again, because you know the config will be generated by a pure function from your database and not other sources of information. This level of isolation will ensure that your config files can be generated correctly as long as CouchDB is running. Because you can't fetch data from other system services, files, or network sources, you can't accidentally write a config file generator that fails due to external factors.

J. Chris got excited about the idea of using list functions to generate config files for the sort of services people usually configure using CouchDB, specifically via Chef, an Apache-licensed infrastructure automation tool. The key feature of infrastructure automation is that deployment scripts are idempotent—that is, running your scripts multiple times will have the same intended effect as running them once, something that becomes critical when a script fails halfway through. This encourages crash-only design, where your scripts can bomb out multiple times but your data remains consistent, because it takes the guesswork out of provisioning and updating servers in the case of previous failures.

Like map, reduce, and show functions, lists are pure functions, from a view query and an HTTP request to an output format. They can't make queries against remote services or otherwise access outside data, so you know they are repeatable. Using a list function to generate an HTTP server configuration file ensures that the configuration is generated repeatably, based on only the state of the database.

Imagine you are running a shared hosting platform, with one name-based virtual host per user. You'll need a config file that starts out with some node configuration (which modules to use, etc.) and is followed by one config section per user, setting things like the user's HTTP directory, subdomain, forwarded ports, etc.

```
function(head, req) {
  // helper function definitions would be here...
  var row, userConf, configHeader, configFoot;
  configHeader = renderTopOfApacheConf(head, req.query.hostname);
  send(configHeader);
```

In the first block of the function, we're rendering the top of the config file using the function `renderTopOfApacheConf(head, req.query.hostname)`. This may include information that's posted into the function, like the internal name of the server that is being configured or the root directory in which user HTML files are organized. We won't show the function body, but you can imagine that it would return a long multi-line string that handles all the global configuration for your server and sets the stage for the per-user configuration that will be based on view data.

The call to send(configHeader) is the heart of your ability to render text using list functions. Put simply, it just sends an HTTP chunk to the client, with the content of the strings pasted to it. There is some batching behind the scenes, as CouchDB speaks with the JavaScript runner with a synchronous protocol, but from the perspective of a programmer, send() is how HTTP chunks are born.

Now that we've rendered and sent the file's head, it's time to start rendering the list itself. Each list item will be the result of converting a view row to a virtual host's configuration element. The first thing we do is call getRow() to get a row of the view.

```
while (row = getRow()) {
  var userConf = renderUserConf(row);
  send(userConf)
}
```

The while loop used here will continue to run until getRow() returns null, which is how CouchDB signals to the list function that all valid rows (based on the view query parameters) have been exhausted. Before we get ahead of ourselves, let's check out what happens when we do get a row.

In this case, we simply render a string based on the row and send it to the client. Once all rows have been rendered, the loop is complete. Now is a good time to note that the function has the option to return early. Perhaps it is programmed to stop iterating when it sees a particular user's document or is based on a tally it's been keeping of some resource allocated in the configuration. In those cases, the loop can end early with a break statement or other method. There's no requirement for the list function to render every row that is sent to it.

```
configFoot = renderConfTail();
  return configFoot;
}
```

Finally, we close out the configuration file and return the final string value to be sent as the last HTTP chunk. The last action of a list function is always to return a string, which will be sent as the final HTTP chunk to the client.

To use our config file generation function in practice, we might run a command-line script that looks like:

```
curl http://localhost:5984/config_db/_design/files/_list/apache/users?hostname=foobar
> apache.conf
```

This will render our Apache config based on data in the user's view and save it to a file. What a simple way to build a reliable configuration generator!

List Theory

Now that we've seen a complete list function, it's worth mentioning some of the helpful properties they have.

The most obvious thing is the iterator-style API. Because each row is loaded independently by calling getRow(), it's easy not to leak memory. The list function API is capable of rendering lists of arbitrary length without error, when used correctly.

On the other hand, this API gives you the flexibility to bundle a few rows in a single chunk of output, so if you had a view of, say, user accounts, followed by subdomains owned by that account, you could use a slightly more complex loop to build up some state in the list function for rendering more complex chunks. Let's look at an alternate loop section:

```
var subdomainOwnerRow, subdomainRows = [];
while (row = getRow()) {
```

We've entered a loop that will continue until we have reached the **endkey** of the view. The view is structured so that a user profile row is emitted, followed by all of that user's subdomains. We'll use the profile data and the subdomain information to template the configuration for each individual user. This means we can't render any subdomain configuration until we know we've received all the rows for the current user.

```
if (!subdomainOwnerRow) {
  subdomainOwnerRow = row;
```

This case is true only for the first user. We're merely setting up the initial conditions.

```
} else if (row.value.user != subdomainOwnerRow.value.user) {
```

This is the end case. It will be called only after all the subdomain rows for the current user have been exhausted. It is triggered by a row with a mismatched user, indicating that we have all the subdomain rows.

```
send(renderUserConf(subdomainOwnerRow, subdomainRows));
```

We know we are ready to render everything for the current user, so we pass the profile row and the subdomain rows to a render function (which nicely hides all the gnarly nginx config details from our fair reader). The result is sent to the HTTP client, which writes it to the config file.

```
subdomainRows = [];
subdomainOwnerRow = row;
```

We've finished with that user, so let's clear the rows and start working on the next user.

```
} else {
  subdomainRows.push(row);
```

Ahh, back to work, collecting rows.

```
    }
  }
  send(renderUserConf(subdomainOwnerRow, subdomainRows));
```

This last bit is tricky—after the loop is finished (we've reached the end of the view query), we've still got to render the last user's config. Wouldn't want to forget that!

The gist of this loop section is that we collect rows that belong to a particular user until we see a row that belongs to another user, at which point we render output for the first user, clear our state, and start working with the new user. Techniques like this show how much flexibility is allowed by the list iterator API.

More uses along these lines include filtering rows that should be hidden from a particular result set, finding the top N grouped reduce values (e.g., to sort a tag cloud by popularity), and even writing custom reduce functions (as long as you don't mind that reductions are not stored incrementally).

Querying Lists

We haven't looked in detail at the ways list functions are queried. Just like show functions, they are resources available on the design document. The basic path to a list function is as follows:

```
/db/_design/foo/_list/list-name/view-name
```

Because the list name and the view name are both specified, this means it is possible to render a list against more than one view. For instance, you could have a list function that renders blog comments in the Atom XML format, and then run it against both a global view of recent comments as well as a view of recent comments by blog post. This would allow you to use the same list function to provide an Atom feed for comments across an entire site, as well as individual comment feeds for each post.

After the path to the list comes the view query parameter. Just like a regular view, calling a list function without any query parameters results in a list that reflects every row in the view. Most of the time you'll want to call it with query parameters to limit the returned data.

You're already familiar with the view query options from Chapter 6. The same query options apply to the `_list` query. Let's look at URLs side by side; see Example 9-1.

Example 9-1. A JSON view query

```
GET /db/_design/sofa/_view/recent-posts?descending=true&limit=10
```

This view query is just asking for the 10 most recent blog posts. Of course, this query could include parameters like **startkey** or **skip**—we're leaving them out for simplicity. To run the same query through a list function, we access it via the list resource, as shown in Example 9-2.

Example 9-2. The HTML list query

```
GET /db/_design/sofa/_list/index/recent-posts?descending=true&limit=10
```

The `index` list here is a function from JSON to HTML. Just like the preceding view query, additional query parameters can be applied to paginate through the list. As we'll see in Part III, once you have a working list, adding pagination is trivial. See Example 9-3.

Example 9-3. The Atom list query

```
GET /db/_design/sofa/_list/index/recent-posts?descending=true&limit=10&format=atom
```

The list function can also look at the query parameters and do things like switch that output to render based on parameters. You can even do things like pass the username into the list using a query parameter (but it's not recommended, as you'll ruin cache efficiency).

Lists, Etags, and Caching

Just like show functions and view queries, lists are sent with proper HTTP Etags, which makes them cacheable by intermediate proxies. This means that if your server is starting to bog down in list-rendering code, it should be possible to relieve load by using a caching reverse proxy like Squid. We won't go into the details of Etags and caching here, as they were covered in Chapter 8.

PART III

Example Application

CHAPTER 10

Standalone Applications

CouchDB is useful for many areas of an application. Because of its incremental MapReduce and replication characteristics, it is especially well suited to online interactive document and data management tasks. These are the sort of workloads experienced by the majority of web applications. This coupled with CouchDB's HTTP interface make it a natural fit for the web.

In this part, we'll tour a document-oriented web application—a basic blog implementation. As a lowest common denominator, we'll be using plain old HTML and JavaScript. The lessons learned should apply to Django/Rails/Java-style middleware applications and even to intensive MapReduce data mining tasks. CouchDB's API is the same, regardless of whether you're running a small installation or an industrial cluster.

There is no right answer about which application development framework you should use with CouchDB. We've seen successful applications in almost every commonly used language and framework. For this example application, we'll use a two-layer architecture: CouchDB as the data layer and the browser for the user interface. We think this is a viable model for many document-oriented applications, and it makes a great way to teach CouchDB, because we can easily assume that all of you have a browser at hand without having to ensure that you're familiar with a particular server-side scripting language.

Use the Correct Version

This part is interactive, so be prepared to follow along with your laptop and a running CouchDB database. We've made the full example application and all of the source code examples available online, so you'll start by downloading the current version of the example application and installing it on your CouchDB instance.

A challenge of writing this book and preparing it for production is that CouchDB is evolving at a rapid pace. The basics haven't changed in a long time, and probably won't change much in the future, but things around the edges are moving forward rapidly for CouchDB's 1.0 release.

This book is going to press as CouchDB version 0.10.0 is about to be released. Most of the code was written against 0.9.1 and the development trunk that is becoming version 0.10.0. In this part we'll work with two other software packages: CouchApp, which is a set of tools for editing and sharing CouchDB application code; and Sofa, the example blog itself.

 See *http://couchapp.org* for the latest information about the CouchApp model.

As a reader, it is your responsibility to use the correct versions of these packages. For CouchApp, the correct version is always the latest. The correct version of Sofa depends on which version of CouchDB you are using. To see which version of CouchDB you are using, run the following command:

```
curl http://127.0.0.1:5984
```

You should see something like one of these three examples:

```
{"couchdb":"Welcome","version":"0.9.1"}
```

```
{"couchdb":"Welcome","version":"0.10.0"}
```

```
{"couchdb":"Welcome","version":"0.11.0a858744"}
```

These three correspond to versions 0.9.1, 0.10.0, and trunk. If the version of CouchDB you have installed is 0.9.1 or earlier, you should upgrade to at least 0.10.0, as Sofa makes use of features not present until 0.10.0. There is an older version of Sofa that will work, but this book covers features and APIs that are part of the 0.10.0 release of CouchDB. It's conceivable that there will be a 0.9.2, 0.10.1 and even a 0.10.2 release by the time you read this. Please use the latest release of whichever version you prefer.

Trunk refers to the latest development version of CouchDB available in the Apache Subversion repository. We recommend that you use a released version of CouchDB, but as developers, we often use trunk. Sofa's master branch will tend to work on trunk, so if you want to stay on the cutting edge, that's the way to do it.

Portable JavaScript

If you're not familiar with JavaScript, we hope the source examples are given with enough context and explanation so that you can keep up. If you are familiar with JavaScript, you're probably already excited that CouchDB supports view and template rendering JavaScript functions.

One of the advantages of building applications that can be hosted on any standard CouchDB installation is that they are portable via replication. This means your application, if you develop it to be served directly from CouchDB, gets offline mode "for free." Local data makes a big difference for users in a number of ways we won't get into here. We call applications that can be hosted from a standard CouchDB *CouchApps*.

CouchApps are a great vehicle for teaching CouchDB because we don't need to worry about picking a language or framework; we'll just work directly with CouchDB so that readers get a quick overview of a familiar application pattern. Once you've worked through the example app, you'll have seen enough to know how to apply CouchDB to your problem domain. If you don't know much about Ajax development, you'll learn a little about jQuery as well, and we hope you find the experience relaxing.

Applications Are Documents

Applications are stored as design documents (Figure 10-1). You can replicate design documents just like everything else in CouchDB. Because design documents can be replicated, whole CouchApps are replicated. CouchApps can be updated via replication, but they are also easily "forked" by the users, who can alter the source code at will.

Figure 10-1. CouchDB executes application code stored in design documents

Because applications are just a special kind of document, they are easy to edit and share.

J. Chris says: Thinking of peer-based application replication takes me back to my first year of high school, when my friends and I would share little programs between the TI-85 graphing calculators we were required to own. Two calculators could be connected via a small cable and we'd share physics cheat sheets, Hangman, some multi-player text-based adventures, and, at the height of our powers, I believe there may have been a Doom clone running.

The TI-85 programs were in Basic, so everyone was always hacking each other's hacks. Perhaps the most ridiculous program was a version of Spy Hunter that you controlled with your mind. The idea was that you could influence the pseudorandom number generator by concentrating hard enough, and thereby control the game. Didn't work. Anyway, the point is that when you give people access to the source code, there's no telling what might happen.

If people don't like the aesthetics of your application, they can tweak the CSS. If people don't like your interface choices, they can improve the HTML. If they want to modify the functionality, they can edit the JavaScript. Taken to the extreme, they may want to completely fork your application for their own purposes. When they show the modified version to their friends and coworkers, and hopefully you, there is a chance that more people may want to make improvements.

As the original developer, you have the control over your version and can accept or reject changes as you see fit. If someone messes around with the source code for a local application and breaks things beyond repair, they can replicate the original copy from your server, as illustrated in Figure 10-2.

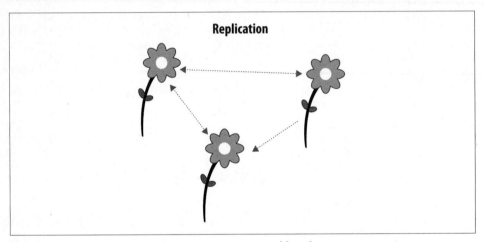

Figure 10-2. Replicating application changes to a group of friends

Of course, this may not be your cup of tea. Don't worry; you can be as restrictive as you like with CouchDB. You can restrict access to data however you wish, but beware of the opportunities you might be missing. There is a middle ground between open collaboration and restricted access controls.

Once you've finished the installation procedure, you'll be able to see the full application code for Sofa, both in your text editor and as a design document in Futon.

Standalone

What happens if you add an HTML file as a document attachment? Exactly the same thing. We can serve web pages directly with CouchDB. Of course, we might also need images, stylesheets, or scripts. No problem; just add these resources as document attachments and link to them using relative URIs.

Let's take a step back. What do we have so far? A way to serve HTML documents and other static files on the Web. That means we can build and serve traditional websites using CouchDB. Fantastic! But isn't this a little like reinventing the wheel? Well, a very important difference is that we also have a document database sitting in the background. We can talk to this database using the JavaScript served up with our web pages. Now we're really cooking with gas!

CouchDB's features are a foundation for building standalone web applications backed by a powerful database. As a proof of concept, look no further than CouchDB's built-in administrative interface. Futon is a fully functional database management application built using HTML, CSS, and JavaScript. Nothing else. CouchDB and web applications go hand in hand.

In the Wild

There are plenty of examples of CouchApps in the wild. This section includes screenshots of just a few sites and applications that use a standalone CouchDB architecture.

Damien Katz, inventor of CouchDB and writer of this book's Foreword, decided to see how long it would take to implement a shared calendar with real-time updates as events are changed on the server. It took about an afternoon, thanks to some amazing open source jQuery plug-ins. The calendar demo is still running on J. Chris's server (*http://jchrisa.net/cal/_design/cal/index.html*). See Figure 10-3.

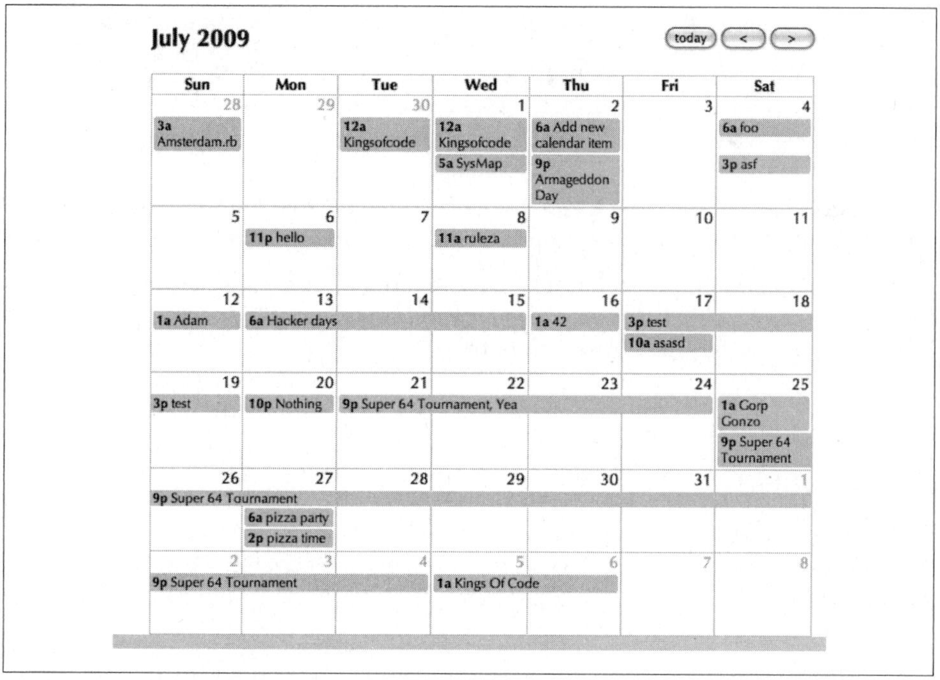

Figure 10-3. Group calendar

Jason Davies swapped out the backend of the Ely Service website (*http://www.elyservice.co.uk/*) with CouchDB, without changing anything visible to the user. The technical details are covered on his blog (*http://www.jasondavies.com/blog/2009/05/08/couchdb-on-wheels/*). See Figure 10-4.

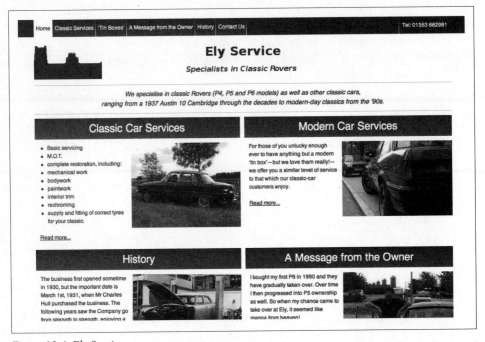

Figure 10-4. Ely Service

Jason also converted his mom's ecommerce website, Bet Ha Bracha, to a CouchApp. It uses the `_update` handler to hook into different transaction gateways. See Figure 10-5.

Processing JS (*http://processingjs.org/*) is a toolkit for building animated art that runs in the browser. Processing JS Studio (*http://github.com/hpoydar/processing-js-studio*) is a gallery for Processing JS sketches. See Figure 10-6.

Figure 10-5. Bet Ha Bracha

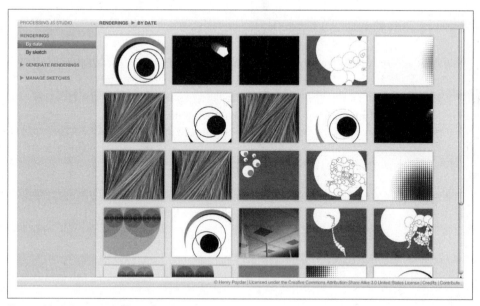

Figure 10-6. Processing JS Studio

Swinger (*http://github.com/quirkey/swinger*) is a CouchApp for building and sharing presentations. It uses the Sammy (*http://www.quirkey.com/blog/2009/09/15/sammy-js -couchdb-and-the-new-web-architecture/*) JavaScript application framework. See Figure 10-7.

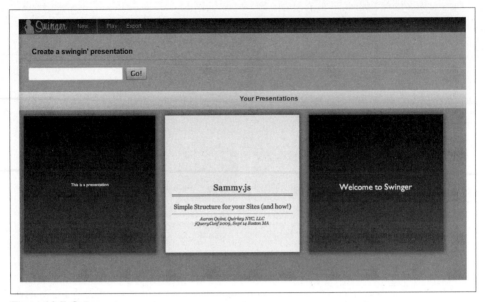

Figure 10-7. Swinger

Nymphormation (*http://nymphormation.org*) is a link sharing and tagging site by Benoît Chesneau. It uses CouchDB's cookie authentication and also makes it possible to share links using replication. See Figure 10-8.

Boom Amazing (*http://github.com/langalex/boom_amazing*) is a CouchApp by Alexander Lang that allows you to zoom, rotate, and pan around an SVG file, record the different positions, and then replay those for a presentation or something else (from the Boom Amazing README). See Figure 10-9.

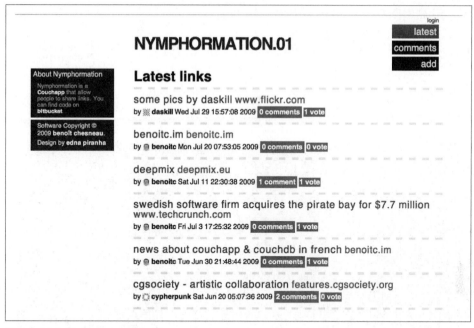

Figure 10-8. Nymphormation

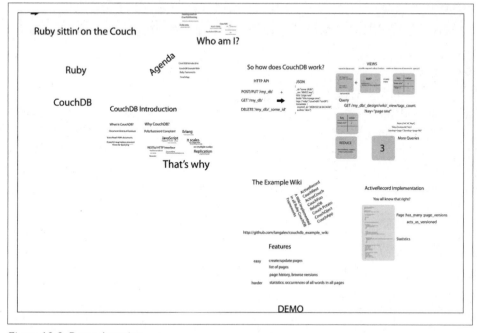

Figure 10-9. Boom Amazing

The CouchDB Twitter Client (*http://github.com/jchris/couchdb-twitter-client*) was one of the first standalone CouchApps to be released. It's documented in J. Chris's blog post, "My Couch or Yours, Shareable Apps are the Future" (*http://jchrisa.net/drl/_design/sofa/_show/post/my_couch_or_yours__shareable_ap*). The screenshot in Figure 10-10 shows the word cloud generated from a MapReduce view of CouchDB's archived tweets. The cloud is normalized against the global view, so universally common words don't dominate the chart.

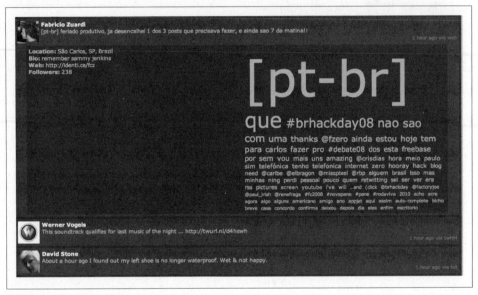

Figure 10-10. Twitter Client

Toast (*http://github.com/jchris/toast*) is a chat application that allows users to create channels and then invite others to real-time chat. It was initially a demo of the _changes event loop, but it started to take off as a way to chat. See Figure 10-11.

Sofa is the example application for this part, and it has been deployed by a few different authors around the web. The screenshot in Figure 10-12 is from Jan's Tumblelog. To see Sofa in action, visit J. Chris's site (*http://jchrisa.net*), which has been running Sofa since late 2008.

Toast - Couch Time

Message _____

Name [J Chris Anderson] Email (for *Gravatar*) [jchris@apache.org] URL [_____] (Go →)

J Chris Anderson: Hello hello
2009/09/21 19:44:17 +0000

Darryl: Hi
2009/09/20 11:00:05 +0000

: blahrg
2009/09/18 18:27:56 +0000

: test
2009/09/18 18:22:47 +0000

Tank: Hi.HI..
2009/09/18 02:19:02 +0000

Giancarlo: Ciao a tutti !!!
2009/09/15 16:36:46 +0000

R4ph4: Cheers Mates!
2009/09/15 04:15:37 +0000

sam: Hi there
2009/09/14 11:38:49 +0000

zz: gdxg
2009/09/13 13:09:50 +0000

Figure 10-11. Toast

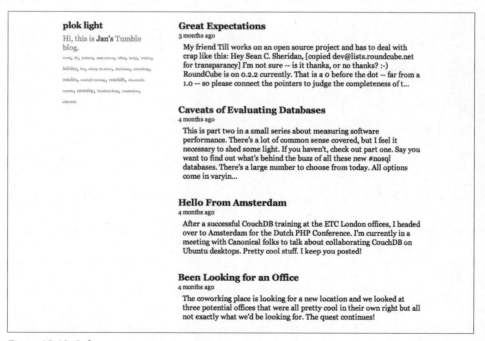

plok light

Hi, this is **Jan's** Tumble blog.

travel, sto, jealous, open source, office, nosql, london,
holiday, fun, erlang via error, databases, coworking,
couchio, couchdb training, couchdb, chocolate
express, carousing, benchmarking, amsterdam,
aberrath

Great Expectations
3 months ago

My friend Till works on an open source project and has to deal with crap like this: Hey Sean C. Sheridan, [copied dev@lists.roundcube.net for transparancy] I'm not sure -- is it thanks, or no thanks? :-) RoundCube is on 0.2.2 currently. That is a 0 before the dot -- far from a 1.0 -- so please connect the pointers to judge the completeness of t...

Caveats of Evaluating Databases
4 months ago

This is part two in a small series about measuring software performance. There's a lot of common sense covered, but I feel it necessary to shed some light. If you haven't, check out part one. Say you want to find out what's behind the buzz of all these new #nosql databases. There's a large number to choose from today. All options come in varyin...

Hello From Amsterdam
4 months ago

After a successful CouchDB training at the ETC London offices, I headed over to Amsterdam for the Dutch PHP Conference. I'm currently in a meeting with Canonical folks to talk about collaborating CouchDB on Ubuntu desktops. Pretty cool stuff. I keep you posted!

Been Looking for an Office
4 months ago

The coworking place is looking for a new location and we looked at three potential offices that were all pretty cool in their own right but all not exactly what we'd be looking for. The quest continues!

Figure 10-12. Sofa

Wrapping Up

J. Chris decided to port his blog from Ruby on Rails to CouchDB. He started by exporting Rails ActiveRecord objects as JSON documents, paring away some features, and adding others as he converted to HTML and JavaScript.

The resulting blog engine features access-controlled posting, open comments with the possibility of moderation, Atom feeds, Markdown formatting, and a few other little goodies. This book is not about jQuery, so although we use this JavaScript library, we'll refrain from dwelling on it. Readers familiar with using asynchronous XMLHttpRequest (XHR) should feel right at home with the code. Keep in mind that the figures and code samples in this part omit many of the bookkeeping details.

We will be studying this application and learning how it exercises all the core features of CouchDB. The skills learned in this part should be broadly applicable to any CouchDB application domain, whether you intend to build a self-hosted CouchApp or not.

CHAPTER 11

Managing Design Documents

Applications can live in CouchDB—nice. You just attach a bunch of HTML and Java-Script files to a design document and you are good to go. Spice that up with view-powered queries and show functions that render any media type from your JSON documents, and you have all it takes to write self-contained CouchDB applications.

Working with the Example Application

If you want to install and hack on your own version of Sofa while you read the following chapters, we'll be using CouchApp to upload the source code as we explore it.

We're particularly excited by the prospect of deploying applications to CouchDB because, depending on a least-common denominator environment, that encourages users to control not just the data but also the source code, which will let more people build personal web apps. And when the web app you've hacked together in your spare time hits the big time, the ability of CouchDB to scale to larger infrastructure sure doesn't hurt.

In a CouchDB design document, there are a mix of development languages (HTML, JS, CSS) that go into different places like attachments and design document attributes. Ideally, you want your development environment to help you as much as possible. More important, you're already used to proper syntax highlighting, validation, integrated documentation, macros, helpers, and whatnot. Editing HTML and JavaScript code as the string attributes of a JSON object is not exactly modern computing.

Lucky for you, we've been working on a solution. Enter *CouchApp*. CouchApp lets you develop CouchDB applications in a convenient directory hierarchy—views and shows are separate, neatly organized *.js* files; your static assets (CSS, images) have their place; and with the simplicity of a couchapp push, you save your app to a design document in CouchDB. Make a change? couchapp push and off you go.

This chapter guides you through the installation and moving parts of CouchApp. You will learn what other neat helpers it has in store to make your life easier. Once we have CouchApp, we'll use it to install and deploy Sofa to a CouchDB database.

Installing CouchApp

The CouchApp Python script and JavaScript framework we'll be using grew out of the work designing this example application. It's now in use for a variety of applications, and has a mailing list, wiki, and a community of hackers. Just search the Internet for "couchapp" to find the latest information. Many thanks to Benoît Chesneau for building and maintaining the library (and contributing to CouchDB's Erlang codebase and many of the Python libraries).

CouchApp is easiest to install using the Python `easy_install` script, which is part of the `setuptools` package. If you are on a Mac, `easy_install` should already be available. If `easy_install` is not installed and you are on a Debian variant, such as Ubuntu, you can use the following command to install it:

```
sudo apt-get install python-setuptools
```

Once you have `easy_install`, installing CouchApp should be as easy as:

```
sudo easy_install -U couchapp
```

Hopefully, this works and you are ready to start using CouchApp. If not, read on....

The most common problem people have installing CouchApp is with old versions of dependencies, especially `easy_install` itself. If you got an installation error, the best next step is to attempt to upgrade `setuptools` and then upgrade CouchApp by running the following commands:

```
sudo easy_install -U setuptools
sudo easy_install -U couchapp
```

If you have other problems installing CouchApp, have a look at **setuptools** (*http://pypi .python.org/pypi/setuptools*) for Python's easy install troubleshooting, or visit the CouchApp mailing list (*http://groups.google.com/group/couchapp*).

Using CouchApp

Installing CouchApp via `easy_install` should, as they say, be easy. Assuming all goes according to plan, it takes care of any dependencies and puts the **couchapp** utility into your system's PATH so you can immediately begin by running the help command:

```
couchapp --help
```

We'll be using the `clone` and `push` commands. `clone` pulls an application from a running instance in the cloud, saving it as a directory structure on your filesystem. `push` deploys a standalone CouchDB application from your filesystem to any CouchDB over which you have administrative control.

Download the Sofa Source Code

There are three ways to get the Sofa source code. They are all equally valid; it's just a matter of personal preference and how you plan to use the code once you have it. The easiest way is to use CouchApp to clone it from a running instance. If you didn't install CouchApp in the previous section, you can read the source code (but not install and run it) by downloading and extracting the ZIP or TAR file. If you are interested in hacking on Sofa and would like to join the development community, the best way to get the source code is from the official Git repository. We'll cover these three methods in turn. First, enjoy Figure 11-1.

Figure 11-1. A happy bird to ease any install-induced frustration

CouchApp Clone

One of the easiest ways to get the Sofa source code is by cloning directly from J. Chris's blog using CouchApp's `clone` command to download Sofa's design document to a collection of files on your local hard drive. The `clone` command operates on a design document URL, which can be hosted in any CouchDB database accessible via HTTP. To clone Sofa from the version running on J. Chris's blog, run the following command:

```
couchapp clone http://jchrisa.net/drl/_design/sofa
```

You should see this output:

```
[INFO] Cloning sofa to ./sofa
```

Now that you've got Sofa on your local filesystem, you can skip to "Deploying Sofa" on page 115 to make a small local change and push it to your own CouchDB.

ZIP and TAR Files

If you merely want to peruse the source code while reading along with this book, it is available as standard ZIP or TAR downloads. To get the ZIP version, access the following URL from your browser, which will redirect to the latest ZIP file of Sofa: *http://github.com/couchapp/couchapp/zipball/master*. If you prefer, a TAR file is available as well: *http://github.com/couchapp/couchapp/tarball/master*.

Join the Sofa Development Community on GitHub

The most up-to-date version of Sofa will always be available at its public code repository (*http://github.com/jchris/sofa*). If you are interested in staying up-to-date with development efforts and contributing patches back to the source, the best way to do it is via Git and GitHub.

Git is a form of distributed version control that allows groups of developers to track and share changes to software. If you are familiar with Git, you'll have no trouble using it to work on Sofa. If you've never used Git before, it has a bit of a learning curve, so depending on your tolerance for new software, you might want to save learning Git for another day—or you might want to dive in head first! For more information about Git and how to install it, see the official Git home page (*http://git-scm.com/*). For other hints and help using Git, see the GitHub guides (*http://github.com/guides*).

To get Sofa (including all development history) using Git, run the following command:

```
git clone git://github.com/jchris/sofa.git
```

Now that you've got the source, let's take a quick tour.

The Sofa Source Tree

Once you've succeeded with any of these methods, you'll have a copy of Sofa on your local disk. The following text is generated by running the `tree` command on the Sofa directory to reveal the full set of files it contains. Sections of the text are annotated to make it clear how various files and directories correspond to the Sofa design document.

```
sofa/
|-- README.md
|-- THANKS.txt
```

The source tree contains some files that aren't necessary for the application—the README and THANKS files are among those.

```
|-- _attachments
|   |-- LICENSE.txt
|   |-- account.html
|   |-- blog.js
|   |-- jquery.scrollTo.js
|   |-- md5.js
|   |-- screen.css
```

```
|   |-- showdown-licenese.txt
|   |-- showdown.js
|   |-- tests.js
|   `-- textile.js
```

The _attachments_ directory contains files that are saved to the Sofa design document as binary attachments. CouchDB serves attachments directly (instead of including them in a JSON wrapper), so this is where we store JavaScript, CSS, and HTML files that the browser will access directly.

 Making your first edit to the Sofa source code will show you how easy it is to modify the application.

```
|-- blog.json
```

The _blog.json_ file contains JSON used to configure individual installations of Sofa. Currently, it sets one value, the title of the blog. You should open this file now and personalize the title field—you probably don't want to name your blog "Daytime Running Lights," so now's your chance to come up with something more fun!

You could add other blog configurations to this file—maybe things like how many posts to show per page and a URL for an About page for the author. Working changes like these into the application will be easy once you've walked through later chapters.

```
|-- couchapp.json
```

We'll see later that `couchapp` outputs a link to Sofa's home page when `couchapp push` is run. The way this works is pretty simple: CouchApp looks for a JSON field on the design document at the address _design_doc.couchapp.index_. If it finds it, it appends the value to the location of the design document itself to build the URL. If there is no CouchApp index specified, but the design document has an attachment called _index.html_, then it is considered the index page. In Sofa's case, we use the index value to point to a list of the most recent posts.

```
|-- helpers
|   `-- md5.js
```

The _helpers_ directory here is just an arbitrary choice—CouchApp will push any files and folders to the design document. In this case, the source code to `md5.js` is JSON-encoded and stored on the `design_document.helpers.md5` element.

```
|-- lists
|   `-- index.js
```

The _lists_ directory contains a JavaScript function that will be executed by CouchDB to render view rows as Sofa's HTML and Atom indexes. You could add new list functions by creating new files within this directory. Lists are covered in depth in Chapter 14.

```
|-- shows
|    |-- edit.js
|    `-- post.js
```

The *shows* directory holds the functions CouchDB uses to generate HTML views of blog posts. There are two views: one for reading posts and the other for editing. We'll look at these functions in the next few chapters.

```
|-- templates
|    |-- edit.html
|    |-- index
|    |    |-- head.html
|    |    |-- row.html
|    |    `-- tail.html
|    `-- post.html
```

The *templates* directory is like the *helpers* directory and unlike the *lists*, *shows*, or *views* directories in that the code stored is not directly executed on CouchDB's server side. Instead, the templates are included into the body of the list and show functions using macros run by CouchApp when pushing code to the server. These CouchApp macros are covered in Chapter 12. The key point is that the *templates* name could be anything. It is not a special member of the design document; just a convenient place to store and edit our template files.

```
|-- validate_doc_update.js
```

This file corresponds to the JavaScript validation function used by Sofa to ensure that only the blog owner can create new posts, as well as to ensure that the comments are well formed. Sofa's validation function is covered in detail in Chapter 12.

```
|-- vendor
|    `-- couchapp
|         |-- README.md
|         |-- _attachments
|         |    `-- jquery.couchapp.js
|         |-- couchapp.js
|         |-- date.js
|         |-- path.js
|         `-- template.js
```

The *vendor* directory holds code that is managed independently of the Sofa application itself. In Sofa's case, the only vendor package used is couchapp, which contains JavaScript code that knows how to do things like link between *list* and *show* URLs and render templates.

During couchapp push, files within a *vendor/**/_attachments/** path are pushed as design document attachments. In this case, *jquery.couchapp.js* will be pushed to an attachment called *couchapp/jquery.couchapp.js* (so that multiple vendor packages can have the same attachment names without worry of collisions).

```
`-- views
    |-- comments
    |    |-- map.js
```

```
|    `-- reduce.js
|-- recent-posts
|    `-- map.js
`-- tags
     |-- map.js
     `-- reduce.js
```

The *views* directory holds MapReduce view definitions, with each view represented as a directory, holding files corresponding to map and reduce functions.

Deploying Sofa

The source code is safely on your hard drive, and you've even been able to make minor edits to the *blog.json* file. Now it's time to deploy the blog to a local CouchDB. The push command is simple and should work the first time, but two other steps are involved in setting up an admin account on your CouchDB and for your CouchApp deployments. By the end of this chapter you'll have your own running copy of Sofa.

Pushing Sofa to Your CouchDB

Any time you make edits to the on-disk version of Sofa and want to see them in your browser, run the following command:

```
couchapp push . sofa
```

This deploys the Sofa source code into CouchDB. You should see output like this:

```
[INFO] Pushing CouchApp in /Users/jchris/sofa to design doc:
http://127.0.0.1:5984/sofa/_design/sofa
[INFO] Visit your CouchApp here:
http://127.0.0.1:5984/sofa/_design/sofa/_list/index/recent-posts?descending=
true&limit=5
```

If you get an error, make sure your target CouchDB instance is running by making a simple HTTP request to it:

```
curl http://127.0.0.1:5984
```

The response should look like:

```
{"couchdb":"Welcome","version":"0.10.1"}
```

If CouchDB is not running yet, go back to Chapter 3 and follow the "Hello World" instructions there.

Visit the Application

If CouchDB was running, then couchapp push should have directed you to visit the application's index URL (*http://127.0.0.1:5984/sofa/_design/sofa/_list/index/recent -posts?descending=true&limit=5*). Visiting the URL should show you something like Figure 11-2.

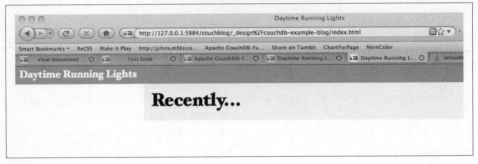

Figure 11-2. Empty index page

We're not done yet—there are a couple of steps remaining before you've got a fully functional Sofa instance.

Set Up Your Admin Account

Sofa is a single-user application. You, the author, are the administrator and the only one who can add and edit posts. To make sure no one else goes in and messes with your writing, you must create an administrator account in CouchDB. This is a straight-forward task. Find your *local.ini* file and open it in your text editor. (By default, it's stored at */usr/local/etc/couchdb/local.ini*.) If you haven't already, uncomment the [admins] section at the end of the file. Next, add a line right below the [admins] section with your preferred username and password:

```
[admins]
jchris = secretpass
```

Now that you've edited your *local.ini* configuration file, you need to restart CouchDB for changes to take effect. Depending on how you started CouchDB, there are different methods of restarting it. If you started in a console, then hitting Ctrl-C and rerunning the same command you used to start it is the simplest way.

If you don't like your passwords lying around in plain-text files, don't worry. When CouchDB starts up and reads this file, it takes your password and changes it to a secure hash, like this:

```
[admins]
jchris = -hashed-207b1b4f8434dc604206c2c0c2aa3aae61568d6c,964 \
    06178007181395cb72cb4e8f2e66e
```

CouchDB will now ask you for your credentials when you try to create databases or change documents—exactly the things you want to keep to yourself.

Deploying to a Secure CouchDB

Now that we've set up admin credentials, we'll need to supply them on the command line when running `couchapp push`. Let's try it:

```
couchapp push . http://jchris:secretpass@localhost:5984/sofa
```

Make sure to replace `jchris` and `secretpass` with your actual values or you will get a "permission denied" error. If all works according to plan, everything will be set up in CouchDB and you should be able to start using your blog.

At this point, we are technically ready to move on, but you'll be much happier if you make use of the *.couchapprc* file as documented in the next section.

Configuring CouchApp with .couchapprc

If you don't want to have to put the full URL (potentially including authentication parameters) of your database onto the command line each time you push, you can use the *.couchapprc* file to store deployment settings. The contents of this file are not pushed along with the rest of the app, so it can be a safe place to keep credentials for uploading your app to secure servers.

The *.couchapprc* file lives in the source directory of your application, so you should look to see if it is at */path/to/the/directory/of/sofa/.couchapprc* (or create it there if it is missing). Dot files (files with names that start with a period) are left out of most directory listings. Use whatever tricks your OS has to "show hidden files." The simplest one in a standard command shell is to list the directory using `ls -a`, which will show all hidden files as well as normal files.

```
{
  "env": {
    "default": {
      "db": "http://jchris:secretpass@localhost:5984/sofa"
    },
    "staging": {
      "db": "http://jchris:secretpass@jchrisa.net:5984/sofa-staging"
    },
    "drl": {
      "db": "http://jchris:secretpass@jchrisa.net/drl"
    }
  }
}
```

With this file set up, you can push your CouchApp with the command `couchapp push`, which will push the application to the "default" database. CouchApp also supports alternate environments. To push your application to a development database, you could use `couchapp push dev`. In our experience, taking the time to set up a good *.couchapprc* is always worth it. Another benefit is that it keeps your passwords off the screen when you are working.

CHAPTER 12

Storing Documents

Documents are CouchDB's central data structure. To best understand and use CouchDB, you need to *think in documents*. This chapter walks you though the lifecycle of designing and saving a document. We'll follow up by reading documents and aggregating and querying them with views. In the next section, you'll see how CouchDB can also transform documents into other formats.

Documents are self-contained units of data. You might have heard the term *record* to describe something similar. Your data is usually made up of small native types such as integers and strings. Documents are the first level of abstraction over these native types. They provide some structure and logically group the primitive data. The height of a person might be encoded as an integer (`176`), but this integer is usually part of a larger structure that contains a label (`"height": 176`) and related data (`{"name":"Chris", "height": 176}`).

How many data items you put into your documents depends on your application and a bit on how you want to use views (later), but generally, a document roughly corresponds to an object instance in your programming language. Are you running an online shop? You will have *items* and *sales* and *comments* for your items. They all make good candidates for objects and, subsequently, documents.

Documents differ subtly from garden-variety objects in that they usually have authors and CRUD operations (create, read, update, delete). Document-based software (like the word processors and spreadsheets of yore) builds its storage model around saving documents so that authors get back what they created. Similarly, in a CouchDB application you may find yourself giving greater leeway to the presentation layer. If, instead of adding timestamps to your data in a controller, you allow the user to control them, you get draft status and the ability to publish articles in the future for free (by viewing published documents using an `endkey` of *now*).

Validation functions are available so that you don't have to worry about bad data causing errors in your system. Often in document-based software, the client application edits and manipulates the data, saving it back. As long as you give the user the document she asked you to save, she'll be happy.

Say your users can comment on the item ("lovely book"); you have the option to store the comments as an array, on the item document. This makes it trivial to find the item's comments, but, as they say, "it doesn't scale." A popular item could have tens of comments, or even hundreds or more.

Instead of storing a list on the item document, in this case it may be better to model comments into a collection of documents. There are patterns for accessing collections, which CouchDB makes easy. You likely want to show only 10 or 20 at a time and provide *previous* and *next* links. By handling comments as individual entities, you can group them with views. A group could be the entire collection or slices of 10 or 20, sorted by the item they apply to so that it's easy to grab the set you need.

A rule of thumb: break up into documents everything that you will be handling separately in your application. Items are single, and comments are single, but you don't need to break them into smaller pieces. Views are a convenient way to group your documents in meaningful ways.

Let's go through building our example application to show you in practice how to work with documents.

JSON Document Format

The first step in designing any application (once you know what the program is for and have the user interaction nailed down) is deciding on the format it will use to represent and store data. Our example blog is written in JavaScript. A few lines back we said documents roughly represent your data objects. In this case, there is a an exact correspondence. CouchDB borrowed the JSON data format from JavaScript; this allows us to use documents directly as native objects when programming. This is really convenient and leads to fewer problems down the road (if you ever worked with an ORM system, you might know what we are hinting at).

Let's draft a JSON format for blog posts. We know we'll need each post to have an author, a title, and a body. We know we'd like to use document IDs to find documents so that URLs are search engine–friendly, and we'd also like to list them by creation date.

It should be pretty straightforward to see how JSON works. Curly braces ({}) wrap objects, and objects are key/value lists. Keys are strings that are wrapped in double quotes (""). Finally, a value is a string, an integer, an object, or an array ([ ]). Keys and values are separated by a colon (:), and multiple keys and values by comma (,). That's it. For a complete description of the JSON format, see Appendix E.

Figure 12-1 shows a document that meets our requirements. The cool thing is we just made it up on the spot. We didn't go and define a schema, and we didn't define how things should look. We just created a document with whatever we needed. Now, requirements for objects change all the time during the development of an application. Coming up with a different document that meets new, evolved needs is just as easy.

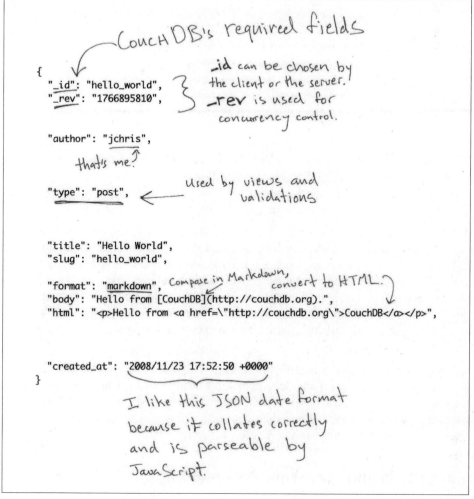

Figure 12-1. The JSON post format

> Do I really look like a guy with a plan? You know what I am? I'm a dog chasing cars. I wouldn't know what to do with one if I caught it. You know, I just do things. The mob has plans, the cops have plans, Gordon's got plans. You know, they're schemers. Schemers trying to control their little worlds. I'm not a schemer. I try to show the schemers how pathetic their attempts to control things really are.
>
> —The Joker, *The Dark Knight*

Let's examine the document in a little more detail. The first two members (_id and _rev) are for CouchDB's housekeeping and act as identification for a particular *instance* of a document. _id is easy: if I store something in CouchDB, it creates the _id and returns it to me. I can use the _id to build the URL where I can get my something back.

Your document's `_id` defines the URL the document can be found under. Say you have a database `movies`. All documents can be found somewhere under the URL `/movies`, but where exactly?

If you store a document with the `_id` Jabberwocky (`{"_id":"Jabberwocky"}`) into your `movies` database, it will be available under the URL `/movies/Jabberwocky`. So if you send a GET request to `/movies/Jabberwocky`, you will get back the JSON that makes up your document (`{"_id":"Jabberwocky"}`).

The `_rev` (or *revision ID*) describes a version of a document. Each change creates a new document version (that again is self-contained) and updates the `_rev`. This becomes useful because, when saving a document, you must provide an up-to-date `_rev` so that CouchDB knows you've been working against the latest document version.

We touched on this in Chapter 2. The revision ID acts as a gatekeeper for writes to a document in CouchDB's MVCC system. A document is a shared resource; many clients can read and write them at the same time. To make sure two writing clients don't step on each other's feet, each client must provide what it believes is the latest revision ID of a document along with the proposed changes. If the on-disk revision ID matches the provided `_rev`, CouchDB will accept the change. If it doesn't, the update will be rejected. The client should read the latest version, integrate the changes, and try saving again.

This mechanism ensures two things: a client can only overwrite a version it knows, and it can't trip over changes made by other clients. This works without CouchDB having to manage explicit *locks* on any document. This ensures that no client has to wait for another client to complete any work. Updates are serialized, so CouchDB will never attempt to write documents faster than your disk can spin, and it also means that two mutually conflicting writes can't be written at the same time.

Beyond _id and _rev: Your Document Data

Now that you thoroughly understand the role of `_id` and `_rev` on a document, let's look at everything else we're storing.

```
{
    "_id":"Hello-Sofa",
    "_rev":"2-2143609722",
    "type":"post",
```

The first thing is the type of the document. Note that this is an application-level parameter, not anything particular to CouchDB. The type is just an arbitrarily named key/value pair as far as CouchDB is concerned. For us, as we're adding blog posts to Sofa, it has a little deeper meaning. Sofa uses the `type` field to determine which validations to apply. It can then rely on documents of that type being valid in the views and the user interface. This removes the need to check for every field and nested JSON value before using it. This is purely by convention, and you can make up your own or infer the type of a document by its structure ("has an array with three elements"—a.k.a. *duck typing*). We just thought this was easy to follow and hope you agree.

```
"author":"jchris",
"title":"Hello Sofa",
```

The `author` and `title` fields are set when the post is created. The `title` field can be changed, but the `author` field is locked by the validation function for security. Only the author may edit the post.

```
"tags":["example","blog post","json"],
```

Sofa's tag system just stores them as an array on the document. This kind of denormalization is a particularly good fit for CouchDB.

```
"format":"markdown",
"body":"some markdown text",
"html":"<p>the html text</p>",
```

Blog posts are composed in the Markdown HTML format (*http://daringfireball.net/ projects/markdown/*) to make them easy to author. The Markdown format as typed by the user is stored in the **body** field. Before the blog post is saved, Sofa converts it to HTML in the client's browser. There is an interface for previewing the Markdown conversion, so you can be sure it will display as you like.

```
"created_at":"2009/05/25 06:10:40 +0000"
}
```

The `created_at` field is used to order blog posts in the Atom feed and on the HTML index page.

The Edit Page

The first page we need to build in order to get one of these blog entries into our post is the interface for creating and editing posts.

Editing is more complex than just rendering posts for visitors to read, but that means once you've read this chapter, you'll have seen most of the techniques we touch on in the other chapters.

The first thing to look at is the *show function* used to render the HTML page. If you haven't already, read Chapter 8 to learn about the details of the API. We'll just look at this code in the context of Sofa, so you can see how it all fits together.

```
function(doc, req) {
    // !json templates.edit
    // !json blog
    // !code vendor/couchapp/path.js
    // !code vendor/couchapp/template.js
```

Sofa's edit page show function is very straightforward. In the previous section, we showed the important templates and libraries we'll use. The important line is the `!json` macro, which loads the *edit.html* template from the *templates* directory. These macros are run by CouchApp, as Sofa is being deployed to CouchDB. For more information about the macros, see Chapter 13.

```
// we only show html
return template(templates.edit, {
  doc : doc,
  docid : toJSON((doc && doc._id) || null),
  blog : blog,
  assets : assetPath(),
  index : listPath('index','recent-posts',{descending:true,limit:8})
});
}
```

The rest of the function is simple. We're just rendering the HTML template with data culled from the document. In the case where the document does not yet exist, we make sure to set the `docid` to `null`. This allows us to use the same template both for creating new blog posts as well as editing existing ones.

The HTML Scaffold

The only missing piece of this puzzle is the HTML that it takes to save a document like this.

In your browser, visit *http://127.0.0.1:5984/blog/_design/sofa/_show/edit* and, using your text editor, open the source file *templates/edit.html* (or view source in your browser). Everything is ready to go; all we have to do is wire up CouchDB using in-page JavaScript. See Figure 12-2.

Just like any web application, the important part of the HTML is the form for accepting edits. The edit form captures a few basic data items: the post title, the body (in Markdown format), and any tags the author would like to apply.

```
<!-- form to create a Post -->
<form id="new-post" action="new.html" method="post">
  <h1>Create a new post</h1>
  <p><label>Title</label>
    <input type="text" size="50" name="title"></p>
  <p><label for="body">Body</label>
    <textarea name="body" rows="28" cols="80">
    </textarea></p>
  <p><input id="preview" type="button" value="Preview"/>
    <input type="submit" value="Save &rarr;"/></p>
</form>
```

We start with just a raw HTML document, containing a normal HTML form. We use JavaScript to convert user input into a JSON document and save it to CouchDB. In the spirit of focusing on CouchDB, we won't dwell on the JavaScript here. It's a combination of Sofa-specific application code, CouchApp's JavaScript helpers, and jQuery for interface elements. The basic story is that it watches for the user to click "Save," and then applies some callbacks to the document before sending it to CouchDB.

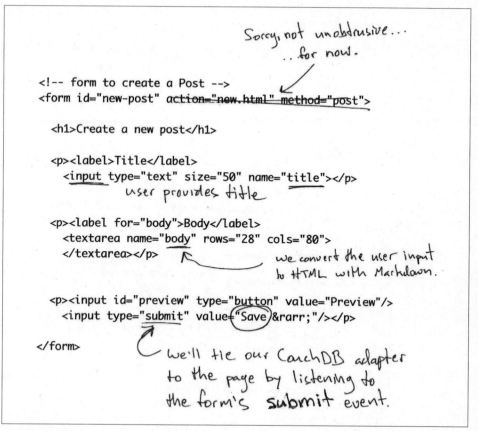

Figure 12-2. HTML listing for edit.html

Saving a Document

The JavaScript that drives blog post creation and editing centers around the HTML form from Figure 12-2. The CouchApp jQuery plug-in provides some abstraction, so we don't have to concern ourselves with the details of how the form is converted to a JSON document when the user hits the submit button. $.CouchApp also ensures that the user is logged in and makes her information available to the application. See Figure 12-3.

```
$.CouchApp(function(app) {
    app.loggedInNow(function(login) {
```

The first thing we do is ask the CouchApp library to make sure the user is logged in. Assuming the answer is yes, we'll proceed to set up the page as an editor. This means we apply a JavaScript event handler to the form and specify callbacks we'd like to run on the document, both when it is loaded and when it saved.

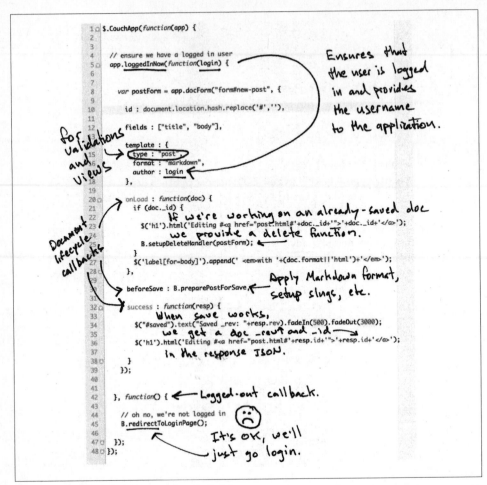

```
1   $.CouchApp(function(app) {
2
3
4       // ensure we have a logged in user
5       app.loggedInNow(function(login) {
6
7
8           var postForm = app.docForm("form#new-post", {
9
10              id : document.location.hash.replace('#',''),
11
12              fields : ["title", "body"],
13
14              template : {
15                  type : "post",
16                  format : "markdown",
17                  author : login
18              },
19
20              onLoad : function(doc) {
21                  if (doc._id) {
22
23                      $('h1').html('Editing #<a href="post.html#'+doc._id+'">'+doc._id+'</a>');
24                      B.setupDeleteHandler(postForm);
25
26                  }
27                  $('label[for=body]').append(' <em>with '+(doc.format||'html')+'</em>');
28              },
29
30              beforeSave : B.preparePostForSave,
31
32              success : function(resp) {
33
34                  $("#saved").text("Saved _rev: "+resp.rev).fadeIn(500).fadeOut(3000);
35
36                  $('h1').html('Editing #<a href="post.html#'+resp.id+'">'+resp.id+'</a>');
37
38              }
39          });
40
41
42      }, function() {
43
44          // oh no, we're not logged in
45          B.redirectToLoginPage();
46
47      });
48  });
```

Handwritten annotations:
- "Ensures that the user is logged in and provides the username to the application." (pointing to line 5)
- "for validations and views" (pointing to line 15)
- "type: "post"" circled
- "author: login" underlined
- "Document lifecycle callbacks" (pointing to lines 20, 30, 32)
- "If we're working on an already-saved doc we provide a delete function." (pointing to lines 22-24)
- "Apply Markdown format, setup slugs, etc." (pointing to line 30)
- "When save works, we get a doc _rev and _id in the response JSON." (pointing to lines 32-36)
- "Logged-out callback." (pointing to line 42)
- "It's OK, we'll just go login." (pointing to line 45)

Figure 12-3. JavaScript callbacks for edit.html

```
// w00t, we're logged in (according to the cookie)
$("#header").prepend('<span id="login">'+login+'</span>');
// setup CouchApp document/form system, adding app-specific callbacks
var B = new Blog(app);
```

Now that we know the user is logged in, we can render his username at the top of the page. The variable B is just a shortcut to some of the Sofa-specific blog rendering code. It contains methods for converting blog post bodies from Markdown to HTML, as well as a few other odds and ends. We pulled these functions into *blog.js* so we could keep them out of the way of main code.

```
var postForm = app.docForm("form#new-post", {
  id : <%= docid %>,
  fields : ["title", "body", "tags"],
  template : {
```

```
        type : "post",
        format : "markdown",
        author : login
    },
```

CouchApp's `app.docForm()` helper is a function to set up and maintain a correspondence between a CouchDB document and an HTML form. Let's look at the first three arguments passed to it by Sofa. The `id` argument tells `docForm()` where to save the document. This can be null in the case of a new document. We set `fields` to an array of form elements that will correspond directly to JSON fields in the CouchDB document. Finally, the `template` argument is given a JavaScript object that will be used as the starting point, in the case of a new document. In this case, we ensure that the document has a type equal to "post," and that the default format is Markdown. We also set the author to be the login name of the current user.

```
    onLoad : function(doc) {
        if (doc._id) {
            B.editing(doc._id);
            $('h1').html('Editing <a href="../post/'+doc._id+'">'+doc._id+'</a>');
            $('#preview').before('<input type="button" id="delete"
                value="Delete Post"/> ');
            $("#delete").click(function() {
                postForm.deleteDoc({
                    success: function(resp) {
                        $("h1").text("Deleted "+resp.id);
                        $('form#new-post input').attr('disabled', true);
                    }
                });
                return false;
            });
        }
        $('label[for=body]').append(' <em>with '+(doc.format||'html')+'</em>');
```

The `onLoad` callback is run when the document is loaded from CouchDB. It is useful for decorating the document before passing it to the form, or for setting up other user interface elements. In this case, we check to see if the document already has an ID. If it does, that means it's been saved, so we create a button for deleting it and set up the callback to the delete function. It may look like a lot of code, but it's pretty standard for Ajax applications. If there is one criticism to make of this section, it's that the logic for creating the delete button could be moved to the *blog.js* file so we can keep more user-interface details out of the main flow.

```
    },
    beforeSave : function(doc) {
        doc.html = B.formatBody(doc.body, doc.format);
        if (!doc.created_at) {
            doc.created_at = new Date();
        }
        if (!doc.slug) {
            doc.slug = app.slugifyString(doc.title);
            doc._id = doc.slug;
        }
```

```
        if(doc.tags) {
          doc.tags = doc.tags.split(",");
          for(var idx in doc.tags) {
            doc.tags[idx] = $.trim(doc.tags[idx]);
          }
        }
      },
```

The beforeSave() callback to docForm is run after the user clicks the submit button. In Sofa's case, it manages setting the blog post's timestamp, transforming the title into an acceptable document ID (for prettier URLs), and processing the document tags from a string into an array. It also runs the Markdown-to-HTML conversion in the browser so that once the document is saved, the rest of the application has direct access to the HTML.

```
      success : function(resp) {
        $("#saved").text("Saved _rev: "+resp.rev).fadeIn(500).fadeOut(3000);
        B.editing(resp.id);
      }
    });
```

The last callback we use in Sofa is the success callback. It is fired when the document is successfully saved. In our case, we use it to flash a message to the user that lets her know she's succeeded, as well as to add a link to the blog post so that when you create a blog post for the first time, you can click through to see its permalink page.

That's it for the docForm() callbacks.

```
    $("#preview").click(function() {
      var doc = postForm.localDoc();
      var html = B.formatBody(doc.body, doc.format);
      $('#show-preview').html(html);
      // scroll down
      $('body').scrollTo('#show-preview', {duration: 500});
    });
```

Sofa has a function to preview blog posts before saving them. Since this doesn't affect how the document is saved, the code that watches for events from the "preview" button is not applied within the docForm() callbacks.

```
    }, function() {
      app.go('<%= assets %>/account.html#'+document.location);
    });
  });
```

The last bit of code here is triggered when the user is not logged in. All it does is redirect him to the account page so that he can log in and try editing again.

Validation

Hopefully, you can see how the previous code will send a JSON document to CouchDB when the user clicks save. That's great for creating a user interface, but it does nothing to protect the database from unwanted updates. This is where validation functions come into play. With a proper validation function, even a determined hacker cannot get unwanted documents into your database. Let's look at how Sofa's works. For more on validation functions, see Chapter 7.

```
function (newDoc, oldDoc, userCtx) {
    // !code lib/validate.js
```

This line imports a library from Sofa that makes the rest of the function much more readable. It is just a wrapper around the basic ability to mark requests as either `forbidden` or `unauthorized`. In this chapter, we've concentrated on the business logic of the validation function. Just be aware that unless you use Sofa's *validate.js*, you'll need to work with the more primitive logic that the library abstracts.

```
unchanged("type");
unchanged("author");
unchanged("created_at");
```

These lines do just what they say. If the document's `type`, `author`, or `created_at` fields are changed, they throw an error saying the update is forbidden. Note that these lines make no assumptions about the content of these fields. They merely state that updates must not change the content from one revision of the document to the next.

```
if (newDoc.created_at) dateFormat("created_at");
```

The `dateFormat` helper makes sure that the date (if one is provided) is in the format that Sofa's views expect.

```
// docs with authors can only be saved by their author
// admin can author anything...
if (!isAdmin(userCtx) && newDoc.author && newDoc.author != userCtx.name) {
    unauthorized("Only "+newDoc.author+" may edit this document.");
}
```

If the person saving the document is an admin, let the edit proceed. Otherwise, make certain that the author and the person saving the document are the same. This ensures that authors may edit only their own posts.

```
// authors and admins can always delete
if (newDoc._deleted) return true;
```

The next block of code will check the validity of various types of documents. However, deletions will normally not be valid according to those specifications, because their content is just `_deleted: true`, so we short-circut the validation function here.

```
if (newDoc.type == 'post') {
    require("created_at", "author", "body", "html", "format", "title", "slug");
    assert(newDoc.slug == newDoc._id, "Post slugs must be used as the _id.")
}
}
```

Finally, we have the validation for the actual post document itself. Here we require the fields that are particular to the post document. Because we've validated that they are present, we can count on them in views and user interface code.

Save Your First Post

Let's see how this all works together! Fill out the form with some practice data, and hit "save" to see a success response.

Figure 12-4 shows how JavaScript has used HTTP to *PUT* the document to a URL constructed of the database name plus the document ID. It also shows how the document is just sent as a JSON string in the body of the PUT request. If you were to *GET* the document URL, you'd see the same set of JSON data, with the addition of the _rev parameter as applied by CouchDB.

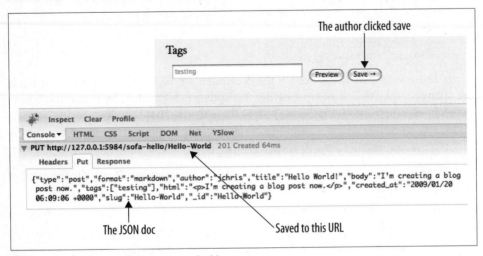

Figure 12-4. JSON over HTTP to save the blog post

To see the JSON version of the document you've saved, you can also browse to it in Futon. Visit *http://127.0.0.1:5984/_utils/database.html?blog/_all_docs* and you should see a document with an ID corresponding to the one you just saved. Click it to see what Sofa is sending to CouchDB.

Wrapping Up

We've covered how to design JSON formats for your application, how to enforce those designs with validation functions, and the basics of how documents are saved. In the next chapter, we'll show how to load documents from CouchDB and display them in the browser.

CHAPTER 13

Showing Documents in Custom Formats

CouchDB's show functions are a RESTful API inspired by a similar feature in Lotus Notes. In a nutshell, they allow you to serve documents to clients, in any format you choose.

A show function builds an HTTP response with any Content-Type, based on a stored JSON document. For Sofa, we'll use them to show the blog post permalink pages. This will ensure that these pages are indexable by search engines, as well as make the pages more accessible. Sofa's show function displays each blog post as an HTML page, with links to stylesheets and other assets, which are stored as attachments to Sofa's design document.

Hey, this is great—we've rendered a blog post! See Figure 13-1.

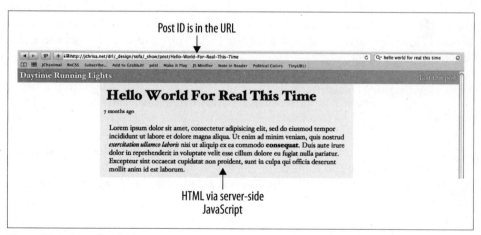

Figure 13-1. A rendered post

The complete show function and template will render a static, cacheable resource that does not depend on details about the current user or anything else aside from the requested document and Content-Type. Generating HTML from a show function will not cause any side effects in the database, which has positive implications for building simple scalable applications.

Rendering Documents with Show Functions

Let's look at the source code. The first thing we'll see is the JavaScript function body, which is very simple—it simply runs a template function to generate the HTML page. Let's break it down:

```
function(doc, req) {
  // !json templates.post
  // !json blog
  // !code vendor/couchapp/template.js
  // !code vendor/couchapp/path.js
```

We're familiar with the !code and !json macros from Chapter 12. In this case, we're using them to import a template and some metadata about the blog (as JSON data), as well as to include link and template rendering functions as inline code.

Next, we render the template:

```
return template(templates.post, {
  title : doc.title,
  blogName : blog.title,
  post : doc.html,
  date : doc.created_at,
  author : doc.author,
```

The blog post title, HTML body, author, and date are taken from the document, with the blog's title included from its JSON value. The next three calls all use the *path.js* library to generate links based on the request path. This ensures that links within the application are correct.

```
  assets : assetPath(),
  editPostPath : showPath('edit', doc._id),
  index : listPath('index','recent-posts',{descending:true, limit:5})
});
}
```

So we've seen that the function body itself just calculates some values (based on the document, the request, and some deployment specifics, like the name of the database) to send to the template for rendering. The real action is in the HTML template. Let's take a look.

The Post Page Template

The template defines the output HTML, with the exception of a few tags that are replaced with dynamic content. In Sofa's case, the dynamic tags look like `<%= replace_me %>`, which is a common templating tag delimiter.

The template engine used by Sofa is adapted from John Resig's blog post, "JavaScript Micro-Templating" (*http://ejohn.org/blog/javascript-micro-templating/*). It was chosen as the simplest one that worked in the server-side context without modification. Using a different template engine would be a simple exercise.

Let's look at the template string. Remember that it is included in the JavaScript using the CouchApp `!json` macro, so that CouchApp can handle escaping it and including it to be used by the templating engine.

```
<!DOCTYPE html>
<html>
  <head>
    <title><%= title %> : <%= blogName %></title>
```

This is the first time we've seen a template tag in action—the blog post title, as well as the name of the blog as defined in *blog.json* are both used to craft the HTML `<title>` tag.

```
<link rel="stylesheet" href="../../screen.css" type="text/css">
```

Because show functions are served from within the design document path, we can link to attachments on the design document using relative URIs. Here we're linking to *screen.css*, a file stored in the *_attachments* folder of the Sofa source directory.

```
  </head>
  <body>
    <div id="header">
      <a id="edit" href="<%= editPostPath %>">Edit this post</a>
      <h2><a href="<%= index %>"><%= blogName %></a></h2>
```

Again, we're seeing template tags used to replace content. In this case, we link to the edit page for this post, as well as to the index page of the blog.

```
    </div>
    <div id="content">
      <h1><%= title %></h1>
      <div id="post">
        <span class="date"><%= date %></span>
```

The post title is used for the `<h1>` tag, and the date is rendered in a special tag with a class of `date`. See "Dynamic Dates" on page 134 for an explanation of why we output static dates in the HTML instead of rendering a user-friendly string like "3 days ago" to describe the date.

```
        <div class="body"><%= post %></div>
      </div>
    </div>
  </body>
</html>
```

In the close of the template, we render the post HTML (as converted from Markdown and saved from the author's browser).

Dynamic Dates

When running CouchDB behind a caching proxy, this means each show function should have to be rendered only once per updated document. However, it also explains why the timestamp looks like 2008/12/25 23:27:17 +0000 instead of "9 days ago."

It also means that for presentation items that depend on the current time, or the identity of the browsing user, we'll need to use client-side JavaScript to make dynamic changes to the final HTML.

```
$('.date').each(function() {
  $(this).text(app.prettyDate(this.innerHTML));
});
```

We include this detail about the browser-side JavaScript implementation not to teach you about Ajax, but because it epitomizes the kind of thinking that makes sense when you are presenting documents to client applications. CouchDB should provide the most useful format for the document, as requested by the client. But when it comes time to integrate information from other queries or bring the display up-to-date with other web services, by asking the client's application to do the lifting, you move computing cycles and memory costs from CouchDB to the client. Since there are typically many more clients than CouchDBs, pushing the load back to the clients means each CouchDB can serve more users.

CHAPTER 14

Viewing Lists of Blog Posts

The last few chapters dealt with getting data into and out of CouchDB. You learned how to model your data into documents and retrieve it via the HTTP API. In this chapter, we'll look at the views used to power Sofa's index page, and the list function that renders those views as HTML or XML, depending on the client's request.

Now that we've successfully created a blog post and rendered it as HTML, we'll be building the front page where visitors will land when they've found your blog. This page will have a list of the 10 most recent blog posts, with titles and short summaries. The first step is to write the MapReduce query that constructs the index used by CouchDB at query time to find blog posts based on when they were written.

In Chapter 6, we noted that reduce isn't needed for many common queries. For the index page, we're only interested in an ordering of the posts by date, so we don't need to use a reduce function, as the map function alone is enough to order the posts by date.

Map of Recent Blog Posts

You're now ready to write the map function that builds a list of all blog posts. The goals for this view are simple: sort all blog posts by date.

Here is the source code for the view function. I'll call out the important bits as we encounter them.

```
function(doc) {
  if (doc.type == "post") {
```

The first thing we do is ensure that the document we're dealing with is a post. We don't want comments or anything other than blog posts getting on the front page. The expression `doc.type == "post"` evaluates to true for posts but no other kind of document. In Chapter 7, we saw that the validation function gives us certain guarantees about posts, designed to make us comfortable about putting them on the front page of our blog.

```
var summary = (doc.html.replace(/<(.|\n)*?>/g, '').substring(0,350) + '...');
```

This line shortens the blog post's HTML (generated from Markdown before saving) and strips out most tags and images, at least well enough to keep them from showing up on the index page, for brevity.

The next section is the crux of the view. We're emitting for each document a key (`doc.created_at`) and a value. The key is used for sorting, so that we can pull out all the posts in a particular date range efficiently.

```
emit(doc.created_at, {
  html : doc.html,
  summary : summary,
  title : doc.title,
  author : doc.author
});
```

The value we've emitted is a JavaScript object, which copies some fields from the document (but not all), and the summary string we've just generated. It's preferable to avoid emitting entire documents. As a general rule, you want to keep your views as lean as possible. Only emit data you plan to use in your application. In this case we emit the summary (for the index page), the HTML (for the Atom feed), the blog post title, and its author.

```
  }
};
```

You should be able to follow the definition of the previous map function just fine by now. The `emit()` call creates an entry for each blog post document in our view's result set. We'll call the view `recent-posts`. Our design document looks like this now:

```
{
  "_design/sofa",
  "views": {
    "recent-posts": {
      "map": "function(doc) { if (doc.type == "post") { ... code to emit posts ... }"
    }
  }
  "_attachments": {
    ...
  }
}
```

CouchApp manages aggregating the filesystem files into our JSON design document, so we can edit our view in a file called *views/recent-posts/map.js*. Once the map function is stored on the design document, our view is ready to be queried for the latest 10 posts. Again, this looks very similar to displaying a single post. The only real difference now is that we get back an array of JSON objects instead of just a single JSON object.

The GET request to the URI is:

```
/blog/_design/sofa/_view/recent-posts
```

A view defined in the document */database/_design/designdocname* in the `views` field ends up being callable under */database/_design/designdocname/_view/viewname*.

You can pass in HTTP query arguments to customize your view query. In this case, we pass in:

```
descending: true, limit: 5
```

This gets the latest post first and only the first five posts in all.

The actual view request URL is:

```
/blog/_design/sofa/_view/recent-posts?descending=true&limit=5
```

Rendering the View as HTML Using a List Function

The `_list` function was covered in detail in Chapter 5. In our example application, we'll use a JavaScript list function to render a view of recent blog posts as both XML and HTML formats. CouchDB's JavaScript view server also ships with the ability to respond appropriately to HTTP content negotiation and Accept headers.

The essence of the `_list` API is a function that is fed one row at a time and sends the response back one chunk at a time.

Sofa's List Function

Let's take a look at Sofa's list function. This is a rather long listing, and it introduces a few new concepts, so we'll take it slow and be sure to cover everything of interest.

```
function(head, req) {
  // !json templates.index
  // !json blog
  // !code vendor/couchapp/path.js
  // !code vendor/couchapp/date.js
  // !code vendor/couchapp/template.js
  // !code lib/atom.js
```

The top of the function declares the arguments `head` and `req`. Our function does not use `head`, just `req`, which contains information about the request such as the headers sent by the client and a representation of the query string as sent by the client. The first lines of the function are CouchApp macros that pull in code and data from elsewhere in the design document. As we've described in more detail in Chapter 11, these macros allow us to work with short, readable functions that pull in library code from elsewhere in the design document. Our list function uses the CouchApp JavaScript helpers for generating URLs (*path.js*), for working with date objects (*date.js*), and the template function we're using to render HTML.

```
var indexPath = listPath('index','recent-posts',{descending:true, limit:5});
var feedPath = listPath('index','recent-posts',{descending:true, limit:5,
    format:"atom"});
```

The next two lines of the function generate URLs used to link to the index page itself, as well as the XML Atom feed version of it. The `listPath` function is defined in *path.js*—

the upshot is that it knows how to link to lists generated by the same design document it is run from.

The next section of the function is responsible for rendering the HTML output of the blog. Refer to Chapter 8 for details about the API we use here. In short, clients can describe the format(s) they prefer in the HTTP Accept header, or in a `format` query parameter. On the server, we declare which formats we provide, as well as assign each format a priority. In cases where the client accepts multiple formats, the first declared format is returned. It is not uncommon for browsers to accept a wide range of formats, so take care to put HTML at the top of the list, or else you can end up with browsers receiving alternate formats when they expect HTML.

```
provides("html", function() {
```

The `provides` function takes two arguments: the name of the format (which is keyed to a list of default MIME types) and a function to execute when rendering that format. Note that when using `provides`, all `send` and `getRow` calls must happen within the render function. Now let's look at how the HTML is actually generated.

```
send(template(templates.index.head, {
  title : blog.title,
  feedPath : feedPath,
  newPostPath : showPath("edit"),
  index : indexPath,
  assets : assetPath()
}));
```

The first thing we see is a template being run with an object that contains the blog title and a few relative URLs. The template function used by Sofa is fairly simple; it just replaces some parts of the template string with passed in values. In this case, the template string is stored in the variable `templates.index.head`, which was imported using a CouchApp macro at the top of the function. The second argument to the template function are the values that will be inserted into the template; in this case, `title`, `feedPath`, `newPostPath`, `index`, and `assets`. We'll look at the template itself later in this chapter. For now, it's sufficient to know that the template stored in `templates.index.head` renders the topmost portion of the HTML page, which does not change regardless of the contents of our recent posts view.

Now that we have rendered the top of the page, it's time to loop over the blog posts, rendering them one at a time. The first thing we do is declare our variables and our loop:

```
var row, key;
while (row = getRow()) {
  var post = row.value;
  key = row.key;
```

The `row` variable is used to store each JSON view row as it is sent to our function. The `key` variable plays a different role. Because we don't know ahead of time which of our rows will be the last row to be processed, we keep the key available in its own variable, to be used after all rows are rendered, to generate the link to the next page of results.

```
    send(template(templates.index.row, {
        title : post.title,
        summary : post.summary,
        date : post.created_at,
        link : showPath('post', row.id)
    }));
}
```

Now that we have the row and its key safely stored, we use the template engine again for rendering. This time we use the template stored in `templates.index.row`, with a data item that includes the blog post title, a URL for its page, the summary of the blog post we generated in our map view, and the date the post was created.

Once all the blog posts included in the view result have been listed, we're ready to close the list and finish rendering the page. The last string does not need to be sent to the client using `send()`, but it can be returned from the HTML function. Aside from that minor detail, rendering the tail template should be familiar by now.

```
    return template(templates.index.tail, {
        assets : assetPath(),
        older : olderPath(key)
    });
});
```

Once the tail has been returned, we close the HTML generating function. If we didn't care to offer an Atom feed of our blog, we'd be done here. But we know most readers are going to be accessing the blog through a feed reader or some kind of syndication, so an Atom feed is crucial.

```
    provides("atom", function() {
```

The Atom generation function is defined in just the same way as the HTML generation function—by being passed to `provides()` with a label describing the format it outputs. The general pattern of the Atom function is the same as the HTML function: output the first section of the feed, then output the feed entries, and finally close the feed.

```
    // we load the first row to find the most recent change date
    var row = getRow();
```

One difference is that for the Atom feed, we need to know when it was last changed. This will normally be the time at which the first item in the feed was changed, so we load the first row before outputting any data to the client (other than HTTP headers, which are set when the `provides` function picks the format). Now that we have the first row, we can use the date from it to set the Atom feed's last-updated field.

```
    // generate the feed header
    var feedHeader = Atom.header({
        updated : (row ? new Date(row.value.created_at) : new Date()),
        title : blog.title,
        feed_id : makeAbsolute(req, indexPath),
        feed_link : makeAbsolute(req, feedPath),
    });
```

The `Atom.header` function is defined in *lib/atom.js*, which was imported by CouchApp at the top of our function. This library uses JavaScript's E4X extension to generate feed XML.

```
// send the header to the client
send(feedHeader);
```

Once the feed header has been generated, sending it to the client uses the familiar `send()` call. Now that we're done with the header, we'll generate each Atom entry, based on a row in the view. We use a slightly different loop format in this case than in the HTML case, as we've already loaded the first row in order to use its timestamp in the feed header.

```
// loop over all rows
if (row) {
  do {
```

The JavaScript `do/while` loop is similar to the `while` loop used in the HTML function, except that it's guaranteed to run at least once, as it evaluates the conditional statement after each iteration. This means we can output an entry for the row we've already loaded, before calling `getRow()` to load the next entry.

```
// generate the entry for this row
var feedEntry = Atom.entry({
  entry_id : makeAbsolute(req, '/' +
    encodeURIComponent(req.info.db_name) +
    '/' + encodeURIComponent(row.id)),
  title : row.value.title,
  content : row.value.html,
  updated : new Date(row.value.created_at),
  author : row.value.author,
  alternate : makeAbsolute(req, showPath('post', row.id))
});
// send the entry to client
send(feedEntry);
```

Rendering the entries also uses the Atom library in *atom.js*. The big difference between the Atom entries and the list items in HTML, is that for our HTML screen we only output the summary of the entry text, but for the Atom entries we output the entire entry. By changing the value of `content` from `row.value.html` to `row.value.summary`, you could change the Atom feed to only include shortened post summaries, forcing subscribers to click through to the actual post to read it.

```
  } while (row = getRow());
}
```

As we mentioned earlier, this loop construct puts the loop condition at the end of the loop, so here is where we load the next row of the loop.

```
    // close the loop after all rows are rendered
    return "</feed>";
  });
};
```

Once all rows have been looped over, we end the feed by returning the closing XML tag to the client as the last chunk of data.

The Final Result

Figure 14-1 shows the final result.

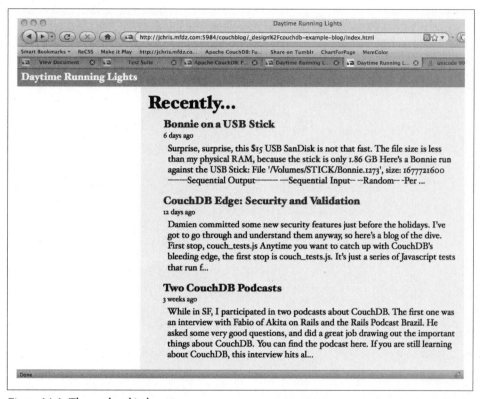

Figure 14-1. The rendered index page

This is our final list of blog posts. That wasn't too hard, was it? We now have the front page of the blog, we know how to query single documents as well as views, and we know how to pass arguments to views.

PART IV

Deploying CouchDB

CHAPTER 15

Scaling Basics

Scaling is an overloaded term. Finding a discrete definition is tricky. Everyone and her grandmother have their own idea of what scaling means. Most definitions are valid, but they can be contradicting. To make things even worse, there are a lot of misconceptions about scaling. To really define it, one needs a scalpel to find out the important bits.

First, scaling doesn't refer to a specific technique or technology; scaling, or *scalability*, is an attribute of a specific architecture. What is being *scaled* varies for nearly every project.

> Scaling is specialization.
>
> —Joe Stump, Lead Architect of Digg.com and SimpleGeo.com

Joe's quote is the one that we find to be the most accurate description of scaling. It is also wishy-washy, but that is the nature of scaling. An example: a website like Facebook.com— with a whole lot of users and data associated with those users and with more and more users coming in every day—might want to scale over user data that typically lives in a database. In contrast, Flickr.com at its core is like Facebook with users and data for users, but in Flickr's case, the data that grows fastest is images uploaded by users. These images do not necessarily live in a database, so scaling image storage is Flickr's path to growth.

 It is common to think of scaling as *scaling out*. This is shortsighted. Scaling can also mean *scaling in*—that is, being able to use fewer computers when demand declines. More on that later.

These are just two services. There are a lot more, and every one has different things they want to scale. CouchDB is a database; we are not going to cover every aspect of scaling any system. We concentrate on the bits that are interesting to you, the CouchDB user. We have identified three general properties that you can scale with CouchDB:

- Read requests
- Write requests
- Data

Scaling Read Requests

A read request retrieves a piece of information from the database. It passes the following stations within CouchDB. First, the HTTP server module needs to accept the request. For that, it opens a socket to send data over. The next station is the HTTP request handle module that analyzes the request and directs it to the appropriate submodule in CouchDB. For single documents, the request then gets passed to the database module where the data for the document is looked up on the filesystem and returned all the way up again.

All this takes processing time and enough sockets (or file descriptors) must be available. The storage backend of the server must be able to fulfill all read requests. There are a few more things that can limit a system to accept more read requests; the basic point here is that a single server can process only so many concurrent requests. If your applications generate more requests, you need to set up a second server that your application can read from.

The nice thing about read requests is that they can be cached. Often-used items can be held in memory and can be returned at a much higher level than the one that is your bottleneck. Requests that can use this cache don't ever hit your database and are thus virtually toll-free. Chapter 18 explains this scenario.

Scaling Write Requests

A write request is like a read request, only a little worse. It not only reads a piece of data from disk, it writes it back after modifying it. Remember, the nice thing about reads is that they're cacheable. Writes: not so much. A cache must be notified when a write changes data, or clients must be told to not use the cache. If you have multiple servers for scaling reads, a write must occur on all servers. In any case, you need to work harder with a write. Chapter 19 covers methods for scaling write requests across servers.

Scaling Data

The third way of scaling is scaling data. Today's hard drives are cheap and have a lot of capacity, and they will only get better in the future, but there is only so much data a single server can make sensible use of. It must maintain one more indexes to the data that uses disk space again. Creating backups will take longer and other maintenance tasks become a pain.

The solution is to chop the data into manageable chunks and put each chunk on a separate server. All servers with a chunk now form a *cluster* that holds all your data. Chapter 19 takes a look at creating and using these clusters.

While we are taking separate looks at scaling of reads, writes, and data, these rarely occur isolated. Decisions to scale one will affect the others. We will describe individual as well as combined solutions in the following chapters.

Basics First

Replication is the basis for all of the three scaling methods. Before we go scaling, Chapter 16 will familiarize you with CouchDB's excellent replication feature.

Replication

This chapter introduces CouchDB's world-class replication system. Replication synchronizes two copies of the same database, allowing users to have low latency access data no matter where they are. These databases can live on the same server or on two different servers—CouchDB doesn't make a distinction. If you change one copy of the database, replication will send these changes to the other copy.

Replication is a one-off operation: you send an HTTP request to CouchDB that includes a *source* and a *target* database, and CouchDB will send the changes from the source to the target. That is all. Granted, calling something world-class and then only needing one sentence to explain it does seem odd. But part of the reason why CouchDB's replication is so powerful lies in its simplicity.

Let's see what replication looks like:

```
POST /_replicate HTTP/1.1
{"source":"database","target":"http://example.org/database"}
```

This call sends all the documents in the local database `database` to the remote database `http://example.org/database`. A database is considered "local" when it is on the same CouchDB instance you send the `POST /_replicate` HTTP request to. All other instances of CouchDB are "remote."

If you want to send changes from the target to the source database, you just make the same HTTP requests, only with source and target database swapped. That is all.

```
POST /_replicate HTTP/1.1
{"source":"http://example.org/database","target":"database"}
```

A remote database is identified by the same URL you use to talk to it. CouchDB replication works over HTTP using the same mechanisms that are available to you. This example shows that replication is a *unidirectional* process. Documents are copied from one database to another and not automatically vice versa. If you want *bidirectional* replication, you need to trigger two replications with *source* and *target* swapped.

The Magic

When you ask CouchDB to replicate one database to another, it will go and compare the two databases to find out which documents on the source differ from the target and then submit a batch of the changed documents to the target until all changes are transferred. Changes include new documents, changed documents, and deleted documents. Documents that already exist on the target in the same revision are not transferred; only newer revisions are.

Databases in CouchDB have a *sequence number* that gets incremented every time the database is changed. CouchDB remembers what changes came with which sequence number. That way, CouchDB can answer questions like, "What changed in database A between sequence number 212 and now?" by returning a list of new and changed documents. Finding the differences between databases this way is an efficient operation. It also adds to the robustness of replication.

 CouchDB views use the same mechanism when determining when a view needs updating and which documents to replication. You can use this to build your own solutions as well.

You can use replication on a single CouchDB instance to create snapshots of your databases to be able to test code changes without risking data loss or to be able to refer back to older states of your database. But replication gets really fun if you use two or more different computers, potentially geographically spread out.

With different servers, potentially hundreds or thousands of miles apart, problems are bound to happen. Servers crash, network connections break off, things go wrong. When a replication process is interrupted, it leaves two replicating CouchDBs in an inconsistent state. Then, when the problems are gone and you trigger replication again, it continues where it left off.

Simple Replication with the Admin Interface

You can run replication from your web browser using Futon, CouchDB's built-in administration interface. Start CouchDB and open your browser to *http://127.0.0.1:5984/ _utils/*. On the righthand side, you will see a list of things to visit in Futon. Click on "Replication."

Futon will show you an interface to start replication. You can specify a source and a target by either picking a database from the list of local databases or filling in the URL of a remote database.

Click on the Replicate button, wait a bit, and have a look at the lower half of the screen where CouchDB gives you some statistics about the replication run or, if an error occurred, an explanatory message.

Congratulations—you ran your first replication.

Replication in Detail

So far, we've skipped over the result from a replication request. Now is a good time to look at it in detail. Here's a nicely formatted example:

```
{
  "ok": true,
  "source_last_seq": 10,
  "session_id": "c7a2bbbf9e4af774de3049eb86eaa447",
  "history": [
    {
      "session_id": "c7a2bbbf9e4af774de3049eb86eaa447",
      "start_time": "Mon, 24 Aug 2009 09:36:46 GMT",
      "end_time": "Mon, 24 Aug 2009 09:36:47 GMT",
      "start_last_seq": 0,
      "end_last_seq": 1,
      "recorded_seq": 1,
      "missing_checked": 0,
      "missing_found": 1,
      "docs_read": 1,
      "docs_written": 1,
      "doc_write_failures": 0,
    }
  ]
}
```

The `"ok": true` part, similar to other responses, tells us everything went well. `source_last_seq` includes the source's `update_seq` value that was considered by this replication. Each replication request is assigned a `session_id`, which is just a UUID; you can also talk about a *replication session* identified by this ID.

The next bit is the replication *history*. CouchDB maintains a list of history sessions for future reference. The history array is currently capped at 50 entries. Each unique replication trigger object (the JSON string that includes the source and target databases as well as potential options) gets its own history. Let's see what a history entry is all about.

The `session_id` is recorded here again for convenience. The start and end time for the replication session are recorded. The `_last_seq` denotes the `update_seq`s that were valid at the beginning and the end of the session. `recorded_seq` is the `update_seq` of the target again. It's different from `end_last_seq` if a replication process dies in the middle and is restarted. `missing_checked` is the number of docs on the target that are already there and don't need to be replicated. `missing_found` is the number of missing documents on the source.

The last three—`docs_read`, `docs_written`, and `doc_write_failures`—show how many documents we read from the source, wrote to the target, and how many failed. If all is well, `_read` and `_written` are identical and `doc_write_failures` is 0. If not, you know something went wrong during replication. Possible failures are a server crash on either side, a lost network connection, or a `validate_doc_update` function rejecting a document write.

One common scenario is triggering replication on nodes that have admin accounts enabled. Creating design documents is restricted to admins, and if the replication is triggered without admin credentials, writing the design documents during replication will fail and be recorded as `doc_write_failures`. If you have admins, be sure to include the credentials in the replication request:

```
> curl -X POST http://127.0.0.1:5984/_replicate \
  -d '{"source":"http://example.org/database", \
      "target":"http://admin:password@e127.0.0.1:5984/database"}'
```

Continuous Replication

Now that you know how replication works under the hood, we share a neat little trick. When you add `"continuous":true` to the replication trigger object, CouchDB will not stop after replicating all missing documents from the source to the target. It will listen on CouchDB's `_changes` API (see Chapter 20) and automatically replicate over any new docs as they come into the source to the target. In fact, they are not replicated right away; there's a complex algorithm determining the ideal moment to replicate for maximum performance. The algorithm is complex and is fine-tuned every once in a while, and documenting it here wouldn't make much sense.

```
> curl -X POST http://127.0.0.1:5984/_replicate \
  -d '{"source":"db", "target":"db-replica", "continuous":true}'
```

At the time of writing, CouchDB doesn't remember continuous replications over a server restart. For the time being, you are required to trigger them again when you restart CouchDB. In the future, CouchDB will allow you to define permanent continuous replications that survive a server restart without you having to do anything.

That's It?

Replication is the foundation on which the following chapters build on. Make sure you have understood this chapter. If you don't feel comfortable yet, just read it again and play around with the replication interface in Futon.

We haven't yet told you everything about replication. The next chapters show you how to manage replication conflicts (see Chapter 17), how to use a set of synchronized CouchDB instances for load balancing (see Chapter 18), and how to build a cluster of CouchDBs that can handle more data or write requests than a single node (see Chapter 19).

Conflict Management

Suppose you are sitting in a coffee shop working on your book. J. Chris comes over and tells you about his new phone. The new phone came with a new number, and you have J. Chris dictate it while you change it using your laptop's address book application.

Luckily, your address book is built on CouchDB, so when you come home, all you need to do to get your home computer up-to-date with J. Chris's number is replicate your address book from your laptop. Neat, eh? What's more, CouchDB has a mechanism to maintain continuous replication, so you can keep a whole set of computers in sync with the same data, whenever a network connection is available.

Let's change the scenario a little bit. Since J. Chris didn't anticipate meeting you at the coffee shop, he also sent you an email with the new number. At the time you weren't using WiFi because you wanted concentrate on your work, so you didn't read his email until you got home. But it was a long day and by then you had forgotten that you changed the number in the address book on your laptop. When you read the email at home, you simply copy-and-pasted the number into the address book on your home computer. Now—and here's the twist—it turns out you entered the wrong number in your laptop's address book.

You now have a document in each of the databases that has different information. This situation is called a *conflict*. Conflicts occur in distributed systems. They are a natural state of your data. How does CouchDB's replication system deal with conflicts?

When you replicate two databases in CouchDB and you have conflicting changes, CouchDB will detect this and will flag the affected document with the special attribute `"_conflicts":true`. Next, CouchDB determines which of the changes will be stored as the latest revision (remember, documents in CouchDB are versioned). The version that gets picked to be the latest revision is the *winning revision*. The *losing revision* gets stored as the previous revision.

CouchDB does not attempt to merge the conflicting revision. Your application dictates how the merging should be done. The choice of picking the winning revision is arbitrary. In the case of the phone number, there is no way for a computer to decide on the *right* revision. This is not specific to CouchDB; no other software can do this (ever had your phone's sync-contacts tool ask you which contact from which source to take?).

Replication guarantees that conflicts are detected and that each instance of CouchDB makes the same choice regarding winners and losers, independent of all the other instances. There is no group decision made; instead, a deterministic algorithm determines the order of the conflicting revision. After replication, all instances taking part have the same data. The data set is said to be in a *consistent state*. If you ask any instance for a document, you will get the same answer regardless which one you ask.

Whether or not CouchDB picked the version that your application needs, you need to go and resolve the conflict, just as you need to resolve a conflict in a version control system like Subversion. Simply create a version that you want to be the latest by either picking the latest, or the previous, or both (by merging them) and save it as the now latest revision. Done. Replicate again and your resolution will populate over to all other instances of CouchDB. Your conflict resolving on one node could lead to further conflicts, all of which will need to be addressed, but eventually, you will end up with a conflict-free database on all nodes.

The Split Brain

This is an interesting conflicts scenario in that we helped a BBC build a solution for it that is now in production. The basic setup is this: to guarantee that the company's website is online 24/7, even in the event of the loss of a data center, it has multiple data centers backing up the website. The "loss" of a data center is a rare occasion, but it can be as simple as a network outage, where the data center is still alive and well but can't be reached by anyone.

The "split brain" scenario is where two (for simplicity's sake we'll stick to two) data centers are up and well connected to end users, but the connection between the data centers—which is most likely not the same connection that end users use to talk to the computers in the data center—fails.

The inter data center connection is used to keep both centers *in sync* so that either one can take over for the other in case of a failure. If that link goes down, you end up with two halves of a system that act independently—the split brain.

As long as all end users can get to their data, the split brain is not scary. Resolving the split brain situation by bringing up the connection that links the data centers and starting synchronization again is where it gets hairy. Arbitrary conflict resolution, like CouchDB does by default, can lead to unwanted effects on the user's side. Data could revert to an earlier stage and leave the impression that changes weren't reliably saved, when in fact they were.

Conflict Resolution by Example

Let's go through an illustrated example of how conflicts emerge and how to solve them in super slow motion. Figure 17-1 illustrates the basic setup: we have two CouchDB databases, and we are replicating from database A to database B. To keep this simple, we assume triggered replication and not continuous replication, and we don't replicate back from database B to A. All other replication scenarios can be reduced to this setup, so this explains everything we need to know.

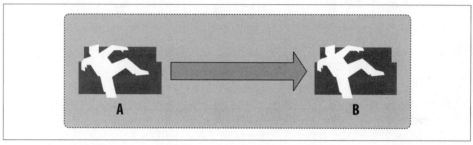

Figure 17-1. Conflict management by example: step 1

We start out by creating a document in database A (Figure 17-2). Note the clever use of imagery to identify a specific revision of a document. Since we are not using continuous replication, database B won't know about the new document for now.

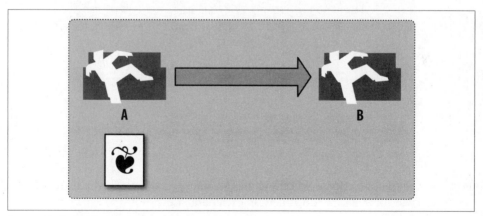

Figure 17-2. Conflict management by example: step 2

We now trigger replication and tell it to use database A as the source and database B as the target (Figure 17-3). Our document gets copied over to database B. To be precise, the latest revision of our document gets copied over.

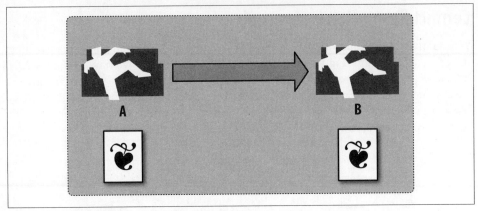

Figure 17-3. Conflict management by example: step 3

Now we go to database B and update the document (Figure 17-4). We change some values and upon change, CouchDB generates a new revision for us. Note that this revision has a new image. Node A is ignorant of any activity.

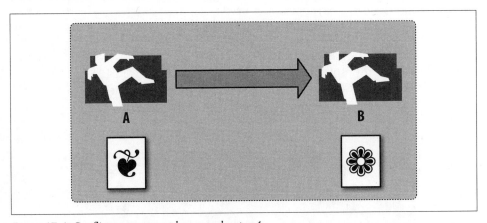

Figure 17-4. Conflict management by example: step 4

Now we make a change to our document in database A by changing some other values (Figure 17-5). See how it makes a different image for us to see the difference? It is important to note that this is still the same document. It's just that there are two different revisions of that same document in each database.

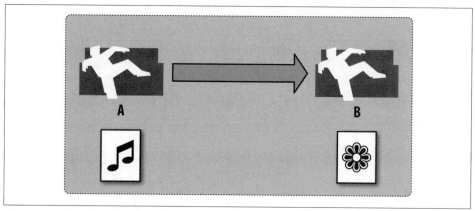

Figure 17-5. Conflict management by example: step 5

Now we trigger replication again from database A to database B as before (Figure 17-6). By the way, it doesn't make a difference if the two databases live in the same CouchDB server or on different servers connected over a network.

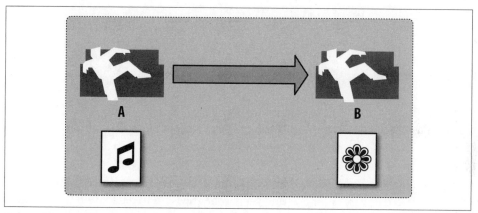

Figure 17-6. Conflict management by example: step 6

When replicating, CouchDB detects that there are two different revisions for the same document, and it creates a conflict (Figure 17-7). A document conflict means that there are now two latest revisions for this document.

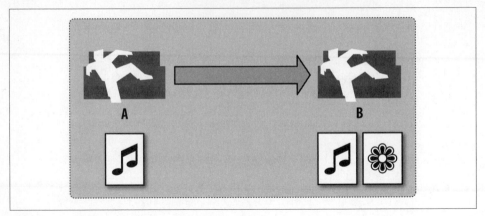

Figure 17-7. Conflict management by example: step 7

Finally, we tell CouchDB which version we would like to be the latest revision by resolving the conflict (Figure 17-8). Now both databases have the same data.

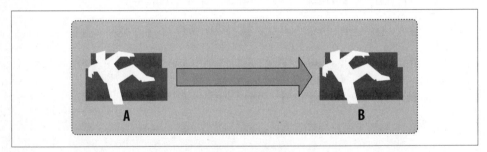

Figure 17-8. Conflict management by example: step 8

Other possible outcomes include choosing the other revision and replicating that decision back to database A, or creating yet another revision in database B that includes parts of both conflicting revisions (a *merge*) and replicating that back to database A.

Working with Conflicts

Now that we've walked through replication with pretty pictures, let's get our hands dirty and see what the API calls and responses for this and other scenarios look like. We'll be continuing Chapter 4 by using `curl` on the command line to make raw API requests.

First, we create two databases that we can use for replication. These live on the same CouchDB instance, but they might as well live on a remote instance—CouchDB doesn't care. To save us some typing, we create a shell variable for our CouchDB base URL that we want to talk to. We then create two databases, `db` and `db-replica`:

```
HOST="http://127.0.0.1:5984"

> curl -X PUT $HOST/db
{"ok":true}

> curl -X PUT $HOST/db-replica
{"ok":true}
```

In the next step, we create a simple document {"count":1} in db and trigger replication to db-replica:

```
curl -X PUT $HOST/db/foo -d '{"count":1}'
{"ok":true,"id":"foo","rev":"1-74620ecf527d29daaab9c2b465fbce66"}

curl -X POST $HOST/_replicate
-d '{"source":"db","target":"http://127.0.0.1:5984/db-replica"}'
{"ok":true,...,"docs_written":1,"doc_write_failures":0}]}
```

We skip a bit of the output of the replication session (see Chapter 16 for details). If you see "docs_written":1 and "doc_write_failures":0, our document made it over to db-replica. We now update the document to {"count":2} in db-replica. Note that we now need to include the correct _rev property.

```
> curl -X PUT $HOST/db-replica/foo
-d '{"count":2,"_rev":"1-74620ecf527d29daaab9c2b465fbce66"}'
{"ok":true,"id":"foo","rev":"2-de0ea16f8621cbac506d23a0fbbde08a"}
```

Next, we create the conflict! We change our document on db to {"count":3}. Our document is now logically in conflict, but CouchDB doesn't know about it until we replicate again:

```
> curl -X PUT $HOST/db/foo
-d '{"count":3,"_rev":"1-74620ecf527d29daaab9c2b465fbce66"}'
{"ok":true,"id":"foo","rev":"2-7c971bb974251ae8541b8fe045964219"}

> curl -X POST $HOST/_replicate
-d '{"source":"db","target":"http://127.0.0.1:5984/db-replica"}'
{"ok":true,..."docs_written":1,"doc_write_failures":0}]}
```

To see that we have a conflict, we create a simple view in db-replica. The map function looks like this:

```
function(doc) {
  if(doc._conflicts) {
    emit(doc._conflicts, null);
  }
}
```

When we query this view, we get this result:

```
{"total_rows":1,"offset":0,"rows":[
{"id":"foo","key":["2-7c971bb974251ae8541b8fe045964219"],"value":null}
]}
```

The key here corresponds to the doc._conflicts property of our document in db-replica. It is an array listing all *conflicting revisions*. We see that the revision we wrote on db (`{"count":3}`) is in conflict. CouchDB's automatic promotion of one revision to be the winning revision chose our first change (`{"count":2}`). To verify that, we just request that document from `db-replica`:

```
> curl -X GET $HOST/db-replica/foo
{"_id":"foo","_rev":"2-de0ea16f8621cbac506d23a0fbbde08a","count":2}
```

To resolve the conflict, we need to determine which one we want to keep.

How Does CouchDB Decide Which Revision to Use?

CouchDB guarantees that each instance that sees the same conflict comes up with the same winning and losing revisions. It does so by running a deterministic algorithm to pick the winner. The application should not rely on the details of this algorithm and must always resolve conflicts. We'll tell you how it works anyway.

Each revision includes a list of previous revisions. The revision with the longest revision history list becomes the winning revision. If they are the same, the `_rev` values are compared in ASCII sort order, and the highest wins. So, in our example, `2-de0ea16f8621cbac506d23a0fbbde08a` beats `2-7c971bb974251ae8541b8fe045964219`.

One advantage of this algorithm is that CouchDB nodes do not have to talk to each other to agree on winning revisions. We already learned that the network is prone to errors and avoiding it for conflict resolution makes CouchDB very robust.

Let's say we want to keep the highest value. This means we don't agree with CouchDB's automatic choice. To do this, we first overwrite the target document with our value and then simply delete the revision we don't like:

```
curl -X DELETE $HOST/db-replica/foo?rev=2-de0ea16f8621cbac506d23a0fbbde08a
{"ok":true,"id":"foo","rev":"3-bfe83a296b0445c4d526ef35ef62ac14"}

curl -X PUT $HOST/db-replica/foo
-d '{"count":3,"_rev":"2-7c971bb974251ae8541b8fe045964219"}'
{"ok":true,"id":"foo","rev":"3-5d0319b075a21b095719bc561def7122"}
```

CouchDB creates yet another revision that reflects our decision. Note that the 3- didn't get incremented this time. We didn't create a new version of the document body; we just deleted a conflicting revision. To see that all is well, we check whether our revision ended up in the document.

```
curl GET $HOST/db-replica/foo
{"_id":"foo","_rev":"3-5d0319b075a21b095719bc561def7122","count":3}
```

We also verify that our document is no longer in conflict by querying our conflicts view again, and we see that there are no more conflicts:

```
{"total_rows":0,"offset":0,"rows":[]}
```

Finally, we replicate from `db-replica` back to `db` by simply swapping `source` and `target` in our request to `_replicate`:

```
curl -X POST $HOST/_replicate
-d '{"target":"db","source":"http://127.0.0.1:5984/db-replica"}'
```

We see that our revision ends up in **db**, too:

```
curl GET $HOST/db/foo
{"_id":"foo","_rev":"3-5d0319b075a21b095719bc561def7122","count":3}
```

And we're done.

Deterministic Revision IDs

Let's have a look at this revision ID: **3-5d0319b075a21b095719bc561def7122**. Parts of the format might look familiar. The first part is an integer followed by a dash (**3-**). The integer increments for each new revision the document receives. Updates to the same document on multiple instances create their own independent increments. When replicating, CouchDB knows that there are two different revisions (like in our previous example) by looking at the second part.

The second part is an md5-hash over a set of document properties: the JSON body, the attachments, and the **_deleted** flag. This allows CouchDB to save on replication time in case you make the same change to the same document on two instances. Earlier versions (0.9 and back) used random integers to specify revisions, and making the same change on two instances would result in two different revision IDs, creating a conflict where it was not really necessary. CouchDB 0.10 and above uses deterministic revision IDs using the md5 hash.

For example, let's create two documents, **a** and **b**, with the same contents:

```
curl -X PUT $HOST/db/a -d '{"a":1}'
{"ok":true,"id":"a","rev":"1-23202479633c2b380f79507a776743d5"}

> curl -X PUT $HOST/db/b -d '{"a":1}'
{"ok":true,"id":"b","rev":"1-23202479633c2b380f79507a776743d5"}
```

Both revision IDs are the same, a consequence of the deterministic algorithm used by CouchDB.

Wrapping Up

This concludes our tour of the conflict management system. You should now be able to create distributed setups that deal with conflicts in a proper way.

CHAPTER 18

Load Balancing

Jill is woken up at 4:30 a.m. by her mobile phone. She receives text message after text message, one every minute. Finally, Joe calls. Joe is furious, and Jill has trouble understanding what Joe is saying. In fact, Jill has a hard time figuring out why Joe would call her in the middle of the night. Then she remembers: Joe is running an online shop selling sports gear on one of her servers, and he is furious because the server went down and now his customers in New Zealand are angry because they can't get to the online shop.

This is a typical scenario, and you have probably seen many variations of it, being in the role of Jill, Joe, or both. If you are Jill, you want to sleep at night, and if you are Joe, you want your customers to buy from you whenever it pleases them.

Having a Backup

The problems persist: computers fail, and in many ways. There are hardware problems, power outages, bugs in the operating system or application software, etc. Only CouchDB doesn't have any bugs. (Well, of course, that's not true. All software has bugs, with the possible exception of things written by Daniel J. Bernstein and Donald Knuth.)

Whatever the cause is, you want to make sure that the service you are providing (in Jill and Joe's case, the database for an online store) is resilient against failure. The road to resilience is a road of finding and removing single points of failure. A server's power supply can fail. To keep the server from turning off during such an event, most come with at least two power supplies. To take this further, you could get a server where everything is duplicated (or more), but that would be a highly specialized (and expensive) piece of hardware. It is much cheaper to get two similar servers where the one can take over if the other has a problem. However, you need to make sure both servers have the same set of data in order to switch them without a user noticing.

Removing all single points of failure will give you a highly available or a fault-tolerant system. The order of tolerance is restrained only by your budget. If you can't afford to lose a customer's shopping cart in any event, you need to store it on at least two servers in at least two far apart geographical locations.

 Amazon does this for the Amazon.com website. If one data center is the victim of an earthquake, a user will still be able to shop.

It is likely, though, that Amazon's problems are not your problems and that you will have a whole set of new problems when your data center goes away. But you still want to be able to live through a server failure.

Before we dive into setting up a highly available CouchDB system, let's look at another situation. Joe calls Jill during regular business hours and relays his customers' complaints that loading the online shop takes "forever." Jill takes a quick look at the server and concludes that this is a lucky problem to have, leaving Joe puzzled. Jill explains that Joe's shop is suddenly attracting many more users who are buying things. Joe chimes in, "I got a great review on that blog. That's where they must be coming from." A quick referrer check reveals that indeed many of the new customers are coming from a single site. The blog post already includes comments from unhappy customers voicing their frustration with the slow site. Joe wants to make his customers happy and asks Jill what to do. Jill advises that they set up a second server that can take half of the load of the current server, making sure all requests get answered in a reasonable amount of time. Joe agrees, and Jill begins to set things up.

The solution to the outlined problem looks a lot like the earlier one for providing a fault-tolerant setup: install a second server and synchronize all data. The difference is that with fault tolerance, the second server just sits there and waits for the first one to fail. In the server-overload case, a second server helps answer all incoming requests. This case is not fault-tolerant: if one server crashes, the other will get all the requests and will likely break down, or at least provide very slow service, either of which is not acceptable.

Keep in mind that although the solutions look similar, high availability and fault tolerance are not the same. We'll get back to the second scenario later on, but first we will take a look at how to set up a fault-tolerant CouchDB system.

We already gave it away in the previous chapters: the solution to synchronizing servers is replication.

CHAPTER 19

Clustering

OK, you've made it this far. I'm assuming you more or less understand what CouchDB is and how the application API works. Maybe you've deployed an application or two, and now you're dealing with enough traffic that you need to think about scaling. "Scaling" is an imprecise word, but in this chapter we'll be dealing with the aspect of putting together a partitioned or sharded cluster that will have to grow at an increasing rate over time from day one.

We'll look at request and response dispatch in a CouchDB cluster with stable nodes. Then we'll cover how to add redundant hot-failover twin nodes, so you don't have to worry about losing machines. In a large cluster, you should plan for 5–10% of your machines to experience some sort of failure or reduced performance, so cluster design must prevent node failures from affecting reliability. Finally, we'll look at adjusting cluster layout dynamically by splitting or merging nodes using replication.

Introducing CouchDB Lounge

CouchDB Lounge (*http://tilgovi.github.com/couchdb-lounge/*) is a proxy-based partitioning and clustering application, originally developed for Meebo (*http://www.meebo .com*), a web-based instant messaging service. Lounge comes with two major components: one that handles simple GET and PUT requests for documents, and another that distributes view requests.

The *dumbproxy* handles simple requests for anything that isn't a CouchDB view. This comes as a module for nginx (*http://nginx.net/*), a high-performance reverse HTTP proxy. Because of the way reverse HTTP proxies work, this automatically allows configurable security, encryption, load distribution, compression, and, of course, aggressive caching of your database resources.

The *smartproxy* handles only CouchDB view requests, and dispatches them to all the other nodes in the cluster so as to distribute the work, making view performance a function of the cluster's cumulative processing power. This comes as a daemon for

Twisted, a popular and high-performance event-driven network programming framework for Python.

Consistent Hashing

CouchDB's storage model uses unique IDs to save and retrieve documents. Sitting at the core of Lounge is a simple method of hashing your document IDs. Lounge then uses the first few characters of this hash to determine which shard to dispatch the request to. You can configure this behavior by writing a *shard map* for Lounge, which is just a simple text configuration file.

Because Lounge allocates a portion of the hash (known as a keyspace) to each node, you can add as many nodes as you like. Because the hash function produces hexidecimal strings that bare no apparent relation to your DocIDs, and because we dispatch requests based on the first few characters, we ensure that all nodes see roughly equal load. And because the hash function is consistent, Lounge will take any arbitrary DocID from an HTTP request URI and point it to the same node each time.

This idea of splitting a collection of shards based on a keyspace is commonly illustrated as a ring, with the hash wrapped around the outside. Each tic mark designates the boundaries in the keyspace between two partitions. The hash function maps from document IDs to positions on the ring. The ring is continuous so that you can always add more nodes by splitting a single partition into pieces. With four physical servers, you allocate the keyspace into 16 independent partitions by distributing them across the servers like so:

A	0,1,2,3
B	4,5,6,7
C	8,9,a,b
D	c,d,e,f

If the hash of your DocID starts with 0, it would be dispatched to shard A. Similarly for 1, 2, or 3. Whereas, if the hash started with c, d, e, or f, it would be dispatched to shard D. As a full example, the hash 71db329b58378c8fa8876f0ec04c72e5 is mapped to the node B, database 7 in the table just shown. This could map to *http://B.couches.local/db-7/* on your backend cluster. In this way, the hash table is just a mapping from hashes to backend database URIs. Don't worry if this all sounds very complex; all you have to do is provide a mapping of shards to nodes and Lounge will build the hash ring appropriately—so no need to get your hands dirty if you don't want to.

To frame the same concept with web architecture, because CouchDB uses HTTP, the proxy can partition documents according to the request URL, without inspecting the body. This is a core principle behind REST and is one of the many benefits using HTTP affords us. In practice, this is accomplished by running the hash function against the request URI and comparing the result to find the portion of the keyspace allocated. Lounge then looks up the associated shard for the hash in a configuration table, forwarding the HTTP request to the backend CouchDB server.

Consistent hashing is a simple way to ensure that you can always find the documents you saved, while balancing storage load evenly across partitions. Because the hash function is simple (it is based on CRC32), you are free to implement your own HTTP intermediaries or clients that can similarly resolve requests to the correct physical location of your data.

Redundant Storage

Consistent hashing solves the problem of how to break up a single logical database evenly across a set of partitions, which can then be distributed across multiple servers. It does not address the problem of how to ensure that data you've stored is safe from loss due to hardware or software failure. If you are serious about your data, you can't consider it saved until you have at least two copies of it, preferably in different geographical locations.

CouchDB replication makes maintaining hot-failover redundant slaves or load-balanced multi-master databases relatively painless. The specifics of how to manage replication are covered in Chapter 16. What is important in this context is to understand that maintaining redundant copies is orthogonal to the harder task of ensuring that the cluster consistently chooses the same partition for a particular document ID.

For data safety, you'll want to have at least two or three copies of everything. However, if you encapsulate redundancy, the higher layers of the cluster can treat each partition as a single unit and let the logical partitions themselves manage redundancy and failover.

Redundant Proxies

Just as we can't accept the possibility of hardware failure leading to data loss, we'll need to run multiple instances of the proxy nodes to avoid the chance that a proxy node crash could leave portions of the cluster unavailable. By running redundant proxy instances, and load balancing across them, we can increase cluster throughput as well as reliability.

View Merging

Consistent hashing leaves documents on the proper node, but documents can still emit() any key. The point of incremental MapReduce is to bring the function to the data, so we shoudn't redistribute the emitted keys; instead, we send the queries to the CouchDB nodes via HTTP proxy, and merge the results using the Twisted Python Smartproxy.

Smartproxy sends each view request to every node, so it needs to merge the responses before returning them to the client. Thankfully, this operation is not resource-intensive, as merging can be done in constant memory space no matter how many rows are returned. The Smartproxy receives the first row from each cluster node and compares them. We sort the nodes according to their row key using CouchDB's collation rules. Smartproxy pops the top row from the first sorted node and returns it to the client.

This process can be repeated as long as the clients continue to send rows, but if a limit is imposed by the client, Smartproxy must end the response early, discarding any extra rows sent by the nodes.

This layout is simple and loosely coupled. It has the advantage that it's simple, which helps in understanding topology and diagnosing failures. There is work underway to move the behavior to Erlang, which ought to make managing dynamic clusters possible as well as let us integrate cluster control into the CouchDB runtime.

Growing the Cluster

Using CouchDB at web scale likely requires CouchDB clusters that can be scaled dynamically. Growing sites must continuously add more storage capacity, so we need a strategy to increase the size of our cluster without taking it down. Some workloads can result in temporary growth in data size, in which case we'll also need a process for shrinking the cluster without an interruption in service.

In this section, we'll see how we can use CouchDB's replication filters to split one database into several partitions, and how to use that technique to grow the cluster without downtime. There are simple steps you can take to avoid partitioning databases while growing the cluster.

Oversharding is a technique where you partition the cluster so that there are multiple shards on each physical machine. Moving a partition from one machine to another is simpler than splitting it into smaller partitions, as the configuration map of the cluster used by the proxy only needs to change to point to shards at their new homes, rather than adding new logical shards. It's also less resource-intensive to move a partition than to split it into many.

One question we need to answer is, "How much should we overshard?" The answer depends on your application and deployment, but there are some forces that push us in one direction over another. If we get the number of shards right, we'll end up with a cluster that can grow optimally.

In "View Merging" on page 167, we discussed how merges can be accomplished in constant space, no matter the number of rows returned. The memory space and network resources required to merge views, as well as to map from document IDs to partitions, does, however, grow linearly with the number of partitions under a given proxy. For this reason, we'll want to limit the number of partitions for each proxy. However, we can't accept an upper limit on cluster size. The solution is to use a tree of proxies, where the root proxy partitions to some number of intermediate proxies, which then proxy to database nodes.

The factors that come into play when deciding how many partitions each proxy should manage are: the storage available to each individual server node, the projected growth rate of the data, the network and memory resources available to proxies, and the acceptable latency for requests against the cluster.

Assuming a conservative 64 shards per proxy, and 1 TB of data storage per node (including room for compaction, these nodes will need roughly 2 TB of drive space), we can see that with a single proxy in front of CouchDB data nodes, we'll be able to store at maximum 64 TB of data (on 128 or perhaps 192 server nodes, depending on the level of redundancy required by the system) before we have to increase the number of partitions.

By replacing database nodes with another proxy, and repartitioning each of the 64 partitions into another 64 partitions, we end up with 4,096 partitions and a tree depth of 2. Just as the initial system can hold 64 partitions on just a few nodes, we can transition to the 2-layer tree without needing thousands of machines. If we assume each proxy must be run on its own node, and that at first database nodes can hold 16 partitions, we'll see that we need 65 proxies and 256 database machines (not including redundancy factors, which should typically multiply the cluster size by two or three times). To get started with a cluster that can grow smoothly from 64 TB to 4 PB, we can begin with roughly 600 to 1,000 server nodes, adding new ones as data size grows and we move partitions to other machines.

We've seen that even a cluster with a depth of 2 can hold a vast amount of data. Basic arithmetic shows us that by applying the same process to create a cluster with three layers of proxies, we can manage 262 petabytes on thousands of machines. Conservative estimates for the latency introduced by each layer is about 100 ms, so even without performance tuning we should see overall response times of 300 ms even with a tree depth of 3, and we should be able to manage queries over exabyte datasets in less than a second.

By using oversharding and iteratively replacing full shards (database nodes that host only one partition) with proxy nodes that point to another set of oversharded partitions, we can grow the cluster to very large sizes while incurring a minimum of latency.

Now we need to look at the mechanics of the two processes that allow the cluster to grow: moving a partition from an overcrowded node to an empty node, and splitting a large partition into many subpartitions. Moving partitions is simpler, which is why it makes sense to use it when possible, running the more resource-intensive repartition process only when partitions get large enough that only one or two can fit on each database server.

Moving Partitions

As we mentioned earlier, each partition is made up of N redundant CouchDB databases, each stored on different physical servers. To keep things easy to conceptualize, any operations should be applied to all redundant copies automatically. For the sake of discussion, we'll just talk about the abstract partition, but be aware that the redundant nodes will all be the same size and so should require the same operations during cluster growth.

The simplest way to move a partition from one node to another is to create an empty database on the target node and use CouchDB replication to fill the new node with data from the old node. When the new copy of the partition is up-to-date with the original, the proxy node can be reconfigured to point to the new machine. Once the proxy points to the new partition location, one final round of replication will bring it up-to-date, and the old partition can be retired, freeing space on the original machine.

Another method for moving partition databases is to rsync the files on disk from the old node to the new one. Depending on how recently the partition was compacted, this should result in efficient, low-CPU initialization of a new node. Replication can then be used to bring the rsynced file up-to-date. See more about rsync and replication in Chapter 16.

Splitting Partitions

The last major thing we need to run a CouchDB cluster is the capability to split an oversized partition into smaller pieces. In Chapter 16, we discussed how to do continuous replication using the _changes API. The _changes API can use filters (see Chapter 20), and replication can be configured to use a filter function to replicate only a subset of a total database. Splitting partitions is accomplished by creating the target partitions and configuring them with the range of hash keys they are interested in. They then apply filtered replication to the source partition database, requesting only documents that meet their hash criteria. The result is multiple partial copies of the source database, so that each new partition has an equal share of the data. In total, they have a complete copy of the original data. Once the replication is complete and the new partitions have also brought their redundant backups up-to-date, a proxy for the new set of partitions is brought online and the top-level proxy is pointed at it instead of the old partition. Just like with moving a partition, we should do one final round of replication after the old partition is no longer reachable by the cluster, so that any last second updates are not lost. Once that is done, we can retire the old partition so that its hardware can be reused elsewhere in the cluster.

PART V

Reference

CHAPTER 20

Change Notifications

Say you are building a message service with CouchDB. Each user has an inbox database and other users send messages by dropping them into the inbox database. When users want to read all messages received, they can just open their inbox databases and see all messages.

So far, so simple, but now you've got your users hitting the Refresh button all the time once they've looked at their messages to see if there are new messages. This is commonly referred to as *polling*. A lot of users are generating a lot of requests that, most of the time, don't show anything new, just the list of all the messages they already know about.

Wouldn't it be nice to ask CouchDB to give you notice when a new message arrives? The `_changes` database API does just that.

The scenario just described can be seen as the *cache invalidation problem*; that is, when do I know that what I am displaying right now is no longer an apt representation of the underlying data store? Any sort of cache invalidation, not only backend/frontend-related, can be built using `_changes`.

`_changes` is also designed and suited to extract an activity stream from a database, whether for simple display or, equally important, to act on a new document (or a document change) when it occurs.

The beauty of systems that use the changes API is that they are *decoupled*. A program that is interested only in latest updates doesn't need to know about programs that create new documents and vice versa.

Here's what a `changes` item looks like:

```
{"seq":12,"id":"foo","changes":[{"rev":"1-23202479633c2b380f79507a776743d5"}]}
```

There are three fields:

`seq`

> The `update_seq` of the database that was created when the document with the `id` got created or changed.

`id`

> The document ID.

`changes`

> An array of fields, which by default includes the document's revision ID, but can also include information about document conflicts and other things.

The changes API is available for each database. You can get changes that happen in a single database per request. But you can easily send multiple requests to multiple databases' changes API if you need that.

Let's create a database that we can use as an example later in this chapter:

```
> HOST="http://127.0.0.1:5984"
> curl -X PUT $HOST/db
{"ok":true}
```

There are three ways to request notifications: *polling* (the default), *long polling* and *continuous*. Each is useful in a different scenario, and we'll discuss all of them in detail.

Polling for Changes

In the previous example, we tried to avoid the polling method, but it is very simple and in some cases the only one suitable for a problem. Because it is the simplest case, it is the default for the changes API.

Let's see what the changes for our test database look like. First, the request (we're using `curl` again):

```
curl -X GET $HOST/db/_changes
```

The result is simple:

```
{"results":[

],
"last_seq":0}
```

There's nothing there because we didn't put anything in yet—no surprise. But you can guess where we'd see results—when they start to come in. Let's create a document:

```
curl -X PUT $HOST/db/test -d '{"name":"Anna"}'
```

CouchDB replies:

```
{"ok":true,"id":"test","rev":"1-aaa8e2a031bca334f50b48b6682fb486"}
```

Now let's run the changes request again:

```
{"results":[
{"seq":1,"id":"test","changes":[{"rev":"1-aaa8e2a031bca334f50b48b6682fb486"}]}
],
"last_seq":1}
```

We get a notification about our new document. This is pretty neat! But wait—when we created the document and got information like the revision ID, why would we want to make a request to the changes API to get it again? Remember that the purpose of the changes API is to allow you to build decoupled systems. The program that creates the document is very likely not the same program that requests changes for the database, since it already knows what it put in there (although this is blurry, the same program could be interested in changes made by others).

Behind the scenes, we created another document. Let's see what the changes for the database look like now:

```
{"results":[
{"seq":1,"id":"test","changes":[{"rev":"1-aaa8e2a031bca334f50b48b6682fb486"}]},
{"seq":2,"id":"test2","changes":[{"rev":"1-e18422e6a82d0f2157d74b5dcf457997"}]}
],
"last_seq":2}
```

See how we get a new line in the result that represents the new document? In addition, the first document we put in there got listed again. The default result for the changes API is the history of all changes that the database has seen.

We've already seen the change for `"seq":1`, and we're no longer really interested in it. We can tell the changes API about that by using the `since=1` query parameter:

```
curl -X GET $HOST/db/_changes?since=1
```

This returns all changes *after* the `seq` specified by `since`:

```
{"results":[
{"seq":2,"id":"test2","changes":[{"rev":"1-e18422e6a82d0f2157d74b5dcf457997"}]}
],
"last_seq":2}
```

While we're discussing options, use `style=all_docs` to get more revision and conflict information in the `changes` array for each result row. If you want to specify the default explicitly, the value is `main_only`.

Long Polling

The technique of long polling was invented for web browsers to remove one of the problems with the regular polling approach: it doesn't run any requests if nothing changed. Long polling works like this: when making a request to the long polling API, you open an HTTP connection to CouchDB until a new row appears in the changes result, and both you and CouchDB keep the HTTP connection open. As soon as a result appears, the connection is closed.

This works well for low-frequency updates. If a lot of changes occur for a client, you find yourself opening many new requests, and the usefulness of this approach over regular polling declines. Another general consequence of this technique is that for each client requesting a long polling change notification, CouchDB will have to keep an

HTTP connection open. CouchDB is well capable of doing so, as it is designed to handle many concurrent requests. But you need to make sure your operating system allows CouchDB to use at least as many sockets as you have long polling clients (and a few spare for regular requests, of course).

To make a long polling request, add the `feed=longpoll` query parameter. For this listing, we added timestamps to show you when things happen.

```
00:00: > curl -X GET "$HOST/db/_changes?feed=longpoll&since=2"
00:00: {"results":[
00:10: {"seq":3,"id":"test3","changes":[{"rev":"1-02c6b758b08360abefc383d74ed5973d"}]}
00:10: ],
00:10: "last_seq":3}
```

At `00:10`, we create another document behind your back again, and CouchDB promptly sends us the change. Note that we used `since=2` to avoid getting any of the previous notifications. Also note that we have to use double quotes for the `curl` command because we are using an ampersand, which is a special character for our shell.

The `style` option works for long polling requests just like for regular polling requests.

Networks are a tricky beast, and sometimes you don't know whether there are no changes coming or your network connection went stale. If you add another query parameter, `heartbeat=N`, where N is a number, CouchDB will send you a newline character each N milliseconds. As long as you are receiving newline characters, you know there are no new change notifications, but CouchDB is still ready to send you the next one when it occurs.

Continuous Changes

Long polling is great, but you still end up opening an HTTP request for each change notification. For web browsers, this is the only way to avoid the problems of regular polling. But web browsers are not the only client software that can be used to talk to CouchDB. If you are using Python, Ruby, Java, or any other language really, you have yet another option.

The *continuous changes API* allows you to receive change notifications as they come in using a single HTTP connection. You make a request to the continuous changes API and both you and CouchDB will hold the connection open "forever." CouchDB will send you newlines for notifications when the occur and—as opposed to long polling —will keep the HTTP connection open, waiting to send the next notification.

This is great for both infrequent and frequent notifications, and it has the same consequence as long polling: you're going to have a lot of long-living HTTP connections. But again, CouchDB easily supports these.

Use the `feed=continuous` parameter to make a continuous changes API request. Following is the result, again with timestamps. At `00:10` and `00:15`, we'll create a new document each:

```
00:00: > curl -X GET "$HOST/db/_changes?feed=continuous&since=3"
00:10: {"seq":4,"id":"test4","changes":[{"rev":"1-02c6b758b08360abefc383d74ed5973d"}]}
00:15: {"seq":5,"id":"test5","changes":[{"rev":"1-02c6b758b08360abefc383d74ed5973d"}]}
```

Note that the continuous changes API result doesn't include a wrapping JSON object with a results member with the individual notification results as array items; it includes only a raw line per notification. Also note that the lines are no longer separated by a comma. Whereas the regular and long polling APIs result is a full valid JSON object when the HTTP request returns, the continuous changes API sends individual rows as valid JSON objects. The difference makes it easier for clients to parse the respective results. The style and heartbeat parameters work as expected with the continuous changes API.

Filters

The change notification API and its three modes of operation already give you a lot of options requesting and processing changes in CouchDB. Filters for changes give you an additional level of flexibility. Let's say the messages from our first scenario have priorities, and a user is interested only in notifications about messages with a high priority.

Enter filters. Similar to view functions, a filter is a JavaScript function that gets stored in a design document and is later executed by CouchDB. They live in special member filters under a name of your choice. Here is an example:

```
{
  "_id": "_design/app",
  "_rev": "1-b20db05077a51944afd11dcb3a6f18f1",
  "filters": {
    "important": "function(doc, req) { if(doc.priority == 'high') { return true; }
    else { return false; }}"
  }
}
```

To query the changes API with this filter, use the filter=designdocname/filtername query parameter:

```
curl "$HOST/db/_changes?filter=app/important"
```

The result now includes only rows for document updates for which the filter function returns true—in our case, where the priority property of our document has the value high. This is pretty neat, but CouchDB takes it up another notch.

Let's take the initial example application where users can send messages to each other. Instead of having a database per user that acts as the inbox, we now use a single database as the inbox for all users. How can a user register for changes that represent a new message being put in her inbox?

We can make the filter function using a request parameter:

```
function(doc, req)
{
  if(doc.name == req.query.name) {
    return true;
  }

  return false;
}
```

If you now run a request adding a ?name=Steve parameter, the filter function will only return result rows for documents that have the name field set to "Steve." If you are running a request for a different user, just change the request parameter (name=Joe).

Now, adding a query parameter to a filtered changes request is easy. What would hinder Steve from passing in name=Joe as the parameter and seeing Joe's inbox? Not much. Can CouchDB help with this? We wouldn't bring this up if it couldn't, would we?

The req parameter of the filter function includes a member userCtx, the *user context*. This includes information about the user that has already been authenticated over HTTP earlier in the phase of the request. Specifically, req.userCtx.name includes the username of the user who makes the filtered changes request. We can be sure that the user is who he says he is because he has been authenticated against one of the authenticating schemes in CouchDB. With this, we don't even need the dynamic filter parameter (although it can still be useful in other situations).

If you have configured CouchDB to use authentication for requests, a user will have to make an authenticated request and the result is available in our filter function:

```
function(doc, req)
{
  if(doc.name) {
    if(doc.name == req.userCtx.name) {
      return true;
    }
  }

  return false;
}
```

Wrapping Up

The changes API lets you build sophisticated notification schemes useful in many scenarios with isolated and asynchronous components yet working to the same beat. In combination with replication, this API is the foundation for building distributed, highly available, and high-performance CouchDB clusters.

CHAPTER 21

View Cookbook for SQL Jockeys

This is a collection of some common SQL queries and how to get the same result in CouchDB. The key to remember here is that CouchDB does not work like an SQL database at all and that best practices from the SQL world do not translate well or at all to CouchDB. This chapter's "cookbook" assumes that you are familiar with the CouchDB basics such as creating and updating databases and documents.

Using Views

How you would do this in SQL:

```
CREATE TABLE
```

or:

```
ALTER TABLE
```

Using views is a two-step process. First you *define* a view; then you *query* it. This is analogous to defining a table structure (with indexes) using `CREATE TABLE` or `ALTER TABLE` and querying it using an SQL query.

Defining a View

Defining a view is done by creating a special document in a CouchDB database. The only real specialness is the `_id` of the document, which starts with `_design/`—for example, `_design/application`. Other than that, it is just a regular CouchDB document. To make sure CouchDB understands that you are defining a view, you need to prepare the contents of that design document in a special format. Here is an example:

```
{
  "_id": "_design/application",
  "_rev": "1-C1687D17",
  "views": {
    "viewname": {
      "map": "function(doc) { ... }",
      "reduce": "function(keys, values) { ... }"
```

```
          }
        }
      }
    }
```

We are defining a view `viewname`. The definition of the view consists of two functions: the *map* function and the *reduce* function. Specifying a reduce function is optional. We'll look at the nature of the functions later. Note that `viewname` can be whatever you like: `users`, `by-name`, or `by-date` are just some examples.

A single design document can also include multiple view definitions, each identified by a unique name:

```
{
  "_id": "_design/application",
  "_rev": "1-C1687D17",
  "views": {
    "viewname": {
      "map": "function(doc) { ... }",
      "reduce": "function(keys, values) { ... }"
    },
    "anotherview": {
      "map": "function(doc) { ... }",
      "reduce": "function(keys, values) { ... }"
    }
  }
}
```

Querying a View

The name of the design document and the name of the view are significant for querying the view. To query the view `viewname`, you perform an HTTP GET request to the following URI:

```
/database/_design/application/_view/viewname
```

`database` is the name of the database you created your design document in. Next up is the design document name, and then the view name prefixed with `_view/`. To query `anotherview`, replace `viewname` in that URI with `anotherview`. If you want to query a view in a different design document, adjust the design document name.

MapReduce Functions

MapReduce is a concept that solves problems by applying a two-step process, aptly named the *map* phase and the *reduce* phase. The map phase looks at all documents in CouchDB separately one after the other and creates a *map result*. The map result is an ordered list of key/value pairs. Both `key` and `value` can be specified by the user writing the map function. A map function may call the built-in `emit(key, value)` function 0 to *N* times per document, creating a row in the map result per invocation.

CouchDB is smart enough to run a map function only once for every document, even on subsequent queries on a view. Only changes to documents or new documents need to be processed anew.

Map functions

Map functions run in isolation for every document. They can't modify the document, and they can't talk to the outside world—they can't have *side effects*. This is required so that CouchDB can guarantee correct results without having to recalculate a complete result when only one document gets changed.

The map result looks like this:

```
{"total_rows":3,"offset":0,"rows":[
  {"id":"fc2636bf50556346f1ce46b4bc01fe30","key":"Lena","value":5},
  {"id":"1fb2449f9b9d4e466dbfa47ebe675063","key":"Lisa","value":4},
  {"id":"8ede09f6f6aeb35d948485624b28f149","key":"Sarah","value":6}
}
```

It is a list of rows sorted by the value of `key`. The `id` is added automatically and refers back to the document that created this row. The `value` is the data you're looking for. For example purposes, it's the girl's age.

The map function that produces this result is:

```
function(doc) {
  if(doc.name && doc.age) {
    emit(doc.name, doc.age);
  }
}
```

It includes the `if` statement as a sanity check to ensure that we're operating on the right fields and calls the `emit` function with the name and age as the key and value.

Reduce functions

Reduce functions are explained in "Aggregate Functions" on page 183.

Look Up by Key

How you would do this in SQL:

```
SELECT field FROM table WHERE value="searchterm"
```

Use case: get a *result* (which can be a record or set of records) associated with a *key* (`"searchterm"`).

To look something up quickly, regardless of the storage mechanism, an index is needed. An index is a data structure optimized for quick search and retrieval. CouchDB's map result is stored in such an index, which happens to be a B+ tree.

To look up a value by "searchterm", we need to put all values into the key of a view. All we need is a simple map function:

```
function(doc) {
  if(doc.value) {
    emit(doc.value, null);
  }
}
```

This creates a list of documents that have a value field sorted by the data in the value field. To find all the records that match "searchterm", we query the view and specify the search term as a query parameter:

```
/database/_design/application/_view/viewname?key="searchterm"
```

Consider the documents from the previous section, and say we're indexing on the age field of the documents to find all the five-year-olds:

```
function(doc) {
  if(doc.age && doc.name) {
    emit(doc.age, doc.name);
  }
}
```

Query:

```
/ladies/_design/ladies/_view/age?key=5
```

Result:

```
{"total_rows":3,"offset":1,"rows":[
{"id":"fc2636bf50556346f1ce46b4bc01fe30","key":5,"value":"Lena"}
]}
```

Easy.

Note that you have to emit a value. The view result includes the associated document ID in every row. We can use it to look up more data from the document itself. We can also use the ?include_docs=true parameter to have CouchDB fetch the documents individually for us.

Look Up by Prefix

How you would do this in SQL:

```
SELECT field FROM table WHERE value LIKE "searchterm%"
```

Use case: find all documents that have a field value that starts with searchterm. For example, say you stored a MIME type (like text/html or image/jpg) for each document and now you want to find all documents that are images according to the MIME type.

The solution is very similar to the previous example: all we need is a map function that is a little more clever than the first one. But first, an example document:

```
{
    "_id": "Hugh Laurie",
    "_rev": "1-9fded7deef52ac373119d05435581edf",
    "mime-type": "image/jpg",
    "description": "some dude"
}
```

The clue lies in extracting the prefix that we want to search for from our document and putting it into our view index. We use a regular expression to match our prefix:

```
function(doc) {
  if(doc["mime-type"]) {
    // from the start (^) match everything that is not a slash ([^\/]+) until
    // we find a slash (\/). Slashes needs to be escaped with a backslash (\/)
    var prefix = doc["mime-type"].match(/^[^\/]+\//);
    if(prefix) {
      emit(prefix, null);
    }
  }
}
```

We can now query this view with our desired MIME type prefix and not only find all images, but also text, video, and all other formats:

```
/files/_design/finder/_view/by-mime-type?key="image/"
```

Aggregate Functions

How you would do this in SQL:

```
SELECT COUNT(field) FROM table
```

Use case: calculate a derived value from your data.

We haven't explained reduce functions yet. Reduce functions are similar to aggregate functions in SQL. They compute a value over multiple documents.

To explain the mechanics of reduce functions, we'll create one that doesn't make a whole lot of sense. But this example is easy to understand. We'll explore more useful reductions later.

Reduce functions operate on the output of the map function (also called the *map result* or *intermediate result*). The reduce function's job, unsurprisingly, is to reduce the list that the map function produces.

Here's what our summing reduce function looks like:

```
function(keys, values) {
  var sum = 0;
  for(var idx in values) {
    sum = sum + values[idx];
  }
  return sum;
}
```

Here's an alternate, more idiomatic JavaScript version:

```
function(keys, values) {
  var sum = 0;
  values.forEach(function(element) {
    sum = sum + element;
  });
  return sum;
}
```

This reduce function takes two arguments: a list of keys and a list of values. For our summing purposes we can ignore the keys-list and consider only the value list. We're looping over the list and add each item to a running total that we're returning at the end of the function.

You'll see one difference between the map and the reduce function. The map function uses emit() to create its result, whereas the reduce function returns a value.

For example, from a list of integer values that specify the age, calculate the sum of all years of life for the news headline, "786 life years present at event." A little contrived, but very simple and thus good for demonstration purposes. Consider the documents and the map view we used earlier in this chapter.

The reduce function to calculate the total age of all girls is:

```
function(keys, values) {
  return sum(values);
}
```

Note that, instead of the two earlier versions, we use CouchDB's predefined sum() function. It does the same thing as the other two, but it is such a common piece of code that CouchDB has it included.

The result for our reduce view now looks like this:

```
{"rows":[
{"key":null,"value":15}
]}
```

The total sum of all age fields in all our documents is 15. Just what we wanted. The key member of the result object is null, as we can't know anymore which documents took part in the creation of the reduced result. We'll cover more advanced reduce cases later on.

As a rule of thumb, the reduce function should reduce a single scalar value. That is, an integer; a string; or a small, fixed-size list or object that includes an aggregated value (or values) from the values argument. It should never just return values or similar. CouchDB will give you a warning if you try to use reduce "the wrong way":

```
{"error":"reduce_overflow_error","message":"Reduce output must shrink more rapidly:
Current output: ..."}
```

Get Unique Values

How you would do this in SQL:

```
SELECT DISTINCT field FROM table
```

Getting unique values is not as easy as adding a keyword. But a reduce view and a special query parameter give us the same result. Let's say you want a list of tags that your users have tagged themselves with and no duplicates.

First, let's look at the source documents. We punt on `_id` and `_rev` attributes here:

```
{
  "name":"Chris",
  "tags":["mustache", "music", "couchdb"]
}


{
  "name":"Noah",
  "tags":["hypertext", "philosophy", "couchdb"]
}


{
  "name":"Jan",
  "tags":["drums", "bike", "couchdb"]
}
```

Next, we need a list of all tags. A map function will do the trick:

```
function(dude) {
  if(dude.name && dude.tags) {
    dude.tags.forEach(function(tag) {
      emit(tag, null);
    });
  }
}
```

The result will look like this:

```
{"total_rows":9,"offset":0,"rows":[
{"id":"3525ab874bc4965fa3cda7c549e92d30","key":"bike","value":null},
{"id":"3525ab874bc4965fa3cda7c549e92d30","key":"couchdb","value":null},
{"id":"53f82b1f0ff49a08ac79a9dff41d7860","key":"couchdb","value":null},
{"id":"da5ea89448a4506925823f4d985aabbd","key":"couchdb","value":null},
{"id":"3525ab874bc4965fa3cda7c549e92d30","key":"drums","value":null},
{"id":"53f82b1f0ff49a08ac79a9dff41d7860","key":"hypertext","value":null},
{"id":"da5ea89448a4506925823f4d985aabbd","key":"music","value":null},
{"id":"da5ea89448a4506925823f4d985aabbd","key":"mustache","value":null},
{"id":"53f82b1f0ff49a08ac79a9dff41d7860","key":"philosophy","value":null}
]}
```

As promised, these are all the tags, including duplicates. Since each document gets run through the map function in isolation, it cannot know if the same key has been emitted already. At this stage, we need to live with that. To achieve uniqueness, we need a reduce:

```
function(keys, values) {
  return true;
}
```

This reduce doesn't do anything, but it allows us to specify a special query parameter when querying the view:

```
/dudes/_design/dude-data/_view/tags?group=true
```

CouchDB replies:

```
{"rows":[
{"key":"bike","value":true},
{"key":"couchdb","value":true},
{"key":"drums","value":true},
{"key":"hypertext","value":true},
{"key":"music","value":true},
{"key":"mustache","value":true},
{"key":"philosophy","value":true}
]}
```

In this case, we can ignore the value part because it is always true, but the result includes a list of all our tags and no duplicates!

With a small change we can put the reduce to good use, too. Let's see how many of the non-unique tags are there for each tag. To calculate the tag frequency, we just use the summing up we already learned about. In the map function, we emit a 1 instead of null:

```
function(dude) {
  if(dude.name && dude.tags) {
    dude.tags.forEach(function(tag) {
      emit(tag, 1);
    });
  }
}
```

In the reduce function, we return the sum of all values:

```
function(keys, values) {
  return sum(values);
}
```

Now, if we query the view with the ?group=true parameter, we get back the count for each tag:

```
{"rows":[
{"key":"bike","value":1},
{"key":"couchdb","value":3},
{"key":"drums","value":1},
{"key":"hypertext","value":1},
{"key":"music","value":1},
{"key":"mustache","value":1},
{"key":"philosophy","value":1}
]}
```

Enforcing Uniqueness

How you would do this in SQL:

```
UNIQUE KEY(column)
```

Use case: your applications require that a certain value exists only once in a database.

This is an easy one: within a CouchDB database, each document must have a unique _id field. If you require unique values in a database, just assign them to a document's _id field and CouchDB will enforce uniqueness for you.

There's one caveat, though: in the distributed case, when you are running more than one CouchDB node that accepts write requests, uniqueness can be guaranteed only per node or outside of CouchDB. CouchDB will allow two identical IDs to be written to two different nodes. On replication, CouchDB will detect a conflict and flag the document accordingly.

CHAPTER 22

Security

We mentioned earlier that CouchDB is still in development and that features may have been added since the publication of this book. This is especially true for the security mechanisms in CouchDB. There is rudimentary support in the currently released versions (0.10.0), but as we're writing these lines, additions are being discussed.

In this chapter, we'll look at the basic security mechanisms in CouchDB: the *Admin Party*, *Basic Authentication*, *Cookie Authentication*, and *OAuth*.

The Admin Party

When you start out fresh, CouchDB allows any request to be made by anyone. Create a database? No problem, here you go. Delete some documents? Same deal. CouchDB calls this the *Admin Party*. Everybody has privileges to do anything. Neat.

While it is incredibly easy to get started with CouchDB that way, it should be obvious that putting a default installation into the wild is adventurous. Any rogue client could come along and delete a database.

A note of relief: by default, CouchDB will listen only on your loopback network interface (`127.0.0.1` or `localhost`) and thus only you will be able to make requests to CouchDB, nobody else. But when you start to open up your CouchDB to the public (that is, by telling it to bind to your machine's public IP address), you will want to think about restricting access so that the next bad guy doesn't ruin your admin party.

In our previous discussions, w dropped some keywords about how things without the admin party work. First, there's *admin* itself, which implies some sort of super user. Then there are *privileges*. Let's explore these terms a little more.

CouchDB has the idea of an *admin user* (e.g. an administrator, a super user, or root) that is allowed to do anything to a CouchDB installation. By default, everybody is an admin. If you don't like that, you can create specific admin users with a username and password as their credentials.

CouchDB also defines a set of requests that only admin users are allowed to do. If you have defined one or more specific admin users, CouchDB will ask for identification for certain requests:

- Creating a database (PUT /database)
- Deleting a database (DELETE /database)
- Creating a design document (PUT /database/_design/app)
- Updating a design document (PUT /database/_design/app?rev=1-4E2)
- Deleting a design document (DELETE /database/_design/app?rev=1-6A7)
- Triggering compaction (POST /_compact)
- Reading the task status list (GET /_active_tasks)
- Restarting the server (POST /_restart)
- Reading the active configuration (GET /_config)
- Updating the active configuration (PUT /_config)

Creating New Admin Users

Let's do another walk through the API using curl to see how CouchDB behaves when you add admin users.

```
> HOST="http://127.0.0.1:5984"
> curl -X PUT $HOST/database
{"ok":true}
```

When starting out fresh, we can add a database. Nothing unexpected. Now let's create an admin user. We'll call her anna, and her password is secret. Note the double quotes in the following code; they are needed to denote a string value for the configuration API (as we learned earlier):

```
curl -X PUT $HOST/_config/admins/anna -d '"secret"'
""
```

As per the _config API's behavior, we're getting the previous value for the config item we just wrote. Since our admin user didn't exist, we get an empty string.

When we now sneak over to the CouchDB log file, we find these two entries:

```
[debug] [<0.43.0>] saving to file \
'/Users/jan/Work/couchdb-git/etc/couchdb/local_dev.ini', \
Config: '{{"admins","anna"},"secret"}'

[debug] [<0.43.0>] saving to file \
'/Users/jan/Work/couchdb-git/etc/couchdb/local_dev.ini', Config:\
'{{"admins","anna"}, \
"-hashed-6a1cc3760b4d09c150d44edf302ff40606221526,a69a9e4f0047be899ebfe09a40b2f52c"}'
```

The first is our initial request. You see that our admin user gets written to the CouchDB configuration files. We set our CouchDB log level to debug to see exactly what is going on. We first see the request coming in with a plain-text password and then again with a hashed password.

Hashing Passwords

Seeing the plain-text password is scary, isn't it? No worries; in normal operation when the log level is not set to `debug`, the plain-text password doesn't show up anywhere. It gets hashed right away. The hash is that big, ugly, long string that starts out with `-hashed-`. How does that work?

1. Creates a new 128-bit UUID. This is our *salt*.
2. Creates a sha1 hash of the concatenation of the bytes of the plain-text password and the salt (`sha1(password + salt)`).
3. Prefixes the result with `-hashed-` and appends `,salt`.

To compare a plain-text password during authentication with the stored hash, the same procedure is run and the resulting hash is compared to the stored hash. The probability of two identical hashes for different passwords is too insignificant to mention (c.f. Bruce Schneier). Should the stored hash fall into the hands of an attacker, it is, by current standards, way too inconvenient (i.e., it'd take a lot of money and time) to find the plain-text password from the hash.

But what's with the `-hashed-` prefix? Well, remember how the configuration API works? When CouchDB starts up, it reads a set of *.ini* files with config settings. It loads these settings into an internal data store (not a database). The config API lets you read the current configuration as well as change it and create new entries. CouchDB is writing any changes back to the *.ini* files.

The *.ini* files can also be edited by hand when CouchDB is not running. Instead of creating the admin user as we showed previously, you could have stopped CouchDB, opened your *local.ini*, added `anna = secret` to the `[admins]` section, and restarted CouchDB. Upon reading the new line from *local.ini*, CouchDB would run the hashing algorithm and write back the hash to *local.ini*, replacing the plain-text password. To make sure CouchDB only hashes plain-text passwords and not an existing hash a second time, it prefixes the hash with `-hashed-`, to distinguish between plain-text passwords and hashed passwords. This means your plain-text password can't start with the characters `-hashed-`, but that's pretty unlikely to begin with.

Basic Authentication

Now that we have defined an admin, CouchDB will not allow us to create new databases unless we give the correct admin user credentials. Let's verify:

```
> curl -X PUT $HOST/somedatabase
{"error":"unauthorized","reason":"You are not a server admin."}
```

That looks about right. Now we try again with the correct credentials:

```
> HOST="http://anna:secret@127.0.0.1:5984"
> curl -X PUT $HOST/somedatabase
{"ok":true}
```

If you have ever accessed a website or FTP server that was password-protected, the `username:password@` URL variant should look familiar.

If you are security conscious, the missing `s` in `http://` will make you nervous. We're sending our password to CouchDB in plain text. This is a bad thing, right? Yes, but consider our scenario: CouchDB listens on `127.0.0.1` on a development box that we're the sole user of. Who could possibly sniff our password?

If you are in a production environment, however, you need to reconsider. Will your CouchDB instance communicate over a public network? Even a LAN shared with other colocation customers is public. There are multiple ways to secure communication between you or your application and CouchDB that exceed the scope of this book. We suggest you read up on VPNs and setting up CouchDB behind an HTTP proxy (like Apache httpd's mod_proxy, nginx, or varnish) that will handle SSL for you. CouchDB does not support exposing its API via SSL at the moment. It can, however, replicate with other CouchDB instances that are behind an SSL proxy.

Update Validations Again

Do you remember Chapter 7? We had an update validation function that allowed us to verify that the claimed author of a document matched the authenticated username.

```
function(newDoc, oldDoc, userCtx) {
  if (newDoc.author) {
    if(newDoc.author != userCtx.name) {
      throw("forbidden": "You may only update documents with author " +
        userCtx.name});
    }
  }
}
```

What is this `userCtx` exactly? It is an object filled with information about the current request's authentication data. Let's have a look at what's in there. We'll show you a simple trick how to introspect what's going on in all the JavaScript you are writing.

```
> curl -X PUT $HOST/somedatabase/_design/log \
  -d '{"validate_doc_update":"function(newDoc, oldDoc, userCtx) { log(userCtx); }"}'
{"ok":true,"id":"_design/log","rev":"1-498bd568e17e93d247ca48439a368718"}
```

Let's show the `validate_doc_update` function:

```
function(newDoc, oldDoc, userCtx) {
  log(userCtx);
}
```

This gets called for every future document update and does nothing but print a log entry into CouchDB's log file. If we now create a new document:

```
> curl -X POST $HOST/somedatabase/ -d '{"a":1}'
{"ok":true,"id":"36174efe5d455bd45fa1d51efbcff986",
"rev":"1-23202479633c2b380f79507a776743d5"}
```

we should see this in our *couch.log* file:

```
[info] [<0.9973.0>] OS Process :: {"db": "somedatabase","name": "anna","roles":
["_admin"]}
```

Let's format this again:

```
{
  "db": "somedatabase",
  "name": "anna",
  "roles": ["_admin"]
}
```

We see the current database, the name of the authenticated user, and an array of roles, with one role "_admin". We can conclude that admin users in CouchDB are really just *regular users* with the *admin role* attached to them.

By separating users and roles from each other, the authentication system allows for flexible extension. For now, we'll just look at admin users.

Cookie Authentication

Basic authentication that uses plain-text passwords is nice and convenient, but not very secure if no extra measures are taken. It is also a very poor user experience. If you use basic authentication to identify admins, your application's users need to deal with an ugly, unstylable browser modal dialog that says *non-professional at work* more than anything else.

To remedy some of these concerns, CouchDB supports *cookie authentication*. With cookie authentication your application doesn't have to include the ugly login dialog that the users' browsers come with. You can use a regular HTML form to submit logins to CouchDB. Upon receipt, CouchDB will generate a one-time token that the client can use in its next request to CouchDB. When CouchDB sees the token in a subsequent request, it will authenticate the user based on the token without the need to see the password again. By default, a token is valid for 10 minutes.

To obtain the first token and thus authenticate a user for the first time, the username and password must be sent to the _session API. The API is smart enough to decode HTML form submissions, so you don't have to resort to any smarts in your application.

If you are not using HTML forms to log in, you need to send an HTTP request that looks as if an HTML form generated it. Luckily, this is super simple:

```
> HOST="http://127.0.0.1:5984"
> curl -vX POST $HOST/_session \
  -H 'application/x-www-form-urlencoded' \
  -d 'username=anna&password=secret'
```

CouchDB replies, and we'll give you some more detail:

```
< HTTP/1.1 200 OK
< Set-Cookie: AuthSession=YW5uYTo0QUIzOTdFQjrC4ipN-D-53hw1sJepVzcVxnriEw;
< Version=1; Path=/; HttpOnly
> ...
<
{"ok":true}
```

A `200` response code tells us all is well, a `Set-Cookie` header includes the token we can use for the next request, and the standard JSON response tells us again that the request was successful.

Now we can use this token to make another request as the same user without sending the username and password again:

```
> curl -vX PUT $HOST/mydatabase \
  --cookie AuthSession=YW5uYTo0QUIzOTdFQjrC4ipN-D-53hw1sJepVzcVxnriEw \
  -H "X-CouchDB-WWW-Authenticate: Cookie" \
  -H "Content-Type: application/x-www-form-urlencoded"
{"ok":true}
```

You can keep using this token for 10 minutes by default. After 10 minutes you need to authenticate your user again. The token lifetime can be configured with the `timeout` (in seconds) setting in the `couch_httpd_auth` configuration section.

> Please note that for cookie authentication to work, you need to enable the `cookie_authentication_handler` in your *local.ini*:
>
> ```
> [httpd]
> authentication_handlers = \
>   {couch_httpd_auth, cookie_authentication_handler}, \
>   {couch_httpd_oauth, oauth_authentication_handler}, \
>   {couch_httpd_auth, default_authentication_handler}
> ```
>
> In addition, you need to define a *server secret*:
>
> ```
> [couch_httpd_auth]
> secret = yours3cr37pr4s3
> ```

Network Server Security

CouchDB is a networked server, and there are best practices for securing these that are beyond the scope of this book. Appendix D includes some of those best practices. Make sure to understand the implications.

CHAPTER 23

High Performance

This chapter will teach you the fastest ways to insert and query data with CouchDB. It will also explain why there is a wide range of performance across various techniques.

The take-home message: bulk operations result in lower overhead, higher throughput, and more space efficiency. If you can't work in bulk in your application, we'll also describe other options to get throughput and space benefits. Finally, we describe interfacing directly with CouchDB from Erlang, which can be a useful technique if you want to integrate CouchDB storage with a server for non-HTTP protocols, like SMTP (email) or XMPP (chat).

Good Benchmarks Are Non-Trivial

Each application is different. Performance requirements are not always obvious. Different use cases need to tune different parameters. A classic trade-off is latency versus throughput. Concurrency is another factor. Many database platforms behave very differently with 100 clients than they do with 1,000 or more concurrent clients. Some data profiles require serialized operations, which increase total time (latency) for the client, and load on the server. We think simpler data and access patterns can make a big difference in the cacheability and scalability of your app, but we'll get to that later.

The upshot: *real benchmarks require real-world load.* Simulating load is hard. Erlang tends to perform better under load (especially on multiple cores), so we've often seen test rigs that can't drive CouchDB hard enough to see where it falls over.

Let's take a look at what a typical web app looks like. This is not exactly how Craigslist works (because we don't know how Craigslist works), but it is a close enough approximation to illustrate problems with benchmarking.

You have a web server, some middleware, and a database. A user request comes in, and the web server takes care of the networking and parses the HTTP request. The request gets handed to the middleware layer, which figures out what to run, then it runs whatever is needed to serve the request. The middleware might talk to your database and other external resources like files or remote web services. The request bounces back to the web server, which sends out any resulting HTML. The HTML includes references to other resources living on your web server (like CSS, JS, or image files), and the process starts anew for every resource. A little different each time, but in general, all requests are similar. And along the way there are caches to store intermediate results to avoid expensive recomputation.

That's a lot of moving parts. Getting a top-to-bottom profile of all components to figure out where bottlenecks lie is pretty complex (but nice to have). We start making up numbers now. The absolute values are not important; only numbers relative to each other are. Say a request takes 1.5 seconds (1,500 ms) to be fully rendered in a browser.

In a simple case like Craigslist, there is the initial HTML, a CSS file, a JS file, and the favicon. Except for the HTML, these are all static resources and involve reading some data from a disk (or from memory) and serving it to the browser that then renders it. The most notable things to do for performance are keeping data small (GZIP compression, high JPG compression) and avoiding requests all together (HTTP-level caching in the browser). Making the web server any faster doesn't buy us much (yeah, hand wavey, but we don't want to focus on static resources here). Let's say all static resources take 500 ms to serve and render.

 Read all about improving client experience with proper use of HTTP from Steve Souders, web performance guru. His YSlow tool is indispensable for tuning a website.

That leaves us with 1,000 ms for the initial HTML. We'll chop off 200 ms for network latency (see Chapter 1). Let's pretend HTTP parsing, middleware routing and execution, and database access share equally the rest of the time, 200 ms each.

If you now set out to improve one part of the big puzzle that is your web app and gain 10 ms in the database access time, this is probably time not well spent (unless you have the numbers to prove it).

However, breaking down a single request like this and looking for how much time is spent in each component is also misleading. Even if only a small percentage of the time is spent in your database under normal load, that doesn't teach you what will happen during traffic spikes. If all requests are hitting the same database, then any locking there could block many web requests. Your database may have minimal impact on total query time, under normal load, but under spike load it may turn into a bottleneck, magnifying the effect of the spike on the application servers. CouchDB can minimize this by dedicating an Erlang process to each connection, ensuring that all clients are handled, even if latency goes up a bit.

High Performance CouchDB

Now that you see database performance is only a small part of overall web performance, we'll give you some tips to squeeze the most out of CouchDB.

CouchDB is designed from the ground up to service highly concurrent use cases, which make up the majority of web application load. However, sometimes we need to import a large batch of data into CouchDB or initiate transforms across an entire database. Or maybe we're building a custom Erlang application that needs to link into CouchDB at a lower level than HTTP.

Hardware

Invariably people will want to know what type of disk they should use, how much RAM, what sort of CPU, etc. The real answer is that CouchDB is flexible enough to run on everything from a smart phone to a cluster, so the answers will vary.

More RAM is better because CouchDB makes heavy use of the filesystem cache. CPU cores are more important for building views than serving documents. Solid State Drives (SSDs) are pretty sweet because they can append to a file while loading old blocks, with a minimum of overhead. As they get faster and cheaper, they'll be really handy for CouchDB.

An Implementation Note

We're not going to rehash append-only B-trees here, but understanding CouchDB's data format is key to gaining an intuition about which strategies yield the best performance. Each time an update is made, CouchDB loads from disk the B-tree nodes that point to the updated documents or the key range where a new document's _id would be found.

This loading will normally come from the filesystem cache, except when updates are made to documents in regions of the tree that have not been touched in a long time. In those cases, the disk has to seek, which can block writing and have other ripple effects. Preventing these disk seeks is the name of the game in CouchDB performance.

We'll use some numbers in this chapter that come from a JavaScript test suite. It's not the most accurate, but the strategy it uses (counting the number of documents that can be saved in 10 seconds) makes up for the JavaScript overhead. The hardware the benchmarks were run on is modest: just an old white MacBook Intel Core 2 Duo (remember those?).

You can run the benchmarks yourself by changing to the *bench/* directory of CouchDB's trunk and running *./runner.sh* while CouchDB is running on port 5984.

Bulk Inserts and Mostly Monotonic DocIDs

Bulk inserts are the best way to have seekless writes. Random IDs force seeking after the file is bigger than can be cached. Random IDs also make for a bigger file because in a large database you'll rarely have multiple documents in one B-tree leaf.

Optimized Examples: Views and Replication

If you're curious what a good performance profile is for CouchDB, look at how views and replication are done. Triggered replication applies updates to the database in large batches to minimize disk chatter. Currently the 0.11.0 development trunk boasts an additional 3–5x speed increase over 0.10's view generation.

Views load a batch of updates from disk, pass them through the view engine, and then write the view rows out. Each batch is a few hundred documents, so the writer can take advantage of the bulk efficiencies we see in the next section.

Bulk Document Inserts

The fastest mode for importing data into CouchDB via HTTP is the `_bulk_docs` endpoint. The bulk documents API accepts a collection of documents in a single POST request and stores them all to CouchDB in a single index operation.

Bulk docs is the API to use when you are importing a corpus of data using a scripting language. It can be 10 to 100 times faster than individual bulk updates and is just as easy to work with from most languages.

The main factor that influences performance of bulk operations is the size of the update, both in terms of total data transferred as well as the number of documents included in an update.

Here are sequential bulk document inserts at four different granularities, from an array of 100 documents, up through 1,000, 5,000, and 10,000:

```
bulk_doc_100
4400 docs
437.37574552683895 docs/sec

bulk_doc_1000
17000 docs
1635.4016354016355 docs/sec

bulk_doc_5000
30000 docs
2508.1514923501377 docs/sec

bulk_doc_10000
30000 docs
2699.541078016737 docs/sec
```

You can see that larger batches yield better performance, with an upper limit in this test of 2,700 documents/second. With larger documents, we might see that smaller batches are more useful. For references, all the documents look like this: {"foo":"bar"}

Although 2,700 documents per second is fine, we want more power! Next up, we'll explore running bulk documents in parallel.

With a different script (using bash and *cURL* with *benchbulk.sh* in the same directory), we're inserting large batches of documents in parallel to CouchDB. With batches of 1,000 docs, 10 at any given time, averaged over 10 rounds, I see about 3,650 documents per second on a MacBook Pro. Benchbulk also uses sequential IDs.

We see that with proper use of bulk documents and sequential IDs, we can insert more than 3,000 docs per second just using scripting languages.

Batch Mode

To avoid the indexing and disk sync overhead associated with individual document writes, there is an option that allows CouchDB to build up batches of documents in memory, flushing them to disk when a certain threshold has been reached or when triggered by the user. The batch option does not give the same data integrity guarantees that normal updates provide, so it should only be used when the potential loss of recent updates is acceptable.

Because batch mode only stores updates in memory until a flush occurs, updates that are saved to CouchDB directly proceeding a crash can be lost. By default, CouchDB flushes the in-memory updates once per second, so in the worst case, data loss is still minimal. To reflect the reduced integrity guarantees when batch=ok is used, the HTTP response code is 202 Accepted, as opposed to 201 Created.

The ideal use for batch mode is for logging type applications, where you have many distributed writers each storing discrete events to CouchDB. In a normal logging scenario, losing a few updates on rare occasions is worth the trade-off for increased storage throughput.

There is a pattern for reliable storage using batch mode. It's the same pattern as is used when data needs to be stored reliably to multiple nodes before acknowledging success to the saving client. In a nutshell, the application server (or remote client) saves to Couch A using batch=ok, and then watches update notifications from Couch B, only considering the save successful when Couch B's _changes stream includes the relevant update. We covered this pattern in detail in Chapter 16.

```
batch_ok_doc_insert
4851 docs
485.00299940011996 docs/sec
```

This JavaScript benchmark only gets around 500 documents per second, six times slower than the bulk document API. However, it has the advantage that clients don't need to build up bulk batches.

Single Document Inserts

Normal web app load for CouchDB comes in the form of single document inserts. Because each insert comes from a distinct client, and has the overhead of an entire HTTP request and response, it generally has the lowest throughput for writes.

Probably the slowest possible use case for CouchDB is the case of a writer that has to make many serialized writes against the database. Imagine a case where each write depends on the result of the previous write so that only one writer can run. This sounds like a bad case from the description alone. If you find yourself in this position, there are probably other problems to address as well.

We can write about 258 documents per second with a single writer in serial (pretty much the worst-case scenario writer).

```
single_doc_insert
2584 docs
257.9357157117189 docs/sec
```

Delayed commit (along with sequential UUIDs) is probably the most important CouchDB configuration setting for performance. When it is set to true (the default), CouchDB allows operations to be run against the disk without an explicit fsync after each operation. Fsync operations take time (the disk may have to seek, on some platforms the hard disk cache buffer is flushed, etc.), so requiring an fsync for each update deeply limits CouchDB's performance for non-bulk writers.

Delayed commit should be left set to true in the configuration settings, unless you are in an environment where you absolutely need to know when updates have been received (such as when CouchDB is running as part of a larger transaction). It is also possible to trigger an fsync (e.g., after a few operations) using the _ensure_full_commit API.

When delayed commit is disabled, CouchDB writes data to the actual disk before it responds to the client (except in batch=ok mode). It's a simpler code path, so it has less overhead when running at high throughput levels. However, for individual clients, it can seem slow. Here's the same benchmark in full commit mode:

```
single_doc_insert
46 docs
4.583042741855135 docs/sec
```

Look at how slow single_doc_insert is with full-commit enabled—four or five documents per second! That's 100% a result of the fact that Mac OS X has a real fsync, so be thankful! Don't worry; the full commit story gets better as we move into bulk operations.

On the other hand, we're getting better times for large bulks with delayed commit off, which lets us know that *tuning for your application* will always bring better results than following a cookbook.

Hovercraft

Hovercraft is a library for accessing CouchDB from within Erlang. Hovercraft benchmarks should show the fastest possible performance of CouchDB's disk and index subsystems, as it avoids all HTTP connection and JSON conversion overhead.

Hovercraft is useful primarily when the HTTP interface doesn't allow for enough control, or is otherwise redundant. For instance, persisting Jabber instant messages to CouchDB might use ejabberd and Hovercraft. The easiest way to create a failure-tolerant message queue is probably a combination of RabbitMQ and Hovercraft.

Hovercraft was extracted from a client project that used CouchDB to store massive amounts of email as document attachments. HTTP doesn't have an easy mechanism to allow a combination of bulk updates with binary attachments, so we used Hovercraft to connect an Erlang SMTP server directly to CouchDB, to stream attachments directly to disk while maintaining the efficiency of bulk index updates.

Hovercraft includes a basic benchmarking feature, and we see that we can get many documents per second.

```
> hovercraft:lightning().
Inserted 100000 docs in 9.37 seconds with batch size of 1000.
(10672 docs/sec)
```

Trade-Offs

Tool X might give you 5 ms response times, an order of magnitude faster than anything else on the market. Programming is all about trade-offs, and everybody is bound by the same laws.

On the outside, it might appear that everybody who is not using Tool X is a fool. But speed and latency are only part of the picture. We already established that going from 5 ms to 50 ms might not even be noticeable by anyone using your product. Speed may come at the expense of other things, such as:

Memory
> Instead of doing computations over and over, Tool X might have a cute caching layer that saves recomputation by storing results in memory. If you are CPU bound, that might be good; if you are memory bound, it might not. A trade-off.

Concurrency
> The clever data structures in Tool X are extremely fast when only one request at a time is processed, and because it is so fast most of the time, it appears as if it would

process multiple requests in parallel. Eventually, though, a high number of concurrent requests fill up the request queue and response time suffers. A variation on this is that Tool X might work exceptionally well on a single CPU or core, but not on many, leaving your beefy servers idling.

Reliability

Making sure data is actually stored is an expensive operation. Making sure a data store is in a consistent state and not corrupted is another. There are two trade-offs here. First, buffers store data in memory before committing it to disk to ensure a higher data throughput. In the event of a power loss or crash (of hard- or software), the data is gone. This may or may not be acceptable for your application. Second, a consistency check is required to run after a failure, and if you have a lot of data, this can take days. If you can afford to be offline, that's OK, but maybe you can't afford it.

Make sure to understand what requirements you have and pick the tool that complies instead of picking the one that has the prettiest numbers. Who's the fool when your web application is offline for a fixup for a day while your customers impatiently wait to get their jobs done or, worse, you lose their data?

But…My Boss Wants Numbers!

You want to know which one of these databases, caches, programming languages, language constructs, or tools is faster, harder, or stronger. Numbers are cool—you can draw pretty graphs that management types can compare and make decisions from.

But the first thing a good executive knows is that she is operating on insufficient data, as diagrams drawn from numbers are a very distilled view of reality. And graphs from numbers that are made up by bad profiling are effectively fantasies.

If you are going to produce numbers, make sure you understand how much information is and isn't covered by your results. Before passing the numbers on, make sure the receiving person knows it too. Again, the best thing to do is test with something as close to real-world load as possible. And that isn't easy.

A Call to Arms

We're in the market for databases and key/value stores. Every solution has a sweet spot in terms of data, hardware, setup, and operation, and there are enough permutations that you can pick the one that is closest to your problem. But how to find out? Ideally, you download and install all possible candidates, create a profiling test suite with proper testing data, make extensive tests, and compare the results. This can easily take weeks, and you might not have that much time.

We would like to ask developers of storage systems to compile a set of profiling suites that simulate different usage patterns of their systems (read-heavy and write-heavy loads, fault tolerance, distributed operation, and many more). A fault-tolerance suite should include the steps necessary to get data live again, such as any rebuild or checkup time. We would like users of these systems to help their developers find out how to reliably measure different scenarios.

We are working on CouchDB, and we'd like very much to have such a suite! Even better, developers could agree (a far-fetched idea, to be sure) on a set of benchmarks that objectively measure performance for easy comparison. We know this is a lot of work and the results may still be questionable, but it'll help our users a great deal when figuring out what to use.

CHAPTER 24

Recipes

This chapter shows some common tasks and how to solve them with CouchDB using best practices and easy-to-follow step-by-step instructions.

Banking

Banks are serious business. They need serious databases to store serious transactions and serious account information. They can't lose any money. Ever. They also can't create money. A bank must be in balance. All the time.

Conventional wisdom says a database needs to support *transactions* to be taken seriously. CouchDB does not support transactions in the traditional sense (although it works transactionally), so you could conclude CouchDB is not well suited to store bank data. Besides, would you trust your money to a couch? Well, we would. This chapter explains why.

Accountants Don't Use Erasers

Say you want to give $100 to your cousin Paul for the New York cheesecake he sent to you. Back in the day, you had to travel all the way to New York and hand Paul the money, or you could send it via (paper) mail. Both methods were considerably inconvenient, so people started looking for alternatives. At one point, banks offered to take care of the money and make sure it arrived at Paul's bank safely without headaches. Of course, they'd charge for the convenience, but you'd be happy to pay a little fee if it could save a trip to New York. Behind the scenes, the bank would send somebody with your money to give it to Paul's bank—the same procedure, but another person was dealing with the trouble. Banks could also batch money transfers; instead of sending each order on its own, they could collect all transfers to New York for a week and send them all at once. In case of any problems—say, the recipient was no longer a customer of the bank (remember, it used to take weeks to travel from one coast to the other)—the money was sent back to the originating account.

Eventually, the modern banking system was put in place and the actual sending of money back and forth could be stopped (much to the disdain of highwaymen). Banks had money *on paper*, which they could send around without actually sending valuables. The old concept is stuck in our heads though. To send somebody money from our bank account, the bank needs to take the notes out of the account and bring them to the receiving account. But nowadays we're used to things happen instantaneously. It takes just a few clicks to order goods from Amazon and have them placed into the mail, so why should a banking transaction take any longer?

Banks are all electronic these days (and have been for a while). When we issue a money transfer, we expect it to go through immediately, and we expect it to work in the way it worked back in the day: take money from my account, add it to Paul's account, and if anything goes wrong, put it back in my account. While this is logically what happens, that's not quite how it works behind the scenes, and hasn't since way before computers were used for banking.

When you go to your bank and ask it to send money to Paul, the accountant will *start a transaction* by noting down that you ordered the sending of the money. The transaction will include the date, amount, and recipient. Remember that banks always need to be in balance. The money taken from your account cannot vanish. The accountant will move the money into an *in-transit* account that the bank maintains for you. Your account balance at this point is an aggregation of your current balance and the transactions in the in-transit account. Now the bank checks whether Paul's account is what you say it is and whether the money could arrive there safely. If that's the case, the money is moved in another single transaction from the in-transit account to Paul's account. Everything is in balance. Notice how there are multiple independent transactions, not one big transaction that combines a number of actions.

Now let's consider an error case: say Paul's account no longer exists. The bank finds this out while performing the batch operation of all the in-transit transactions that need to be performed. A second transaction is generated that moves the money back from the in-transit account to your bank account. Note that the transaction that moved the money out of your account is *not* undone. Rather, a second transaction that does the reverse action is created.

Here's another error case: say you don't have sufficient funds to send $100 to Paul. This will be checked by the accountant (or software) before the bank creates any money-deducting transaction. For accountability, a bank cannot pretend an action didn't happen; it has to record every action minutely in a log. Undoing is done explicitly by performing a reverse action, not by reverting or removing an existing transaction. "Accountants don't use erasers" is a quote from Pat Helland, a senior architect of transactional systems who worked at Microsoft and Amazon.

To rehash, a *transaction* can succeed or fail, but nothing in between. The only operation that CouchDB guarantees to have succeed or fail is a single document write. All operations that comprise a transaction need to be combined into a single document. If business logic detects that an error occurred (e.g., not enough funds), a reverse transaction needs to be created.

Let's look at a CouchDB example. We mentioned earlier that your account balance is an aggregated value. If we stick to this picture, things become downright easy. Instead of updating the balance of two accounts (yours and Paul's, or yours and the in-transit account), we simply create a single transaction document that describes what we're doing and use a view to aggregate your account balance.

Let's consider a bunch of transactions:

```
...
{"from":"Jan","to":"Paul","amount":100}
{"from":"Paul","to":"Steve","amount":20}
{"from":"Work","to":"Jan","amount":200}
...
```

Single document writes in CouchDB are atomic. Querying a view forces an update to the view index with all changes to all documents. The view result is always consistent with the data in our documents. This guarantees that our bank is always in balance. There are many more transactions, of course, but these will do for illustration purposes.

How do we read the current account balance? Easy—create a MapReduce view:

```
function(transaction) {
  emit(transaction.from, transaction.amount * -1);
  emit(transaction.to, transaction.amount);
}

function(keys, values) {
  return sum(values);
}
```

Doesn't look too hard, does it? We'll store this in a view `balance` in a `_design/account` document. Let's find out Jan's balance:

```
curl 'http://127.0.0.1:5984/bank/_design/account/_view/balance?key="Jan"'
```

CouchDB replies:

```
{"rows":[
{"key":null,"value":100}
]}
```

Looks good! Now let's see if our bank is actually in balance. The sum of all transactions should be zero:

```
curl http://127.0.0.1:5984/bank/_design/account/_view/balance
```

CouchDB replies:

```
{"rows":[
{"key":null,"value":0}
]}
```

Wrapping Up

This should explain that applications with strong consistency requirements can use CouchDB if it is possible to break up bigger transactions into smaller ones. A bank is a good enough approximation of a serious business, so you can be safe modeling your important business logic into small CouchDB transactions.

Ordering Lists

Views let you sort things by any value of your data—even complex JSON keys are possible, as we've seen in earlier chapters. Sorting by date is very useful for allowing users to find things quickly; a name is much easier to find in a list of names that is sorted alphabetically. Humans naturally resort to a divide-and-conquer algorithm (sound familiar?) and don't consider a large part of the input set because they know the name won't show up there. Likewise, sorting by number and date helps a great deal to let users manage their ever-increasing amounts of data.

There's another sorting type that is a little more fuzzy. Search engines show you results in order of relevance. That relevance is what the search engine thinks is most relevant to you given your search term (and potential search and surfing history). There are other systems trying to infer from earlier data what is most relevant to you, but they have the near-to-impossible task of guessing what a user is interested in. Computers are notoriously bad at guessing.

The easiest way for a computer to figure out what's most relevant for a user is to let the user prioritize things. Take a to-do application: it allows users to reorder to-do items so they know what they need to work on next. The underlying problem—keeping a user-defined sorting order—can be found in a number of other places.

A List of Integers

Let's stick with the to-do application example. The naïve approach is pretty easy: with each to-do item we store an integer that specifies the location in a list. We use a view to get all to-do items in the right order.

First, we need some example documents:

```
{
  "title":"Remember the Milk",
  "date":"2009-07-22T09:53:37",
  "sort_order":2
}

{
  "title":"Call Fred",
  "date":"2009-07-21T19:41:34",
  "sort_order":3
}
```

```
{
  "title":"Gift for Amy",
  "date":"2009-07-19T17:33:29",
  "sort_order":4
}


{
  "title":"Laundry",
  "date":"2009-07-22T14:23:11",
  "sort_order":1
}
```

Next, we create a view with a simple map function that emits rows that are then sorted by the **sort_order** field of our documents. The view's result looks like we'd expect:

```
function(todo) {
  if(todo.sort_order && todo.title) {
    emit(todo.sort_order, todo.title);
  }
}
{
  "total_rows": 4,
  "offset": 0,
  "rows": [
    {
      "key":1,
      "value":"Laundry",
      "id":"..."
    },
    {
      "key":2,
      "value":"Remember the Milk",
      "id":"..."
    },
    {
      "key":3,
      "value":"Call Fred",
      "id":"..."
    },
    {
      "key":4,
      "value":"Gift for Amy",
      "id":"..."
    }
  ]
}
```

That looks reasonably easy, but can you spot the problem? Here's a hint: what do you have to do if getting a gift for Amy becomes a higher priority than remembering the milk? Conceptually, the work required is simple:

1. Assign "Gift for Amy" the **sort_order** of "Remember the Milk."

2. Increment the **sort_order** of "Remember the Milk" and *all* items that follow by one.

Under the hood, this is a lot of work. With CouchDB you'd have to load every document, increment the sort_order, and save it back. If you have a lot of to-do items (I do), then this is some significant work. Maybe there's a better approach.

A List of Floats

The fix is simple: instead of using an integer to specify the sort order, we use a float:

```
{
  "title":"Remember the Milk",
  "date":"2009-07-22T09:53:37",
  "sort_order":0.2
}

{
  "title":"Call Fred",
  "date":"2009-07-21T19:41:34",
  "sort_order":0.3
}

{
  "title":"Gift for Amy",
  "date":"2009-07-19T17:33:29",
  "sort_order":0.4
}

{
  "title":"Laundry",
  "date":"2009-07-22T14:23:11",
  "sort_order":0.1
}
```

The view stays the same. Reading this is as easy as the previous approach. Reordering becomes much easier now. The application frontend can keep a copy of the sort_order values around, so when we move an item and store the move, we not only have available the new position, but also the sort_order value for the two new surrounding items.

Let's move "Gift for Amy" so it's above "Remember the Milk." The surrounding sort_orders in the target position are 0.1 and 0.2. To store "Gift for Amy" with the correct sort_order, we simply use the median of the two surrounding values: (0.1 + 0.2) / 2 = 0.3 / 2 = 0.15.

If we query the view again, we now get the desired result:

```
{
  "total_rows": 4,
  "offset": 0,
  "rows": [
    {
      "key":0.1,
      "value":"Laundry",
      "id":"..."
```

```
    },
    {
      "key":0.15,
      "value":"Gift for Amy",
      "id":"..."
    },
    {
      "key":0.2,
      "value":"Remember the Milk",
      "id":"..."
    },
    {
      "key":0.3,
      "value":"Call Fred",
      "id":"..."
    }
  ]
}
```

The downside of this approach is that with an increasing number of reorderings, float precision can become an issue as digits "grow" infinitely. One solution is not to care and expect that a single user will not exceed any limits. Alternatively, an administrative task can reset the whole list to single decimals when a user is not active.

The advantage of this approach is that you have to touch only a single document, which is efficient for storing the new ordering of a list and updating the view that maintains the ordered index since only the changed document has to be incorporated into the index.

Pagination

This recipe explains how to paginate over view results. Pagination is a user interface (UI) pattern that allows the display of a large number of rows (the *result set*) without loading all the rows into the UI at once. A fixed-size subset, the *page*, is displayed along with *next* and *previous* links or buttons that can move the *viewport* over the result set to an adjacent page.

We assume you're familiar with creating and querying documents and views as well as the multiple view query options.

Example Data

To have some data to work with, we'll create a list of bands, one document per band:

```
{ "name":"Biffy Clyro" }

{ "name":"Foo Fighters" }

{ "name":"Tool" }

{ "name":"Nirvana" }
```

```
{ "name":"Helmet" }

{ "name":"Tenacious D" }

{ "name":"Future of the Left" }

{ "name":"A Perfect Circle" }

{ "name":"Silverchair" }

{ "name":"Queens of the Stone Age" }

{ "name":"Kerub" }
```

A View

We need a simple map function that gives us an alphabetical list of band names. This should be easy, but we're adding extra smarts to filter out "The" and "A" in front of band names to put them into the right position:

```
function(doc) {
  if(doc.name) {
    var name = doc.name.replace(/^(A|The) /, "");
    emit(name, null);
  }
}
```

The views result is an alphabetical list of band names. Now say we want to display band names five at a time and have a link pointing to the next five names that make up one page, and a link for the previous five, if we're not on the first page.

We learned how to use the startkey, limit, and skip parameters in earlier chapters. We'll use these again here. First, let's have a look at the full result set:

```
{"total_rows":11,"offset":0,"rows":[
  {"id":"a0746072bba60a62b01209f467ca4fe2","key":"Biffy Clyro","value":null},
  {"id":"b47d82284969f10cd1b6ea460ad62d00","key":"Foo Fighters","value":null},
  {"id":"45ccde324611f86ad4932555dea7fce0","key":"Tenacious D","value":null},
  {"id":"d7ab24bb3489a9010c7d1a2087a4a9e4","key":"Future of the Left","value":null},
  {"id":"ad2f85ef87f5a9a65db5b3a75a03cd82","key":"Helmet","value":null},
  {"id":"a2f31cfa68118a6ae9d35444fcb1a3cf","key":"Nirvana","value":null},
  {"id":"67373171d0f626b811bdc34e92e77901","key":"Kerub","value":null},
  {"id":"3e1b84630c384f6aef1a5c50a81e4a34","key":"Perfect Circle","value":null},
  {"id":"84a371a7b8414237fad1b6aaf68cd16a","key":"Queens of the Stone Age",
"value":null},
  {"id":"dcdaf08242a4be7da1a36e25f4f0b022","key":"Silverchair","value":null},
  {"id":"fd590d4ad53771db47b0406054f02243","key":"Tool","value":null}
]}
```

Setup

The mechanics of paging are very simple:

- Display first page.
- If there are more rows to show, show *next* link.
- Draw subsequent page
- If this is not the first page, show a *previous* link.
- If there are more rows to show, show *next* link.

Or in a pseudo-JavaScript snippet:

```
var result = new Result();
var page = result.getPage();

page.display();

if(result.hasPrev()) {
  page.display_link('prev');
}

if(result.hasNext()) {
  page.display_link('next');
}
```

Slow Paging (Do Not Use)

Don't use this method! We just show it because it might seem natural to use, and you need to know why it is a bad idea. To get the first five rows from the view result, you use the `?limit=5` query parameter:

```
curl -X GET http://127.0.0.1:5984/artists/_design/artists/_view/by-name?limit=5
```

The result:

```
{"total_rows":11,"offset":0,"rows":[
  {"id":"a0746072bba60a62b01209f467ca4fe2","key":"Biffy Clyro","value":null},
  {"id":"b47d82284969f10cd1b6ea460ad62d00","key":"Foo Fighters","value":null},
  {"id":"45ccde324611f86ad4932555dea7fce0","key":"Tenacious D","value":null},
  {"id":"d7ab24bb3489a9010c7d1a2087a4a9e4","key":"Future of the Left","value":null},
  {"id":"ad2f85ef87f5a9a65db5b3a75a03cd82","key":"Helmet","value":null}
]}
```

By comparing the `total_rows` value to our `limit` value, we can determine if there are more pages to display. We also know by the `offset` member that we are on the first page. We can calculate the value for `skip=` to get the results for the next page:

```
var rows_per_page = 5;
var page = (offset / rows_per_page) + 1; // == 1
var skip = page * rows_per_page; // == 5 for the first page, 10 for the second ...
```

So we query CouchDB with:

```
curl -X GET
'http://127.0.0.1:5984/artists/_design/artists/_view/by-name?limit=5&skip=5'
```

Note we have to use ' (single quotes) to escape the & character that is special to the shell we execute curl in.

The result:

```
{"total_rows":11,"offset":5,"rows":[
  {"id":"a2f31cfa68118a6ae9d35444fcb1a3cf","key":"Nirvana","value":null},
  {"id":"67373171d0f626b811bdc34e92e77901","key":"Kerub","value":null},
  {"id":"3e1b84630c384f6aef1a5c50a81e4a34","key":"Perfect Circle","value":null},
  {"id":"84a371a7b8414237fad1b6aaf68cd16a","key":"Queens of the Stone Age",
"value":null},
  {"id":"dcdaf08242a4be7da1a36e25f4f0b022","key":"Silverchair","value":null}
]}
```

Implementing the hasPrev() and hasNext() method is pretty straightforward:

```
function hasPrev()
{
  return page > 1;
}

function hasNext()
{
  var last_page = Math.floor(total_rows / rows_per_page) +
    (total_rows % rows_per_page);
  return page != last_page;
}
```

The dealbreaker

This all looks easy and straightforward, but it has one fatal flaw. Remember how view results are generated from the underlying B-tree index: CouchDB jumps to the first row (or the first row that matches startkey, if provided) and reads one row after the other from the index until there are no more rows (or limit or endkey match, if provided).

The skip argument works like this: in addition to going to the first row and starting to read, skip will skip as many rows as specified, but CouchDB will still read from the first row; it just won't return any values for the skipped rows. If you specify skip=100, CouchDB will read 100 rows and not create output for them. This doesn't sound too bad, but it is *very* bad, when you use 1000 or even 10000 as skip values. CouchDB will have to look at a lot of rows unnecessarily.

As a rule of thumb, skip should be used only with single digit values. While it's possible that there are legitimate use cases where you specify a larger value, they are a good indicator for potential problems with your solution. Finally, for the calculations to work, you need to add a reduce function and make two calls to the view per page to get all the numbering right, and there's still a potential for error.

Fast Paging (Do Use)

The correct solution is not much harder. Instead of slicing the result set into equally sized pages, we look at 10 rows at a time and use `startkey` to jump to the next 10 rows. We even use `skip`, but only with the value `1`.

Here is how it works:

- Request `rows_per_page` + 1 rows from the view
- Display `rows_per_page` rows, store + 1 row as `next_startkey` and `next_start key_docid`
- As *page information*, keep `startkey` and `next_startkey`
- Use the `next_*` values to create the *next* link, and use the others to create the *previous* link

The trick to finding the next page is pretty simple. Instead of requesting 10 rows for a page, you request 11 rows, but display only 10 and use the values in the 11th row as the `startkey` for the next page. Populating the link to the previous page is as simple as carrying the current `startkey` over to the next page. If there's no previous `startkey`, we are on the first page. We stop displaying the link to the next page if we get `rows_per_page` or less rows back. This is called *linked list pagination*, as we go from page to page, or list item to list item, instead of jumping directly to a pre-computed page. There is one caveat, though. Can you spot it?

CouchDB view keys do not have to be unique; you can have multiple index entries *read*. What if you have more index entries for a key than rows that should be on a page? `startkey` jumps to the first row, and you'd be screwed if CouchDB didn't have an additional parameter for you to use. All view keys with the same value are internally sorted by `docid`, that is, the ID of the document that created that view row. You can use the `startkey_docid` and `endkey_docid` parameters to get subsets of these rows. For pagination, we still don't need `endkey_docid`, but `startkey_docid` is very handy. In addition to `startkey` and `limit`, you also use `startkey_docid` for pagination if, and only if, the extra row you fetch to find the next page has the same key as the current `startkey`.

It is important to note that the `*_docid` parameters only work *in addition* to the `*key` parameters and are only useful to further narrow down the result set of a view for a single key. They do not work on their own (the one exception being the built-in `_all_docs` view that already sorts by document ID).

The advantage of this approach is that all the key operations can be performed on the super-fast B-tree index behind the view. Looking up a page doesn't include scanning through hundreds and thousands of rows unnecessarily.

Jump to Page

One drawback of the linked list style pagination is that you can't pre-compute the rows for a particular page from the page number and the rows per page. Jumping to a specific page doesn't really work. Our gut reaction, if that concern is raised, is, "Not even Google is doing that!" and we tend to get away with it. Google always pretends on the first page to find 10 more pages of results. Only if you click on the second page (something very few people actually do) might Google display a reduced set of pages. If you page through the results, you get links for the previous and next 10 pages, but no more. Pre-computing the necessary `startkey` and `startkey_docid` for 20 pages is a feasible operation and a pragmatic optimization to know the rows for every page in a result set that is potentially tens of thousands of rows long, or more.

If you really do need to jump to a page over the full range of documents (we have seen applications that require that), you can still maintain an integer value index as the view index and take a hybrid approach at solving pagination.

PART VI

Appendixes

Installing on Unix-like Systems

Debian GNU/Linux

You can install the CouchDB package by running:

```
sudo aptitude install couchdb
```

When this completes, you should have a copy of CouchDB running on your machine. Be sure to read through the Debian-specific system documentation that can be found under */usr/share/couchdb*.

Starting with Ubuntu 9.10 ("Karmic"), CouchDB comes preinstalled with every desktop system.

Ubuntu

You can install the CouchDB package by running:

```
sudo aptitude install couchdb
```

When this completes, you should have a copy of CouchDB running on your machine. Be sure to read through the Ubuntu-specific system documentation that can be found under */usr/share/couchdb*.

Gentoo Linux

Enable the development ebuild of CouchDB by running:

```
sudo echo dev-db/couchdb >> /etc/portage/package.keywords
```

Check the CouchDB ebuild by running:

```
emerge -pv couchdb
```

Build and install the CouchDB ebuild by running:

```
sudo emerge couchdb
```

When this completes, you should have a copy of CouchDB running on your machine.

Problems

See Appendix D if your distribution doesn't have a CouchDB package.

Installing on Mac OS X

CouchDBX

The easiest way to get started with CouchDB on Mac OS X is by downloading CouchDBX (*http://janl.github.com/couchdbx/*). This unofficial application doesn't install anything to your system and can be run with a single double-click. Note, however, that for more serious use, it is recommended that you do a traditional installation with something like Homebrew (*http://github.com/mxcl/homebrew/*).

Homebrew

Homebrew is a recent addition to the software management tools on Mac OS X. Its premise is zero configuration, heavy optimizations, and a beer theme. Get Homebrew from *http://github.com/mxcl/homebrew*. The installation instructions are minimal. Once you are set up, run:

```
brew install couchdb
```

in the Terminal and wait until it is done. To start CouchDB, simply run:

```
couchdb
```

to see all the startup options available to you, run:

```
couchdb -h
```

This tells you how to run CouchDB in the background, among other useful hints.

To verify that CouchDB is indeed running, open your browser and visit *http://127.0.0.1:5984/_utils/index.html*.

MacPorts

MacPorts is the de facto package management tool for Mac OS X. While not an official part of the operating system, it can be used to simplify the process of installing FLOSS software on your machine. Before you can install CouchDB with MacPorts, you need to download and install MacPorts (*http://www.macports.org/install.php*).

Make sure your MacPorts installation is up-to-date by running:

```
sudo port selfupdate
```

You can install CouchDB with MacPorts by running:

```
sudo port install couchdb
```

This command will install all of the necessary dependencies for CouchDB. If a dependency was already installed, MacPorts will not take care of upgrading the dependency to the newest version. To make sure that all of the dependencies are up-to-date, you should also run:

```
sudo port upgrade couchdb
```

Mac OS X has a service management framework called `launchd` that can be used to start, stop, or manage system daemons. You can use this to start CouchDB automatically when the system boots up. If you want to add CouchDB to your `launchd` configuration, you should run:

```
sudo launchctl load -w
/opt/local/Library/LaunchDaemons/org.apache.couchdb.plist
```

After running this command, CouchDB should be available at:

http://127.0.0.1:5984/_utils/index.html

CouchDB will also be started and stopped along with the operating system.

Installing on Windows

CouchDB does not officially support Windows. CouchDB intends to provide an official Windows installer at some point in the future, so this may change. At the time this book is going to print, there is, however, an unofficial binary installer (*http://people .apache.org/~mhammond/dist/*).

This is unofficial software, so please remember to exercise additional caution when downloading or installing it, as it may damage your system. Imagine a fearsomely comprehensive disclaimer of author liability. Now fear, comprehensively.

We recommend that you ask on the CouchDB mailing lists for further help.

CouchDB will have official Windows support as part of the 1.0 release.

Installing from Source

Generally speaking, you should avoid installing from source. Many operating systems provide package managers that will allow you to download and install CouchDB with a single command. These package managers usually take care of setting things up correctly, handling security, and making sure that the CouchDB database is started and stopped correctly by your system. The first few appendixes showed you how to install CouchDB packages for Unix-like, Mac OS X, and Windows operating systems. If you are unable to follow those instructions, or you need to install by hand for other reasons, this chapter is for you.

Dependencies

To build and install CouchDB, you will need to install a collection of other software that CouchDB depends on. Without this software properly installed on your system, CouchDB will refuse to work. You'll need to download and install the following:

- Erlang OTP (*http://erlang.org/*) (>=R12B)
- ICU (*http://icu.sourceforge.net/*)
- OpenSSL (*http://www.openssl.org/*)
- Mozilla SpiderMonkey (*http://www.mozilla.org/js/spidermonkey/*)
- libcurl (*http://curl.haxx.se/libcurl/*)
- GNU Make (*http://www.gnu.org/software/make/*)
- GNU Compiler Collection (*http://gcc.gnu.org/*)

It is recommended that you install Erlang OTP R12B-5 or above if possible.

Each of these software packages should provide custom installation instructions, either on the website or in the archive you download. If you're lucky, however, you may be able to use a package manager to install these dependencies.

Debian-Based (Including Ubuntu) Systems

You can install the dependencies by running:

```
apt-get install build-essential erlang libicu-dev libmozjs-dev libcurl4-openssl-dev
```

If you get an error about any of these packages, be sure to check for the current version offered by your distribution. It may be the case that a newer version has been released and the package name has been changed. For example, you can search for the newest ICU package by running:

```
apt-cache search libicu
```

Select and install the highest version from the list available.

Mac OS X

You will need to install the Xcode Tools metapackage by running:

```
open /Applications/Installers/Xcode\ Tools/XcodeTools.mpkg
```

If this is unavailable on your system, you will need to install it from your Mac OS X installation CD. Alternatively, you can download a copy (*http://developer.apple.com/ TOOLS/Xcode/*).

You can then install the other dependencies using MacPorts by running:

```
port install icu erlang spidermonkey curl
```

See Appendix B for more details.

Installing

Once you have installed all of the dependencies, you should download a copy of the CouchDB source (*http://couchdb.apache.org/downloads.html*). This should give you an archive that you'll need to unpack. Open up a terminal and change directory to your newly unpacked archive.

Configure the source by running:

```
./configure
```

We're going to be installing CouchDB into */usr/local*, which is the default location for user-installed software. A ton of options are available for this command, and you can customize everything from the installation location, such as your home directory, to the location of your Erlang or SpiderMonkey installation.

To see what's available, you can run:

```
./configure --help
```

Generally, you can ignore this step if you didn't get any errors the first time you ran it. You'll only need to pass extra options if your setup is a bit weird and the script is having trouble finding one of the dependencies you installed in the last section.

If everything was successful, you should see the following message:

```
You have configured Apache CouchDB, time to relax.
```

Relax.

Build and install the source by running:

```
make && sudo make install
```

If you changed the installation location to somewhere temporary, you may not want to use the sudo command here. If you are having problems running make, you may want to try running gmake if it is available on your system. More options can be found by reading the INSTALL file.

Security Considerations

It is not advisable to run the CouchDB server as the super user. If the CouchDB server is compromised by an attacker while it is being run by a super user, the attacker will get super user access to your entire system. That's not what we want!

We strongly recommend that you create a specific user for CouchDB. This user should have as few privileges on your system as possible, preferably the bare minimum needed to run the CouchDB server, read the configuration files, and write to the data and log directories.

You can use whatever tool your system provides to create a new couchdb user.

On many Unix-like systems you can run:

```
adduser --system \
        --home /usr/local/var/lib/couchdb --no-create-home \
        --shell /bin/bash \
        --group --gecos "CouchDB" couchdb
```

Mac OS X provides the standard Accounts option from the System Preferences application, or you can use the Workgroup Manager application, which can be downloaded as part of the Server Admin Tools (*http://www.apple.com/support/downloads/serverad mintools1047.html*).

You should make sure that the couchdb user has a working login shell. You can test this by logging into a terminal as the couchdb user. You should also make sure to set the home directory to */usr/local/var/lib/couchdb*, which is the CouchDB database directory.

Change the ownership of the CouchDB directories by running:

```
chown -R couchdb:couchdb /usr/local/etc/couchdb
chown -R couchdb:couchdb /usr/local/var/lib/couchdb
```

```
chown -R couchdb:couchdb /usr/local/var/log/couchdb
chown -R couchdb:couchdb /usr/local/var/run/couchdb
```

Change the permission of the CouchDB directories by running:

```
chmod -R 0770 /usr/local/etc/couchdb
chmod -R 0770 /usr/local/var/lib/couchdb
chmod -R 0770 /usr/local/var/log/couchdb
chmod -R 0770 /usr/local/var/run/couchdb
```

This isn't the final word in securing your CouchDB setup. If you're deploying CouchDB on the Web, or any place where untrusted parties can access your sever, it behooves you to research the recommended security measures for your operating system and take any additional steps needed. Keep in mind the network security adage that the only way to properly secure a computer system is to unplug it from the network.

Running Manually

You can start the CouchDB server by running:

```
sudo -i -u couchdb couchdb -b
```

This uses the sudo command to run the couchdb command as the couchdb user.

When CouchDB starts, it should eventually display the following message:

```
Apache CouchDB has started, time to relax.
```

Relax.

To check that everything has worked, point your web browser to:

```
http://127.0.0.1:5984/_utils/index.html
```

This is Futon, the CouchDB web administration console. We covered the basics of Futon in our early chapters. Once you have it loaded, you should select and run the CouchDB Test Suite from the righthand menu. This will make sure that everything is behaving as expected, and it may save you some serious headaches if things turn out to be a bit wonky.

Running As a Daemon

Once you've got CouchDB running nicely, you'll probably want to run it as daemon. A daemon is a software application that runs continually in the background, waiting to handle requests. This is how most production database servers run, and you can configure CouchDB to run like this, too.

When you run CouchDB as a daemon, it logs to a number of files that you'll want to clean up from time to time. Letting your log files fill up a disk is a good way to break your server! Some operating systems come with software that does this for you, and it is important for you to research your options and take the necessary steps to make sure that this doesn't become a problem. CouchDB ships with a `logrotate` configuration that may be useful.

SysV/BSD-Style Systems

Depending on your operating system, the `couchdb` daemon script could be installed into a directory called *init.d* (for SysV-style systems) or *rc.d* (for BSD-style systems) under the */usr/local/etc* directory. The following examples use [`init.d`|`rc.d`] to indicate this choice, and you must replace it with your actual directory before running any of these commands.

You can start the CouchDB daemon by running:

```
sudo /usr/local/etc/[init.d|rc.d]/couchdb start
```

You can stop the CouchDB daemon by running:

```
sudo /usr/local/etc/[init.d|rc.d]/couchdb stop
```

You can get the status of the CouchDB daemon by running:

```
sudo /usr/local/etc/[init.d|rc.d]/couchdb status
```

If you want to configure how the daemon script works, you will find a bunch of options you can edit in the */usr/local/etc/default/couchdb* file.

If you want to run the script without the `sudo` command, you will need to remove the `COUCHDB_USER` setting from this file.

Your operating system will probably provide a way to control the CouchDB daemon automatically, starting and stopping it as a system service. To do this, you will need to copy the daemon script into your system */etc/[init.d|rc.d]* directory, and run a command such as:

```
sudo update-rc.d couchdb defaults
```

Consult your system documentation for more information.

Mac OS X

You can use the `launchd` system to control the CouchDB daemon.

You can load the `launchd` configuration by running:

```
sudo launchctl load /usr/local/Library/LaunchDaemons/org.apache.couchdb.plist
```

You can unload the `launchd` configuration by running:

```
sudo launchctl unload /usr/local/Library/LaunchDaemons/org.apache.couchdb.plist
```

You can start the CouchDB daemon by running:

```
sudo launchctl start org.apache.couchdb
```

You can stop the CouchDB daemon by running:

```
sudo launchctl stop org.apache.couchdb
```

The `launchd` system can control the CouchDB daemon automatically, starting and stopping it as a system service. To do this, you will need to copy the plist file into your system */Library/LaunchDaemons* directory.

Consult the `launchd` documentation for more information.

Troubleshooting

Software being software, you can count on something going wrong every now and then. No need to panic; CouchDB has a great community full of people who will be able to answer your questions and help you get started. Here are a few resources to help you on your way:

- If you're getting a weird error message, see the Error Messages wiki page (*http:// wiki.apache.org/couchdb/Error_messages*).
- For general troubleshooting, try out the Troubleshooting steps (*http://wiki.apache .org/couchdb/Troubleshooting*).
- For other general support, you should visit the mailing lists (*http://couchdb.apache .org/community/lists.html*).

Don't forget to use your favorite search engine when diagnosing problems. If you look around a bit, you're likely to find something. It's very possible that a bunch of other people have had exactly the same problem as you and a solution has been posted somewhere on the Web. Good luck, and remember to relax!

JSON Primer

CouchDB uses *JavaScript Object Notation* (JSON) for data storage, a lightweight format based on a subset of JavaScipt syntax. One of the best bits about JSON is that it's easy to read and write by hand, much more so than something like XML. We can parse it naturally with JavaScript because it shares part of the same syntax. This really comes in handy when we're building dynamic web applications and we want to fetch some data from the server.

Here's a sample JSON document:

```
{
    "Subject": "I like Plankton",
    "Author": "Rusty",
    "PostedDate": "2006-08-15T17:30:12-04:00",
    "Tags": [
        "plankton",
        "baseball",
        "decisions"
    ],
    "Body": "I decided today that I don't like baseball. I like plankton."
}
```

You can see that the general structure is based around key/value pairs and lists of things.

Data Types

JSON has a number of basic data types you can use. We'll cover them all here.

Numbers

You can have positive integers: `"Count": 253`

Or negative integers: `"Score": -19`

Or floating-point numbers: `"Area": 456.31`

There is a subtle but important difference between floating-point numbers and decimals. When you use a number like 15.7, this will be interpreted as 15.699999999999999 by most clients, which may be problematic for your application. For this reason, currency values are usually better represented as strings in JSON. A string like "15.7" will be interpreted as "15.7" by every JSON client.

Or scientific notation: "Density": 5.6e+24

Strings

You can use strings for values:

    "Author": "Rusty"

You have to escape some special characters, like tabs or newlines:[*]

    "poem": "May I compare thee to some\n\tsalty plankton."

Booleans

You can have boolean true values:

    "Draft": true

Or boolean false values:

    "Draft": false

Arrays

An array is a list of values:

    "Tags": ["plankton", "baseball", "decisions"]

An array can contain any other data type, including arrays:

    "Context": ["dog", [1, true], {"Location": "puddle"}]

Objects

An object is a list of key/value pairs:

    {"Subject": "I like Plankton", "Author": "Rusty"}

Nulls

You can have null values:

    "Surname": null

---

[*] The JSON site (*http://www.json.org*) has details on what needs to be escaped.

The Power of B-trees

CouchDB uses a data structure called a B-tree to index its documents and views. We'll look at B-trees enough to understand the types of queries they support and how they are a good fit for CouchDB.

This is our first foray into CouchDB internals. To use CouchDB, you don't need to know what's going on under the hood, but if you understand how CouchDB performs its magic, you'll be able to pull tricks of your own. Additionally, if you understand the consequences of the ways you are using CouchDB, you will end up with smarter systems.

If you weren't looking closely, CouchDB would appear to be a B-tree manager with an HTTP interface.

 CouchDB is actually using a B+ tree, which is a slight variation of the B-tree that trades a bit of (disk) space for speed. When we say *B-tree*, we mean CouchDB's *B+ tree*.

A B-tree is an excellent data structure for storing huge amounts of data for fast retrieval. When there are millions and billions of items in a B-tree, that's when they get fun. B-trees are usually a shallow but wide data structure. While other trees can grow very high, a typical B-tree has a single-digit height, even with millions of entries. This is particularly interesting for CouchDB, where the leaves of the tree are stored on a slow medium such as a hard drive. Accessing any part of the tree for reading or writing requires visiting only a few nodes, which translates to a few head seeks (which are what make a hard drive slow), and because the operating system is likely to cache the upper tree nodes anyway, only the seek to the final leaf node is needed.

> From a practical point of view, B-trees, therefore, guarantee an access time of less than 10 ms even for extremely large datasets.

> —Dr. Rudolf Bayer, inventor of the B-tree

CouchDB's B-tree implementation is a bit different from the original. While it maintains all of the important properties, it adds Multi-Version Concurrency Control (MVCC) and an append-only design. B-trees are used to store the main database file as well as view indexes. One database is one B-tree, and one view index is one B-tree.

MVCC allows concurrent reads and writes without using a locking system. Writes are serialized, allowing only one write operation at any point in time for any single database. Write operations do not block reads, and there can be any number of read operations at any time. Each read operation is guaranteed a consistent view of the database. How this is accomplished is at the core of CouchDB's storage model.

The short answer is that because CouchDB uses append-only files, the B-tree root node must be rewritten every time the file is updated. However, old portions of the file will never change, so every old B-tree root, should you happen to have a pointer to it, will also point to a consistent snapshot of the database.

Early in the book we explained how the MVCC system uses the document's `_rev` value to ensure that only one person can change a document version. The B-tree is used to look up the existing `_rev` value for comparison. By the time a write is accepted, the B-tree can expect it to be an authoritative version.

Since old versions of documents are not overwritten or deleted when new versions come in, requests that are reading a particular version do not care if new ones are written at the same time. With an often changing document, there could be readers reading three different versions at the same time. Each version was the latest one when a particular client started reading it, but new versions were being written. From the point when a new version is *committed*, new readers will read the new version while old readers keep reading the old version.

In a B-tree, data is kept only in leaf nodes. CouchDB B-trees append data only to the database file that keeps the B-tree on disk and grows only at the end. Add a new document? The file grows at the end. Delete a document? That gets recorded at the end of the file. The consequence is a robust database file. Computers fail for plenty of reasons, such as power loss or failing hardware. Since CouchDB does not overwrite any existing data, it cannot corrupt anything that has been written and *committed* to disk already. See Figure F-1.

Committing is the process of updating the database file to reflect changes. This is done in the file footer, which is the last 4k of the database file. The footer is 2k in size and written twice in succession. First, CouchDB appends any changes to the file and then records the file's new length in the first database footer. It then force-flushes all changes to disk. It then copies the first footer over to the second 2k of the file and force-flushes again.

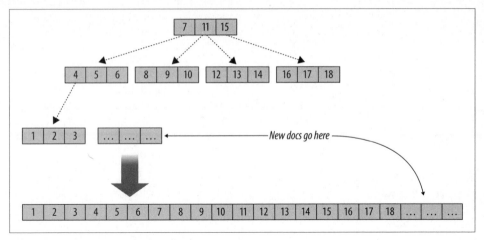

Figure F-1. Flat B-tree and append-only

If anywhere in this process a problem occurs—say, power is cut off and CouchDB is restarted later—the database file is in a consistent state and doesn't need a checkup. CouchDB starts reading the database file backward. When it finds a footer pair, it makes some checks: if the first 2k are corrupt (a footer includes a checksum), CouchDB replaces it with the second footer and all is well. If the second footer is corrupt, CouchDB copies the first 2k over and all is well again. Only once both footers are flushed to disk successfully will CouchDB acknowledge that a write operation was successful. Data is never lost, and data on disk is never corrupted. This design is the reason for CouchDB having no *off* switch. You just terminate it when you are done.

There's a lot more to say about B-trees in general, and if and how SSDs change the runtime behavior. The Wikipedia article on B-trees (*http://en.wikipedia.org/wiki/B -tree*) is a good starting point for further investigations. Scholarpedia includes notes (*http://www.scholarpedia.org/article/B-tree_and_UB-tree*) by Dr. Rudolf Bayer, inventor of the B-tree.

Index

Symbols

! (bang), beginning macros, 81
" (quotation marks), delimiting JSON strings, 22
, (comma), separating multiple keys and values in JSON, 120
. (dot) notation, 82
/ (slashes), in design document URLs, 50
: (colon), separating key/value pairs, 120
<%= replace_me %> templating tags, 133
[ ] (square brackets), enclosing arrays in JSON, 22, 120
{ } (curly braces), enclosing objects in JSON, 22, 120

A

Accept headers, 80
admin accounts
    replication requests and, 152
    setting up for Sofa, 116
admin party, 189
admin role, 193
admin users, 189
    creating new, 190
aggregate functions in SQL, 183
Ajax queries against JSON API, 50
API
    core API (see core CouchDB API)
    exploring bare-bones CouchDB API using curl utility, 21–23
application servers, rendering JSON documents into HTML, 76
arrays, 22, 232
Atom feeds

recent blog posts, 138
    served by CouchDB, 50
Atom list query, 93
Atom.header( ) function, 139
attachments to documents, 41
    Sofa design document, 113
    using in standalone applications, 100
authentication
    basic, 191–193
    cookie, 193–194
authorship, validating, 73
availability, 11, 12
awesome (see Katz, Damien)

B

B-trees
    caching intermediate reduce results, 59
    CouchDB storage engine, 13
    index, reduce view results and, 61–64
    performance and, 197
    power of, 233–235
    view results in, 55
backup server, 163
banking, using CouchDB, 205–208
batch mode, 199
benchmarks, 195
    Hovercraft benchmarking feature, 201
bidirectional replication, 149
blog post template, 85
blog posts
    CouchDB document for, 122
    displaying with Sofa show function, 131
    JSON format for, 120
    rendering with show functions, 132–134
    viewing lists of, 135–141

We'd like to hear your suggestions for improving our indexes. Send email to *index@oreilly.com*.

D

daemon, running CouchDB as, 228–230
data format, performance and, 197
data modeling, 4
data types, 70
    JSON, 231–232
        arrays, 232
        booleans, 232
        nulls, 232
        numbers, 231
        objects, 232
        strings, 232
data, scaling, 6, 147
database management system (DMS), 34
databases, 34–37
    design documents in, 50
    local and remote, 149
    sequence number, 150
dates
    Date header, 36
    dynamic, 134
    outputting static dates in HTML, 133
    sorting blog posts by, 136
DELETE requests, 23
dependencies for CouchDB installed from source, 225
design document resources, 79
design documents, 47–52
    applications as documents, 48
    as applications, 99
    basic, 51
    CouchApps, installation of, 110
    list functions in, 87
    macros pulling data from elsewhere into, 137
    query server, 48
    recent-posts view (example), 136
    show functions in, 78
        linking to attachments, 133
    validation functions in, 69
    view definitions, 179
    view functions in, 54
    working with example application, 109
directory hierarchy, 82
display logic
    required fields and, 71
distributed computing, fallacies of, 8
distributed systems, 11
Django, 76

D (continued column)

DMS (database management system), 34
docForm( ) helper function, 126–128
docs_read field, 152
docs_written field, 152
document IDs, 38
    design documents, 48
    hashing, 166
    monotonic, bulk inserts and, 198
document modeling, 47
documents, 38–42, 119–130
    attachments, 41
    creating, 25
        example document for MapReduce view, 27
    data other than _id and _rev, 122
    edit page, 123–124
        HTML scaffold, 124
    _id field, 121, 187
    JSON format, 120
    _rev field, 121
    revisions, 39
    saving, 125–130
        blog post (example), 130
        validation, 129
    showing in custom formats, 131–134
        dynamic dates, 134
        rendering with show functions, 132–134
    validation functions for, 67
    versioned, in CouchDB, 15
doc_write_failures field, 152
dot (.) notation, 82
duck typing, 70, 123

E

E4X extension (JavaScript), 140
easy_install script, 110
edit page, 123–124
edit.html form, JavaScript callbacks for, 125–128
Ely Service website, 101
emit( ) function, 54
_ensure_full_commit API, 200
equality tests, 72
Erlang, 9, 195
    assessing CouchDB from within, using Hovercraft, 201
    versions, in Server header, 36
Etags, 81

eventual consistency, 16

F

fast paging, 215
fault-tolerant systems, 163
filters for changes, 177
floats, ordered list of, 210
format, render_function function, 80
formats
    specifying for blog output, 138
    XML and HTML for blog posts, 137
fsync, triggering, 200
full commit, 200
functions, 55
    (see also entries for individual function
        names)
    aggregate functions in SQL, replacing with
        views, 183
    function definition in JavaScript, 54
    templates and, 81
Futon, 23
    creating temporary view, 29
    running replication with, 150
    running test suite, 23

G

GET requests
    issuing with curl, 21
    responses to, side effect–free and cacheable,
        78
getRow( ) function, 138
getting started with CouchDB
    bare-bones API, 21–23
    creating a database and document, 24
    Futon administrative interface, 23
    running a query using MapReduce, 27–32
    triggering replication, 32
group_level reduce queries, 59–61
GUIDs (globally unique identifiers), 38

H

hardware, performance and, 197
hashing
    consistent, 166–168
    passwords, 191
hasPrev( ) and hasNext( ) methods, 214
headers
    Accept headers, 80

    custom, setting with show function, 76
    generating header for Atom feed, 140
    response, 36
    Set-Cookie header, 194
    use with list and show functions, 88
    User-Agent header, 36
high availability and fault tolerance, 164
high performance (see performance)
Hovercraft, 201
HTML
    dynamic changes in final HTML, using
        client-side JavaScript, 134
    list query, 92
    listing for edit.html, 124
    Markdown format, 123
    rendering for blog posts (example), 133
    rendering from database records, 75
    rendering in show function results, 83
    rendering recent blog post view as, using list
        function, 137–141
    views of blog posts (in Sofa), 114
    writing templates for HTML pages, 85
HTTP, 3
    proper use of, improving client experience,
        196
HTTP requests, 21, 33, 35
    GET request, 88
    PUT request, 34
        JSON over to save blog post, 130
HTTP responses, 36
HTTP status codes, 36

I

_id field, documents, 25, 39, 121, 187
IDs, document (see document IDs)
incremental replication, 16
indexes
    B-tree, reduce view results and, 61–64
    building efficient indexes for lookups, 56–
        59
    Sofa, 113
.ini files with configuration settings, 191
inserts, single document, 200
    (see also bulk inserts)
installing CouchDB
    from source, 225–230
        installation, 226
        running CouchDB as daemon, 228–230
        running manually, 228

running CouchDB as daemon, 229
MacPorts package, 222
macros, 81
  !code, 82
  !json, 82
    loading edit.html template, 124
  CouchApp, pulling code and data into
      design document, 137
  using in JavaScript show function, 132
manually running CouchDB, 228
map functions, 64, 180
  creating alphabetic list of bands (example),
      212
  defining in JavaScript, 54
  in view definitions, 180
  view getting comments for posts, 59
map result, 183
MapReduce
  running a query using, 27–32
    creating example documents, 28
    editing map function, 29
    modifying view function, 30
    results of running a view in Futon, 30
    temporary view in Futon, 29
  use by CouchDB, 14
Markdown HTML format, 123
memory, performance and, 201
message queue, failure-tolerant, 201
middle-tier application servers, 76
Mimeparse, JavaScript port of, 80
MVCC (Multi-Version Concurrency Control),
    15, 40

N

node admins, 73
null values, 232
numeric types (JSON), 231
Nymphormation link sharing and tagging site,
    104

O

objects, 232
  documents versus, 119
  JSON, 120
  JSON syntax, 22, 120
  recent post documents, 136
ordered lists, 208–211
  in JSON, 22

list of floats, 210
list of integers, 208
oversharding, 168

P

pagination, 211–216
  creating a view, 212
  example data for, 211
  fast paging, 215
  jump to page, 216
  set up, 213
  slow paging, 213
partition tolerance, 11, 12
partitions
  determining number per proxy, 169
  moving, 170
  splitting, 170
passwords
  hashing, 191
  plain-text, 192
performance, 195–203
  bulk document inserts, 198
  bulk inserts and monotonic document IDs,
    198
  data format and, 197
  good benchmarks, 195
  hardware, 197
  single document inserts, 200
  trade-offs, expense for speed, 201
  using batch mode, 199
  using Hovercraft library, 201
polling for changes, 174
POST requests, 25
  issuing with curl, 22
privileges, 189
Processing JS Studio, 102
provides( ) function, 138
proxies
  number of partitions per proxy, 169
  redundant, 167
  setting up CouchDB behind HTTP proxy,
    192
proxy-based partitioning and clustering
    application (Lounge), 165
pull replication, 44
push replication, 44
PUT requests, 22
  JSON over, to save blog post, 130
  sending using curl, 34

Python
  easy_install script, 110
  Twisted framework, 166
  Twisted Smartproxy, 167

Q

query server, 48
querying views, 54, 180

R

RAM for CouchDB, 197
read requests
  reflecting newest information, 13
  scaling, 6, 146
recipes (see tasks and solutions using
    CouchDB)
records, 119
reduce functions, 64
  group_level reduce queries, 59
  overview of, 183
  rereduce parameter, 59, 61–64, 65
  in view definitions, 180
relational databases
  consistency, availability, and partition
    tolerance, 12
reliability, performance and, 202
remote replication, 44
remote target database (for replication), 43
replication, 8, 42–44, 149–152
  conflict detection and resolution, 153
  conflict management by example, 155–158
  continuous, 152
  details of, 151
  incremental, between CouchDB nodes, 16
  performance optimization, 198
  sequence numbers for database changes,
    150
  triggering, 32
  using Futon admin interface, 150
  working with conflicts, 158–161
replication sessions, 43, 151
request headers, 35
requests, 88
  (see also HTTP requests)
  forbidden or unauthorized, 129
  req object (example), 87
require( ) function, 71
required fields, validating, 71

responses
  HTTP, 36
RESTful API, 3, 44
  CouchDB show functions, 131
result set, 211
_rev field, documents, 25, 39, 121
_rev property, 159
reversed view results, 58
revisions, 39
  conflicting, 160
  conflicts in, winning and losing revisions,
    153
  deterministic revision IDs, 161
roles and users, 193
Ruby on Rails, 76

S

scalability, 11
scalar values, 184
scaling, 4, 145–147
  data, 147
  read requests, 146
  read requests, write requests, or data, 6
  write requests, 146
security, 189–194
  admin party, 189–191
  basic authentication, 191–193
  considerations for CouchDB installed from
    source, 227
  cookie authentication, 193–194
self-contained data, 5
seq field, 174
sequence numbers in databases, 150
server secret, 194
servers
  CouchDB, checking if running, 33
  having a backup, 163
  Server header, 36
session history of replications, 43
session_id (replication), 151
Set-Cookie header, 194
setuptools package, 110
shard maps (Lounge), 166
show functions, 50, 75–85, 131–134
  API for, 76
  basic form function, 83
  edit page show function, 123
  Etags and, 81
  free of side effects, 77

About the Authors

J. Chris Anderson is an Apache CouchDB committer and cofounder of Relaxed, Inc. Chris is obsessed with JavaScript CouchApps and bending the physics of the Web to give control back to users.

Jan Lehnardt is an Apache CouchDB committer and cofounder of Relaxed, Inc. Jan hacks on all parts of the web technology stack and focuses on making developers' lives easier.

Noah Slater is an Apache CouchDB committer and release manager. He works with the community to get CouchDB running in as many places as possible.

Colophon

The animal on the cover of *CouchDB: The Definitive Guide* is a Pomeranian dog (*Canis familiaris*), a small variety of the generally larger German Spitz breed, named for the Baltic region of Pomerania (today spilt between northeastern Germany and northern Poland) where it was first bred.

Originally, Pomeranians were closer in size to their German Spitz relatives—weighing 30–50 pounds—and were bred as herding dogs because of their intelligence, energy, and loyalty. From the late 19th century, however, breeders began to favor increasingly smaller dogs, a move caused in large part by Queen Victoria's affinity for that variety. Today, Pomeranians are classed as "toy dogs," weighing only 4–7 pounds, and are particularly kept as small pets and show dogs.

The Pomeranian exhibits many of the physical and behavioral characteristics of its larger ancestors and relatives. It has a short, pointed muzzle, upright and pointed ears, a large bushy tail carried curled over the back, and is especially spirited and friendly. Pomeranians are also particularly noted for their double coat—a soft and dense undercoat and a long, straight and harshly textured outer coat—and come in a wide variety of colors, including white, black, brown, red, orange, sable, spotted, or any combination thereof. Because of their small size, Pomeranians are able to exercise sufficiently in small indoor spaces if taken for a daily walk, and consequently make excellent apartment pets.

The cover image is from Lydekker's *Royal Natural History*. The cover font is Adobe ITC Garamond. The text font is Linotype Birka; the heading font is Adobe Myriad Condensed; and the code font is LucasFont's TheSansMonoCondensed.

Get even more for your money.

Join the O'Reilly Community, and register the O'Reilly books you own.It's free, and you'll get:

- 40% upgrade offer on O'Reilly books
- Membership discounts on books and events
- Free lifetime updates to electronic formats of books
- Multiple ebook formats, DRM FREE
- Participation in the O'Reilly community
- Newsletters
- Account management
- 100% Satisfaction Guarantee

Signing up is easy:

1. **Go to: oreilly.com/go/register**
2. **Create an O'Reilly login.**
3. **Provide your address.**
4. **Register your books.**

Note: English-language books only

To order books online:
oreilly.com/order_new

For questions about products or an order:
orders@oreilly.com

To sign up to get topic-specific email announcements and/or news about upcoming books, conferences, special offers, and new technologies:
elists@oreilly.com

For technical questions about book content:
booktech@oreilly.com

To submit new book proposals to our editors:
proposals@oreilly.com

Many O'Reilly books are available in PDF and several ebook formats. For more information:
oreilly.com/ebooks

O'REILLY®

Spreading the knowledge of innovators   www.oreilly.com

Buy this book and get access to the online edition for 45 days—for free!

CouchDB: The Definitive Guide
By J. Chris Anderson, Jan Lehnardt & Noah Slater
January 2010, $39.99
ISBN 9780596155896

With Safari Books Online, you can:

Access the contents of thousands of technology and business books

- Quickly search over 7000 books and certification guides
- Download whole books or chapters in PDF format, at no extra cost, to print or read on the go
- Copy and paste code
- Save up to 35% on O'Reilly print books
- **New!** Access mobile-friendly books directly from cell phones and mobile devices

Stay up-to-date on emerging topics before the books are published

- Get on-demand access to evolving manuscripts.
- Interact directly with authors of upcoming books

Explore thousands of hours of video on technology and design topics

- Learn from expert video tutorials
- Watch and replay recorded conference sessions

To try out Safari and the online edition of this book FREE for 45 days,
go to **www.oreilly.com/go/safarienabled** and enter the coupon code ULMMPWA.
To see the complete Safari Library, visit safari.oreilly.com.

O'REILLY®

Spreading the knowledge of innovators   safari.oreilly.com